Library Administration and Staff Training

Library Administration and Staff Training

Aditya Rajput

RANDOM

RANDOM PUBLICATIONS

NEW DELHI (INDIA)

Library Administration and Staff Training

ISBN 978-93-5111-563-2

Published in 2015 in India by

RANDOM PUBLICATIONS
4376-A/4B, Gali Murari Lal, Ansari Road
New Delhi-110 002
Phone : +9111-43580356, 011-23289044, 011-43142548
e-mail: sales@randompublications.com,
info@randompublications.com, randomexports@gmail.com

Reprinted 2021

Type Setting by : Friends Media, Delhi-110089
Digitally Printed at : Replika Press Pvt. Ltd.

Preface

The basics of library administration are, division of work, discipline, authority, responsibility and unitary command. In any library work should be properly divided. Management activities should be separated from other jobs and the subordinates should receive orders from one senior only.

Library Administration provides leadership and support for the University Libraries in its mission to enrich the student learning experience, encourage exploration and research at all levels, and contribute to advancements in access to scholarly resources.

Training for new staff should clearly be conducted as soon as possible after they're hired. The ideal is that it be part of their orientation -- if the orientation period is long or comprehensive enough -- or that it at least starts before they begin work, so they'll know what they're doing. But a well-planned training program should run all throughout the life of the organization.

Staff development should be scheduled regularly, as part of the normal operation of the organization. Probably, at minimum, everyone in the organization should have the opportunity for some ongoing training at least once a month. Some organizations may conduct or sponsor ongoing training much more often, sometimes as part of a weekly or biweekly staff meeting. Such training opportunities could be as low-key as a half-hour presentation at a staff meeting, or as formal as a presentation or workshop by a nationally known expert in the field, depending upon the organization's resources.

This book analyses the two aspects of library science in a comprehensive and objective way.I would like to thank my team for standing beside me throughout my career and writing this book. My special thanks go to "Random Publications" who have published the book.

– Aditya Rajput

Contents

1

Leadership and Management in Library Administration

Before waiting of the particular areas of technical services, researcher want to add to the philosophical discussion of administrative issues a specific discussion of personnel administration, simply because there cannot be libraries without librarians, and if the librarians are not infused with "the spirit of the times", libraries will not fulfil the needs of today's library patrons.

Researchers with good reason, is deeply alarmed by the mania for change that has invaded many companies, the mental laziness of the American population that wants everything to be easy and quick, the dependence of many organisations on various management ideologies, the sad phenomenon of extensive job dissatisfaction among workers, the obsession with numbers alone, and the lack of understanding of the very purpose of many organisations by their own leaders. Instead of such ideas and others commonly on the horizon of our management practice, Secor proposes a moderate view based on the revitalisation of certain traditional values and an eagerness to readapt and renew at every turn as the world keeps evolving. Researcher summarises his long essay in the very direction of my defence of "vertical thinking" when he says to his audience, "I've pointed you back to your roots." Before continuing to discuss Secor's ideas let me draw a new tree arrangement of the fundamental terms in personnel administration:

- Human Resources,
- Workers,
- Managers,
- Leaders,
- Company History.

Starting with a strong defence of the need for a true self identity on the part of all members of a company's staff, researcher proposes a new idea of leadership which should make us rethink our notions of the relationship between leaders and followers. Armed with an awareness of the company's origin and nature, leaders are responsible for the introduction of change while watching out for the company's stability, and for the creation of a team in which everybody gets retrained as the changing content of each person's work demands and in which everybody contributes willingly to the total effort according to his or her own abilities.

Researcher writes, "If it's a team sport, then personal and interpersonal training is part of the conditioning." And, "Skills training and personal and interpersonal effectiveness training are critical building blocks for personal and organisational renewal." If one wants to disagree with the idea that a company's life is a "team sport" and prefers to believe it is an individual's privileged domain only, then there is no need to continue this discussion.

But if the fundamental notion of "team sport" is granted, then he point about the radical need to think and learn continuously and to renew oneself, whether we are talking of leaders, managers, or workers, should be at the center of a new theory of management for the contemporary company. Then, more specifically, He neatly distinguishes the concepts of "leader" and "manager" as pertaining to two quite distinct skill sets and personality types, and asserts that any healthy organisation needs to have some of both if it wishes to endure. The leaders are charged with the creation of a credible vision for the future and they must try to understand that human nature means the workers will feel uncomfortable with the tensions that accompany all change.

Capable managers will also be needed to bring about the change involved and help all workers adapt to it. And, of course, old and new workers will have to be employed to carry out the business of the company, following the lead of the leaders, and responding to the management of the competent managers, in a spirit of full participation and never of blind submission. Leaders, managers, and workers should join in the pursuit of the legitimate goal of the organisation and for the good of all, the company itself, and its customers.

It seems to me that researcher must have been thinking about libraries when he wrote, "Most organisations do need to make fundamental changes in how they do business so that they can adapt faster and faster to their changing environments." Our library environments seem truly to change faster and faster, and thus far we librarians have failed to respond faster and faster to such changes.

The reasons for this are obvious. The responsibility for this failure rests with all of us - leaders, managers, and worker alike. First, our leaders often do not know how to lead, do not care for stability but only for abstract change and newness, do not communicate to library managers and workers clear visions that need to be shared by all, do not empower their managers with the proper responsibility, and do not respect the humanity of their workers. Second, many library managers do not care to manage but want to lead only, do not help their workers to adapt to the continuous changes, and do not attempt to understand the organisation's purpose and goal but care only to produce high figures and stay out of trouble.

And, third, too many workers do not want to work but only manage or lead in spite of their lack of qualifications for such tasks, do not join managers in any form to sustain a collective effort, and do not care about the organisation's past or future but are only interested in a self-serving, short-term benefit. To correct this situation, we need to go back to the drawing board, and for that we have the scheme presented by my new tree for the vertical organisation of a library's life.

Researcher would suppose that most persons trying to draw this tree of personnel would have placed the workers at the root level and the leaders at the branch level. We do not call certain powerful employees "top" executives for no reason. However, Since, the role of the leader is the decision-making that provides direction to the life of the organisation, we need to correct our customary incremental thinking and properly situate the "leaders" at the root level. Their work infuses the whole organisation with the vital substance which flows through all its parts. "Managers" do fit in the middle where we draw the tree's trunk. They must be the strongest members of the staff, involved as they always are of necessity in sustaining the company's life, whatever the circumstances.

And the "workers" should be placed at the level of the branches. They can change departments, they sometimes waver in their endeavors, they are visible to outsiders, they grow rather obviously when they educate themselves further, etc. When things are well in a company, we all know it has to do with having good leaders and managers first, but, also and decisively, with having good workers on the front line. Whether these workers are mechanics, programmers, or masons, the point is the same always. So, we do need "top" librarians in all good libraries - "top" reference specialists, "top" catalogers and indexers, "top" searchers, etc. Most companies today have a human resources department to watch over the workers and their human needs and to help with many delicate management issues and help "leaders" communicate with "managers" and "workers" In so doing, they are responding to the true reality of the organic life of a company in spite of our collective faults in thinking.

Without the fundamental direction of the "leaders," there will not be a tree or company at all but, instead, the company will wither away (as it is the case with many in the real world of economic and social competition, and whether or not they have tried "downsizing" or "re-engineering.") Without "managers" who sustain the whole edifice of the organisation, wellrooted in the vision shared by the "leaders" from its roots, there will be chaos in the organisation. And without true "workers" there will not be the product that makes a company recognisable and appreciated. In the case of a library, the "leaders" can be the directors of national associations or consortia as well as the local heads of the largest libraries. The "managers" are, independent of their titles, the directors or head librarians of the smaller (school, public, special, corporate) libraries or the department heads of the sizable academic libraries. And the "workers" are the beginning professional librarians, the best of the paraprofessional staff, and even the expert veterans in all sorts of specialties whether degreed or not. The relationships among all of them, their understanding of the roles they play in library organisations, and their commitment to a vital vision of the place of libraries is what makes or breaks the real and effective existence of libraries in our society.

EARLY LEADERSHIP

Leadership among Greek warriors was based upon "a first among equals" principle. Such leadership was a product of a culture of equality and mutual accountability. In a very tangible sense, cultures are networks of social relationships. Military cultures, especially in battlefield situations, have highly articulated roles and codes of conduct and mutual accountability.

Although an individual may gain prominence and status apart from a group, it is often not the result of individual achievement, but how the individual exemplifies certain traits that represent the best traits of that group, such as sacrifice, decisiveness, courage, initiative, and prowess. In fact, to attribute successes to the individual that derive from the group undermines a core principle of true leadership: the group comes before the individual.

In the following stanzas taken from Alfred Lord Tennyson's ode to Wellington, many of the qualities that continue to make leaders great are captured:

- Mourn for the man of amplest influence, Yet clearest of ambitious crime, *our greatest yet with least pretence,* Great in council and great in war, Foremost captain of his time, *rich in saving common-sence* And, as the greatest only are, In his *simp licity sublim.*
- *Who never sold the truth to serve the hour,* Nor palter'd with Eternal God for power; Who let the turbid streams of rumor flow Thro' either babbling world of high and low; Whose life was work, whose language rife *with rugged maximus hewn from life;* Who never spoke against a foe; Whose eighty winters freeze with one rebuke All great self-seekers trampling on the right. *Truth-teller was our England's Alfred named;* Truth-lover was our English Duke; Whatever record leap to light He never shall be shamed...

By embodying the best qualities of a group, a military leader does not try to elevate himself above his peers, but brings Honour and distinction to them, be they his company, brigade, division, or service. These qualities of "simplicity sublime" and "truth-teller" are parts of the best of military culture. They are hard to transfer from the field of battle into bureaucratic and administrative assignments, where often different kinds of codes of conduct are rewarded. As noted earlier, small networks of 150-200 individuals can still be coordinated by face-to-face relationships and personal codes of Honour and accountability.

At such a scale, combat relationships are more transparent and accountable, and hence, not so easily "gamed" and "politicised" as in hierarchical, formal organisations. It is not surprising that many who succeed on the battlefield fail to adjust to the rules of a bureaucratic organisation, whose codes of success are often at variance with those of the battlefield group.

In bureaucratic organisations, successful leadership can entail the subordination of the interests of the group to the promotion of the individual, as visibility to outside parties is associated with an individual leader who is *personally* credited with a certain policy or success. Under such circumstances, the leader in bureaucratic groups becomes a marker, a kind of shorthand, for the success or failure of an issue, policy, or campaign—not the exemplar of the group.

This kind of leadership can entail taking much of the credit and little of the blame, thereby undermining the very principles of transparency and accountability upon which effective peer networks depend. The systemic failure of corporate leadership and governance in the United States over the last 10 years can be partly attributed to a bureaucratic culture wherein a company's success was almost totally attributed to the skills of the CEO and senior management.

This was reflected in senior executive compensation packages that ballooned to 301 times the average worker's pay package. Yet when the downturn came, and even widespread fraudulent practices were revealed, very few corporate leaders were held accountable, and shareholders and employees assumed the bulk of the losses. These failures were neither personality - nor individually-based, but were systemic in terms of how leaders were selected, cultivated, rewarded, and held accountable. The systemic subversion of governance leadership roles needed to achieve independence, truth telling, and transparency has been its own kind of perverse "network effect." This chapter's treatment of leadership is not founded upon any "great man" leadership model.

This is not to say that individual qualities are not important, but rather that sustainable and replicable qualities of leadership are treated here as a network property, made possible by the combination of the character of the social network and the individuals themselves. Moreover, it will be argued that there are several different types of leadership roles and the relative importance and combination of these roles depends upon the circumstances and structure of the organisational networks involved.

THE CORE OF LEADERSHIP

Leadership is the art of engaging the hearts and minds of ordinary people to achieve extraordinary results. This Isn't the Company I Joined, I've been interviewing gifted leaders from a wide range of industries. Each has his or her unique corporate responsibilities to carry out. Each has to deal with widely different competitive pressures, customer demands, marketing strategies, stockholder expectations, and Workforce requirements.

Each represents an organisation that is affected in specific ways by the new global economy, the IT revolution, the disappearance of stable currency values worldwide, and the collapse of the old Industrial business paradigm as an organising model for their companies. But all share one thing in common: an apparently innate set of emotional and intellectual qualities that make up what I call the Core of Leadership.

The components of that core are:

- Vision,
- Integrity,
- Trust,
- Values,
- Vulnerability,
- Motivation.

Together they produce what we all instantly recognise as leaders. How they do it is easier to note in practice than it is to define in principle. Because we aren't just talking about special skills or strategies these people exercise, we're talking about individual character. Like the force of gravity or the lump of uranium in a nuclear generator, the leadership core works invisibly. And like any living system, it sometimes works intuitively and mysteriously. But its positive effects upon others can be readily observed, and those observations, in turn, can be put to immediate use by anyone charged with leading fellow employees at any level of an organisation.

LEADERSHIP AS VISION

In contrast to control-minded authority of the past, today's leaders must exercise power through a shared purpose and vision. An organisational vision is not the same as long-range or even strategic planning. Planning is a linear process; progression Towards a goal. Vision is more holistic — a sense of direction that combines a good business strategy with a comprehensive organisational purpose that declares its own importance.

A vision describes a business as it could become over the long term and outlines a feasible way of achieving this goal. To transform an organisation, leaders must adopt and communicate a vision of the future that impels people beyond the boundaries and limits of the past. Leaders who articulate such visions aren't mystics, but broad-based thinkers who are willing to take risks. Visionary leaders don't have to be brilliant, highly innovative, or incredibly charismatic. But they do have to be intently focused on what it is they are trying to achieve. Fred Smith, ounder and Chief Executive Officer of Federal Express, put it in these very practical terms: "If there is any indication that the leader is not totally committed to achieving the vision, then all the sweet talk in the world will not get people to support it."

LEADERSHIP AS INTEGRITY

A leader must be seen to stand for something, must act from deep-seated principles, and must rely on strong personal beliefs. Leading with integrity implies a willingness to embody the attitudes and Behaviours you want to see in employees. Steve Wikstrom is the Co-Chief Executive Officer of Reell Precision Manufacturing Corporation, a $35 million company that produces wrap spring clutches and constant torque hinges for foreign and domestic customers. "In our company we try to create relationships that allows us to 'call' one another on Behaviour that doesn't represent our values.

A recent example occurred during the development of our latest strategic plan. Every year we get the top dozen leaders together once a week, for six to eight weeks. At the end of each of the weekly sessions, we have 'homework' assignments to prepare for the next meeting. At the beginning of one session, a participant told us that at the last meeting he had offered to send us information that we had agreed to review and return with our comments.

He went on to say that of the twelve messages he sent out, only three responses had been received. He then asked all of us what we were going to do about this issue of 'irresponsibility.' The meeting stopped and we discussed how to better Honour our commitments. Right at the top of the organisation's leadership, we are aware of the need to mirror whatever Behaviour we expect to receive in kind."

LEADERSHIP AS TRUST

Until recently, managers' primary function has been supervision — telling employees what to do and measuring how well they did it. But the new breed of knowledge workers increasingly don't want or need to be micro-managed. They need to be set free in the sphere of their own authority. They need to be trusted. Trust is an attitude of confidence in another person, a positive set of expectations about that person's competencies and character.

The powerful influence of one person's expectation on another's Behaviour is known as the "Pygmalion Effect." Eliza Doolittle explains it in George Bernard Shaw's play Pygmalion: "You see, really and truly, apart from the things anyone can pick up, the difference between a lady and a flower girl is not how she behaves but how she's treated.

I shall always be a flower girl to Professor Higgins because he always treats me as a flower girl and always will; but I know I can be a lady to you because you always treat me as a lady and always will." The difference between leaders who complain about the lack of responsibility in today's employees and those who speak with pride of the creative contribution and dedication of their staff may lie in the realm of management's expectation.

LEADERSHIP AS VULNERABILITY

Recognition of the potential of the Workforce for contributing solutions to organisational problems has increased while the infallibility of leaders and the certainty of management tasks have declined. The unquestioned authority of leaders in the corporation of the past has been replaced by the need to acknowledge the expertise of those below, and to enlist employees as true partners. Moving from a model in which leadership made all the decisions and knew all the answers to an organisational environment of openness, candor, and empowerment takes a willingness by leaders to become and remain highly vulnerable.

There has never been a time in which our organisations have experienced more uncertainty and chaos. It may sound ironic, but the corporate leader who can say to his or her employees, "Sure, I'm scared too," will have done more for company morale with that single admission than a dozen phony pep talks ever could. Why? Because, as Sue Swenson, president of Leap Wireless, observes: "When leaders are perceived as human and vulnerable, employees identify with those attributes and begin to see the potential for success and leadership in themselves."

LEADERSHIP AS VALUES

Webster defines value as "a principle, standard or quality considered inherently worthwhile or desirable." The root is the Latin valor, which means strength. Values are a source of strength for an enterprise or an individual.

As leadership strategy moves from coercion to cooperation, the key to bonding people to the goals of the organisation automatically becomes the intangibles — relationships, commitments and shared values.Founding President and Chief Operating Officer of Ritz-Carlton Hotels, "Values are the heart and soul of our organisation. It is not enough for people just to fill functions. They have to know what we are all about." Leaders must stay focused on values and keep them energised — which is the hardest part.

For that, you need to find processes that renew and revitalise values. One process that Ritz-Carlton uses is called the "Line Up." Fifteen minutes before shift begins every day, the leader of the line up goes through the basics of that day. Employees of R-C all over the world are reminded of the same "value of the day," as prepared by the corporate office. Added to that is a "teaching" — an issue brought to our awareness, based on customer-service input, and then some comments about the daily value that are customised to the individual hotel.

LEADERSHIP AS MOTIVATION

The secret to being a great motivator is realising that motivation isn't something that can be forced or ordered. Motivation is an intrinsic capacity of human beings that can be tapped, nurtured, and developed — but never coerced. In essence, all motivation is self-motivation.

It manifests when leaders hold a compelling vision of the future, have a strong personal desire to realise the vision, and possess the ability to engage people's individual motivation in the common cause of that vision so that a true interconnection emerges. Motivational leaders inspire exceptional levels of commitment and performance. Prior to forming his own public relations firm, Bob Dilenschneider served as president and CEO of Hill and Knowlton.

He talked with me about his most memorable boss: "Barney Clarke, the CEO of Columbia Gas Systems, was brilliant — a genius who thought way outside the box. Although I suspect he had the answers all the time, he spent hours talking with us, involving us and making us feel as if we were an integral part of a huge change — as if we were making history.

And he got so much out of all of us. We'd work 'round the clock. Working with Barney was exciting, exhausting, incredibly intense, and absolutely thrilling.

DEVELOPMENT OF LEADERSHIP

Leadership development refers to any activity that enhances the quality of leadership within an individual or organisation. These activities have ranged from MBA style Programmes offered at university business schools to action learning, high-ropes courses and executive retreats.

DEVELOPING INDIVIDUAL LEADERS

Traditionally, leadership development has focused on developing the leadership abilities and attitudes of individuals. Just like people aren't all born with the ability to, say, play football like Zinedine Zidane or sing like Luciano Pavarotti, people aren't all born with the ability to lead. Different personal characteristics can help or hinder a person's leadership effectiveness and require formalised programmes for developing leadership competencies. Yet, everyone can develop their leadership effectiveness.

Achieving such development takes focus, practice and persistence more akin to learning a musical instrument than reading a book. Classroom-style training and associated reading is effective in helping leaders to know more about what is involved in leading well.

However, knowing what to do and doing what you know are two very different outcomes; management expert Henry Mintzberg is one person to highlight this dilemma. It is estimated that as little as 15 per cent of learning from traditional classroom style training results in sustained Behavioural change within the workplace. The success of leadership development efforts has been linked to three variables:

- Individual learner characteristics.
- The quality and nature of the leadership development Programme.
- Genuine support for behavioural change from the leader's supervisor.

Military officer training academies, such as the Royal Military Academy Sandhurst, go to great lengths to only accept candidates who show the highest potential to lead well. Personal characteristics that associated with successful leadership development include leader motivation to learn, a high achievement drive and personality traits such as openness to experience, an internal focus of control, and self-monitoring.

Development is also more likely to occur when the design of the development programme:

- Integrates a range of developmental experiences over a set period of time. These experiences may include 360 degree feedback, experiential classroom style Programmes, business school style coursework, executive coaching, reflective journaling, mentoring and more.
- Involve goal setting, following an assessment of key developmental needs and then evaluate the achievement of goals after a given time period.

DEVELOPING LEADERSHIP AT A COLLECTIVE LEVEL

More recently, organisations have come to understand that leadership can also be developed by strengthening the connection between, and alignment of, the efforts of individual leaders and the systems through which they influence organisational operations. This has led to a differentiation between leader development and leadership development. Leader development focuses on the development of the leader, such as the personal attributes desired in a leader, desired ways of behaving, ways of thinking or feeling. In contrast, leadership development focuses on the development of leadership as a process.

This will include the interpersonal relationships, social influence process, and the team dynamics between the leader and his/her team at the dyad level, the contextual factors surrounding the team such as the perception of the organisational climate and the social network linkages between the team and other groups in the organisation. One practical example of developing leadership specifically so as to influence an organisation's safety culture is described by Burman and Evans. Both forms of development may mutually influence each other, as exemplified in the concept of "Deep Change" in Robert E. Quinn 's 1996 book of the same title.

Leadership development can build on the development of individuals to become leaders. In addition, it also needs to focus on the interpersonal linkages between the individuals in the team. In the belief that the most important resource that an organisation possesses is the people that comprise the organisation, some organisations address the development of these resources. In contrast, the concept of "Employeeship" recognises that what it takes to be a good leader is not too dissimilar to what it takes to be a good employee. Therefore, bringing the notional leader together with the team to explore these similarities brings positive results. This approach has been particularly successful in Sweden where the power distance between manager and team is small.

SUCCESSION PLANNING

The development of "high potentials" to effectively take over the current leadership when their time comes to exit their positions is known. This type of leadership development usually requires the extensive transfer of an individual between departments. In many multinationals, it usually requires international transfer and experience to build a future leader. Succession planning requires a sharp focus on organisation's future and vision, in order to align leadership development with the future the firm aspires to create. Thus successive leadership development is based not only on knowledge and history but also on a dream. For such a plan to be successful, a screening of future leadership should be based not only on "what we know and have" but also on "what we aspire to become". Persons involved in succession planning should be current leadership representing the vision and HR executives having to translate it all into a Programme.

Meir Jacob and Amit Cohen three critical dimensions should be considered:

- Skills and knowledge.
- Role perception and degree of acceptance of leading role.
- Self-efficacy.

These three dimensions should be a basis of any leadership succession programme.

TYPES OF NETWORK LEADERSHIP ROLES

There are at least eight different kinds of leadership roles in a networked organisation. Each of these can be associated with specific network *signatures* consisting of patterns of links and nodes and the social rules governing their interactions. For example, some network leaders, such as visionaries, primarily generate new information and typically do not directly request others to perform tasks for them.

They generally work in conjunction with connector and facilitator leaders who help them get their information out. Connectors, unlike visionaries, may have many symmetric dyadic interactions and act as gateways for a variety of sub-networks, whereas truth-teller leaders may only interact weakly with other members, having strong ties with a relatively small number of peers. Many of these roles can coexist in the same person. However, as networks grow in scale and complexity, these roles often become highly differentiated and expressed as Searle's *institutional* facts.

The Exemplar or "Alpha Member"

Most peer networks, whether they are military, technological, recreational, adolescent, criminal, terrorist, artistic, professional, or athletic, are founded by individuals who exemplify the standards and qualities that characterise the best competencies of the peer network. These are the role models that others imitate. Sometimes their role can be simply symbolic, even ceremonial, but they are non-etheless important in setting the tone and culture of the organisation. Successful and charismatic founders of new organisations, from Bill Gates, Steve Jobs, and Sam Walton to Osama Bin Laden and Aum Shinrikyo, all embody values and personalities that become the values of their organisation. These leaders also exemplify the assessment criteria and set the standards for becoming a member of a network. In the military, each Service has its own types of exemplars: pilots and Seals for the Navy; Green Berets, and Rangers for the Army; and fighter pilots for the Air Force. These exemplars embody what is considered the most difficult and admired professional qualities that set that Service apart.

The Gatekeeper

For every network there are membership rules—criteria for being included, retained, elevated, and excluded. The gatekeeper decides who is in and who is out. In Congressional politics, the party leadership plays this role by deciding who gets what committee assignments and whose bills take precedence in a legislative agenda. This is a role that President Johnson as the former majority leader of the Senate understood brilliantly, while President Carter—an outsider, visionary, truth-teller, and moralist—never fully appreciated. In many military organisations, the drill sergeant often plays multiple leadership roles, acting as exemplars, enforcers, and gatekeepers. He weeds out recruits whom he believes fail to meet the standards of his unit. The gatekeeper role is especially important for elite units that seek to achieve a high degree of exclusivity based upon exceptional standards of excellence. Like the doorman to exclusive clubs, the gatekeeper role is a combination of truth-teller, applying the standard for admittance, and enforcer, denying admittance to those parties that fail the test.

The Visionary

The role of the visionary leader is to imagine futures, determine what is limiting about the present, and show what is possible in the future. Visionary leaders such as Steve Jobs, Winston Churchill, Walt Disney, Craig Venter, Billy

Mitchell, and Thomas Edison are a constant fount of new ideas and are "at war with the present." Many high technology startups have been founded by visionaries, but eventually end up being run by operatives or fixers.

The visionary leader imagines new possibilities, creating new institutional facts and realities, and therefore plays a critical role in moving networked organisations in new directions. This is an absolutely critical role in the start-up or crisis phase of an organisation. However, it can also be disruptive in circumstances where continuity and execution are critical to success.

Visionaries play a vital and sometimes contentious role within the military. They are often the first to see weaknesses in prevalent military doctrine, to espouse new technologies and doctrines, and therefore, to challenge current leadership and entrenched interests. Consequently, unless they are able to prove themselves within wartime, their ideas can languish for decades.

Rare are the individuals such as Lord Nelson or Napoleon, who were both visionaries and the senior commanders. In the case of Billy Mitchell, Col. John Boyd, or even Winston Churchill, it was only later in their careers that their innovations were appreciated. However, as the nature of warfare today is in constant transition with respect both to doctrine and new technologies, the visionary will have increased influence. The visionary role is best coevolved with that of the truth-teller.

The Truth-Teller

In every network organisation, someone has to keep the network honest. This entails the very challenging task of identifying free riders and cheaters. In knowledge-based organisations, it is also about ferreting out half-truths, spin, blunders, and lies. Such a leadership role can become easily compromised.

Like the accounting function in a corporation or the judicial function in the legal system, truth-tellers can lose their independence, and Hence, effectiveness. Since, these are often the first roles to go in times of stress, successful leadership is exemplified here by independence, transparency, accuracy, and candor in the face of enormous pressure. As Tennyson's ode to Wellington eloquently and astutely expresses, truth telling and resistance to the lure of fame go hand in hand and are a critical and enduring signature of effective leadership.

One of the arguments for modesty in leadership is that the lure of celebrity and its attendant rewards can compromise independence and hence, credibility. Therefore, if a leader is to be an effective truthteller, he or she must also be credible, and even the hint of self-dealing can undermine his effectiveness. The challenges are especially acute and consequential within military organisations. If credibility breaks down, trust soon becomes the next casualty, and then the overall effectiveness of the chain of command. The admonition "Don't shoot the messenger" is taken from military experience and reflects the high potential cost of reporting unwanted information. In response to such pressures, the military developed the doctrine of "ground truth" after the Vietnam War. The truth telling goal is to provide authenticated and accurate reporting of the outcomes of missions. It can take enormous courage to resist the inevitable pressures of peers and superiors to report what they want to be known, rather then the truth of the matter. Being a truth-teller can be highly unpopular and a long road to advancement.

Even highly established and previously unchallenged military institutions can come under enormous pressure for truth telling. The armed forces newspaper, *stars and stripes*, undertook its own "ground truth investigation" into morale in Iraq in 2003 and was widely censured by some members of Congress and threatened with a reduced budget for its reporting. Similarly, the success and credibility of the enquiry into the alleged tortures within Abu Ghraib and elsewhere within Iraq and Afghanistan will depend upon individuals assuming very strong truth-teller leadership roles.

The Fixer

This is an individual who knows how to get things done and measures him or herself not just by how many people they might know, but rather how they can get things done that others cannot. Such individuals are results oriented. They "know where the bodies are buried" and what "makes people tick." In politics, they are the operatives, the Mr. Fix-its. They are all about opening and closing loops—getting tasks done. In Tennyson's words, they abide by the "rugged maxims hewn from life."

They are without illusions and are inherently pragmatic. They may interact with a range of other network leaders—visionaries, truth-tellers, and connectors—but always with a concrete outcome in mind. Within the military there is the archetype of the "scrounger," an individual who is highly skilled at finding and assembling "found" materials, people, and resources to solve a variety of human and mission needs, from chocolate and silk stockings during WWII, to scrap iron as armor platting for Humvees in Iraq. Fixers are gifted improvisers, what the French call "bricolagers," who take common available materials and repurpose them into something useful.

In contrast to those who work through formal channels and depend upon approved procedures, fixers typically are "rule benders" and work through informal networks. Within the British Army during the late Victorian period, the Quartermaster was famous for the orderly but creative acquisition of supplies under the most trying and unpredictable of circumstances.

The Connector

These network leaders participate in multiple social networks, connecting not only with a large number of members, but a highly diverse number of members as well. They are known for having numerous friends, connections, and contacts—for being consummate networkers. Like the visionary leaders, they can introduce variety and options into a network through the diversity of people with whom they interact.

They are critical for identifying and accessing new resources and helping to get a message out. By building links across network boundaries, they can help a networked organisation break out of the "lock ins" of scale-free networks and introduce greater diversity, and Hence, robustness. During WWII, General Eisenhower as the Supreme Allied Commander developed a reputation as a highly accomplished connector leader by virtue of his ability to relate to the different interests and cultural styles of the allied commanders.

He was able to make and sustain connections among contending parties in order to keep the alliance together and on course. He was also able to exercise significant control over those whose primary allegiances were to different military organisations.

The Enforcer

In smaller networks, this role is often combined with that of the gatekeeper and even the truth-teller. However, in larger networks it is an independent role. Enforcement can mean physical coercion, but more often entails psychological or peer pressure.

Like the truth-teller function, independence and transparency are critical for overall network effectiveness. Clearly, force and military means are the enforcement methods of last resort, but are necessary in order to buttress other forms of enforcement, which can vary from guilt and shame to legal redress. Most networks have their own forms of redress and enforcement that entail exclusion.

The power of ostracism in Greek city-states, for example, was extremely effective because it not only removed an individual's right of protection but destroyed their social identity as well. An exceptional example of a senior commander acting to enforce discipline across all levels of command was the Duke of Wellington's order during the Peninsular Campaign in 1807. Wellington issued an order that any breach in military discipline towards the treatment of the Spanish civilians and military would result in an immediate flogging and hanging. Paul Kennedy, this order was enforced with impartiality and force and was instrumental to Wellington's success.

The Facilitator

In order for a network to grow and evolve, it must be able to add new members and reach across network boundaries in order to do so. The facilitator role is pivotal in creating communities or sub-networks that provide the greatest form of network value. By assuming a leadership role in helping others, facilitators create value that benefits an entire network or community, whereas a connector, while playing a similar value creation role, appropriates value to himself and only indirectly benefits the overall group.

The role of facilitator in many respects resembles that of the "community coordinator" in the development of communities of practice, a method developed for helping to create and leverage knowledge. Within the military, this role is filled primarily as a staff function to a commander, and therefore may not appear to have the caché of the connector or visionary leadership roles. However, in networked organisational structures where decisionmaking is be more distributed and less hierarchical, this leadership role is vital to coordinating and enabling other actors and decisionmakers.

In the case of networked organisation, the facilitator role and the associated skills of enabling cooperation and self-organisation will play a more critical role than within current hierarchical organisations. When self-synchronisation depends upon peer-based cooperation, the facilitator role is a prerequisite for effective operations.

STYLES OF LEADERSHIP

In the past several decades, management experts have undergone a revolution in how they define leadership and what their attitudes are towards it. They have gone from a very classical autocratic approach to a very creative, participative approach. Somewhere along the line, it was determined that not everything old was bad and not everything new was good. Rather, different styles were needed for different situations and each leader needed to know when to exhibit a particular approach.

Four of the most basic leadership styles are:

- Autocratic,
- Bureaucratic,
- Laissez-faire,
- Democratic.

Autocratic Leadership Style

This is often considered the classical approach. It is one in which the manager retains as much power and decision-making authority as possible. The manager does not consult employees, nor are they allowed to give any input. Employees are expected to obey orders without receiving any explanations.

The motivation environment is produced by creating a structured set of rewards and punishments. This leadership style has been greatly criticised during the past 30 years. Some studies say that organisations with many autocratic leaders have higher turnover and absenteeism than other organisations. Certainly Gen X employees have proven to be highly resistant to this management style.

These studies say that autocratic leaders:

- Rely on threats and punishment to influence employees.
- Do not trust employees.
- Do not allow for employee input.

Yet, autocratic leadership is not all bad. Sometimes it is the most effective style to use. These situations can include:

- New, untrained employees who do not know which tasks to perform or which procedures to follow.
- Effective supervision can be provided only through detailed orders and instructions.
- Employees do not respond to any other leadership style.
- There are high-volume production needs on a daily basis.
- There is limited time in which to make a decision.
- A manager's power is challenged by an employee.
- The area was poorly managed.
- Work needs to be coordinated with another department or organisation.

The autocratic leadership style should not be used when:

- Employees become tense, fearful, or resentful.
- Employees expect to have their opinions heard.
- Employees begin depending on their manager to make all their decisions.
- There is low employee morale, high turnover and absenteeism and work stoppage.

Bureaucratic Leadership Style

Bureaucratic leadership is where the manager manages "by the book" Everything must be done according to procedure or policy. This manager is really more of a police officer than a leader. He or she enforces the rules.

This style can be effective when:

- Employees are performing routine tasks over and over.
- Employees need to understand certain standards or procedures.
- Employees are working with dangerous or delicate equipment that requires a definite set of procedures to operate.
- Safety or security training.
- Is being conducted.
- Employees are performing tasks that require handling cash.

This style is ineffective when:

- Work habits form that are hard to break, especially if they are no longer useful.
- Employees lose their interest in their jobs and in their fellow workers.
- Employees do only what is expected of them and no more.

Democratic Leadership Style

The democratic leadership style is also called the participative style as it encourages employees to be a part of the decision making. The democratic manager keeps his or her employees informed about everything that affects their work and shares decision making and problem solving responsibilities. This style requires the leader to be a coach who has the final say, but gathers information from staff members before making a decision. Democratic leadership can produce high quality and high quantity work for long periods of time. Many employees like the trust they receive and respond with cooperation, team spirit, and high morale.

Typically the democratic leader:

- Develops plans to help employees evaluate their own performance.
- Allows employees to establish goals.
- Encourages employees to grow on the job and be promoted.
- Recognises and encourages achievement.

Like the other styles, the democratic style is not always appropriate. It is most successful when used with highly skilled or experienced employees or when implementing operational changes or resolving individual or group problems. The democratic leadership style is most effective when:

- The leader wants to keep employees informed about matters that affect them.
- The leader wants employees to share in decision-making and problem-solving duties.
- The leader wants to provide opportunities for employees to develop a high sense of personal growth and job satisfaction.
- There is a large or complex problem that requires lots of input to solve.
- Changes must be made or problems solved that affect employees or groups of employees.
- You want to encourage team building and participation.

Democratic leadership should not be used when:

- There is not enough time to get everyone's input.
- It's easier and more cost-effective for the manager to make the decision.
- The business can't afford mistakes.
- The manager feels threatened by this type of leadership.
- Employee safety is a critical concern.

Laissez-Faire Leadership Style

The laissez-faire leadership style is also known as the "hands-off" style. It is one in which the manager provides little or no direction and gives employees as much freedom as possible.

All authority or power is given to the employees and they must determine goals, make decisions, and resolve problems on their own.

This is an effective style to use when:

- Employees are highly skilled, experienced, and educate.
- Employees have pride in their work and the drive to do it successfully on their own.
- Outside experts, such as staff specialists or consultants are being used and,
- Employees are trustworthy and experienced.

This style should not be used when:

- It makes employees feel insecure at the unavailability of a manager.
- The manager cannot provide regular feedback to let employees know how well they are doing.
- Managers are unable to thank employees for their good work.
- The manager doesn't understand his or her responsibilities and is hoping the employees can cover for him or her.

VARYING LEADERSHIP STYLE

While the proper leadership style depends on the situation, there are three other factors.

That also influence which leadership style to use:

- The manager's personal background. What personality, knowledge, values, ethics, and experiences does the manager have. What does he or she think will work?
- The employees being supervised. Employees are individuals with different personalities and backgrounds. The leadership style managers use will vary depending upon the individual employee and what he or she will respond best to.
- The company. The traditions, values, philosophy, and concerns of the company will influence how a manager acts.

LEADERSHIP AND SERVICE PROVISION IN PUBLIC LIBRARIES

In USA and Western Europe, we do witness the same types of developments in public libraries and we see very similar themes of discourses independent of the national and local culture in which these libraries operate. Some of the themes concern the manage-ment structure and organisation bur more important is probably the current think about service delivery in a broad sense. Service delivery concerns the activities. It is areas like collection and collection management, the allocation of resources to the different part of the collection, the interplay and relationship between national internet-based delivery and the local service.

Another important theme is the effort concerning the public library and its integration into the community taking up different forms of citizen services, cooperation and partnership with the local community, but also a focus on playing a new and more active role in the cultural scene by for example emphasising learning activities, lifelong learning, internet courses and different forms for events and exhibitions. The ambition is to become a local meeting place, a third room; a common intended to generate social capital.

This discourse and many of the activities resulting from it like 23 thinks, the libraries in the second world and experiments with various forms of social technology appear to have great appeal in the library profession. However, both library statistics and numerous studies of users and their preferences give a more differentiated picture. In most countries, the public libraries face economic hardship. They witness stagnating or decreasing numbers of visitors and the issues of traditional materials also tend to decrease. The public appear to value especially the services and products that suffer due to economic pressures and the internal priority setting in libraries.

Overall, it appears—at least at the surface–that users do have a rather traditional view of the public library and their stated preferences also seems to be very traditional as they are oriented towards books and information and to a lesser degree towards new services and delivery forms. It is of course of paramount interest to investigate possible discrepancies between the discourse and the practices in the professions and the users' preferences, priorities and level of satisfaction.

There is probably no right solution to the problem, but it is of both a practical and theoretical significance to investigate which factors influence the development of the discourse and the activities in the professions and in the public libraries and is also important to be able to measure users perception of the significance and importance of the service delivery and to which degree this is connected with measures of satisfaction. The paper further discusses the factors behind the profession's discourse and practices.

The concept of an organisational recipe is introduced in relation to organisational culture as two factors that have influence on the way libraries tend to adopt different forms of innovations. Of course, leadership plays an important role and the keynote also introduces measures of the personality traits of library directors and discusses this in relation to the innovation and development process but also in relation to the 'sense' or construction the profession is creating of the user.

This paper departs from 2 different theoretical perspectives of pertinent interest for management of institutions. One of the perspectives is concerned with the question about how manage-ment information and management recipes are adopted and interpreted in organisations like libraries. The other perspective concerns the role of the directors' personality in this context especially how they acquire management information and how they value and use management information in relation to organisational change processes. This paper is built on several studies into leadership in libraries in Denmark and United Kingdom. The paper also builds on several user studies.

LEADERSHIP AND PERSONALITY

During the last couple of years, the interest in leadership and management topics has increased very much. This is also the case in library and information science. It is due to the very fundamental changes that takes place overall in the public sector. Many of these changes are connected to requirements concerning accountability, user orientation, outsourcing, quality, information technology and staff-related issues. It is a widespread notion that the requirements in relation to leadership and management have become much more complex.

The complexity is connected to environmental turbulence, change processes and to the amount of vast information that leaders need to deal with. Information in the form of management tools or recipes is one way to confront the organisational problems arising from the changes. Leadership is an important element in the configuration of organisational culture and both leadership styles and the leaders approach to innovation, change, and competency development are of importance in relation to the directions of the organisation. Leaders are both part of an organisational culture but they also have the possibility to be change agents in relation to the culture. The relationship between leadership priorities and organisational culture are important.

One can argue an interesting relationship between the directors' personality and preferences and the direction and change processes in libraries and this is exactly the focus for this paper. The Revised NEO- Personality Inventory is one of the most widespread personality tests based on the Five-Factor model and it was employed in this investigation. Besides allowing for both a general and detailed description of personality, the test is also build up in such a way that it takes into consideration the characteristics of the specific test-person in focus. Specific norms for groups of people and profiles have been developed from research to help validate the testresult.

The NEO--PI-R measures five broad personality factors. Each of these is a summary and an average of six facets. Each of the five factors and their associated 6 facets is measured through 48 statements, implying that all 30 facets are measured through 240 statements. The result of the 240 statements is distributed into low and high scores on the 5 factors and the 30 facets, hence demonstrating a personality profile. As suggested, now turn to a short profiling of the 8 library directors.

The profiles of the directors as a whole are very congruent with modern expectations of leaders and managers. They tend to possess emotional stability. They are extroverted and open to change. They all score high on the facet assertiveness. They score high on conscientiousness. Overall, the profiles of the library directors appear to be very far away from the traditional stereotypes of librarians as shy, introverted, a bit oldfashioned, nervous and timid.

The factor named openness is often considered as an important factor in relation to chance processes and it is clear that all directors except one scores high on this factor. One director is distinct from the others, scoring rather low. It is director B that scores low on 3 of the 6 facets. What is more interesting is probably that all directors score high on some of the more important facets related to get things done. All score from middle to very high on actions, ideas and values indicating openness to new ideas.

Common for all the directors have been the fact that they have been involved in change processes. These change processes have focused on both the provision of services and on organis-ational development implementing more flexible and democratic structures. They have all succeeded to change the libraries both internally and in relation to the users. One of the reasons that change processes have been successful overall can possibly be attributed to the assertiveness of the directors, their overall openness to experience and change and their general high degree of conscientiousness. The organisational culture is a very important mediating factor both in relation to how information in the form of recipes are adopted and translated both also in relation to the actual possibilities the director possess for implementing change. But the style of change management varies. This can be partly explained by situational factors like the local political climate, restrictions due to the building and economy, the organisational culture and other important factors.

The relevant facets or traits that relates to interpretation and adoption of new standards are some of the traits that relate to the factors named openness and conscientiousness. The facets under openness can possibly give an indication of how willing the director is to seek and implement new recipes in the organisation and the facets related to conscientiousness can indicate how through the process of implementation is conducted. These facets will also relate to the directors' sense of the usefulness of own participating in leadership courses and development. We emphasise that it is broad hypotheses. Another more general aspect is how the directors value innovations or changes. A comparison of D with H indicates the usefulness of analysing behaviour using all the facets and not only the factors. It is evident that the profile of H indicates a person oriented towards actions and change. H also possesses a high degree of impulsiveness and a middle orientation towards ideas. H is more of a doer than a thinker and this is also the way H comes forward in the interview and in interviews with the staff.

Things must happen and failures—both own and staff failures—are accepted as inevitable. Some of the change processes are conducted nearly on the spot and many traditional activities are set in motion. In some ways, the change processes runs in a very goal directed manner but there is a high degree of acceptance of a chaotic nature of some of these processes that involves staff very much because the director delegates much based on both trust and on a disposition to take up new challenges.

The change processes that have taken place in D's library are conducted in a very different way. They are just as goal directed and strategic but they are much slower and much more deliberated and it is evident that the D places a very high value on bringing the staff along. The disposition for activity seeking is much less here than in relation to H. It results in a 'flavour' of the library as a bit more old-fashioned and a bit slower or a bit more cautious in change processes.

The implicit formulated hypotheses about the relationship between personality traits and profiles indicated that the director's openness to especially intellectual experiences or practical innovations and changes influenced the process of implementation of both structures and processes of competences. It also influenced the way the recipes and standards were conceptualised in the organisation. The integration of the recipes was influenced by the perseverance of the director with cultural factors as a mediating factor.

DISCOURSES AND ORGANISATIONAL RECIPES

These figures contrast to a certain degree to the dominant discourses in the public library profession. The dominant discourses are concerned with modern topics and issues like library as a place and libraries as generators of social capital and societal trust on a more general level. In relation to services the emphasis in the discourses are on issues like lifelong learning, information literacies and integration of the physical library into the digital services. The discourse also contains strong elements of the need for permanent change for example in relation to continuing professional development.

There is also much debate on phenomena like 23 things, facebook and other digital services. A discourse is characterised by dominant themes but is also delimited by themes that do not occur and these absent themes signifies the themes in the discourse. In the 80'ies and 90'ies, the library profession had focus on collections and collection management and especially the concept of immediate availability was a central topic.

Today, these themes of discussion are missing from the professional debate. There existed also a rather interesting debate or discourse concerning the proper relationship between supply and demand in relation to the collection. It is interesting that these topics seldom are covered in the present discussion because the different digital possibilities emphasise new turns of these central concepts. Just to give a few hopefully illuminating examples one can ask questions about the links on libraries' web sites and enquire if a link is part of the collection or not.

The answer to that question is interesting because if the answer is yes it follows that the libraries have the responsibility for dead links and for the misinformation contained in some of the links. Another interesting question is the transformation of topical needs into specific needs due to the way people search the digital databases. Librarians are not discussing the increase in the selling of books and the reasons behind this interesting fact. Is it because of an increasing affluence in society or is it because of a want for instant gratification?

Many of the elements in a given dominant discourse relates to organisational recipes or standards. A recipe or a standard that becomes a trend has the following characteristics: It often originates in an academic setting but very often it is created in cooperation with the professional world—be it libraries or business. It is blueprinted by leading members of the academic and professional communities and it is taken up also by the consultancy industry.

Prestigious firm and companies use it. The recipe incorporates the promise to solve serious problems in the companies and in the institutions they are interesting to work with. They are marketed and they are frameworks for actions but most of all they are interpretable meaning that institutions can adopt them, change them according to the national and organisational culture. They are very often connected to stories of success and the story behind the recipe often takes the form of a drama.

Successful recipes tend to hit a trend in the time and use this as a kind of vehicle for its travel across boundaries and cultures. Some recipes like the balanced scorecard have a rather long life. Other—not as successful like for example business process re-engineering—have a shorter lifespan. It does not mean that they are not used. It could mean that they are incorporated in the organisational operations but people have stopped talking about it.

Finally, all recipes have dimensions of both content and symbolic aspects. It is of course extremely interesting which recipes become dominating themes in the discourse of a profession. It is also of huge interest which recipes a given profession does not include in its arsenal of themes in the discourse. There is no doubt that the profession as a whole has a very determined focus on change and the need for change. The catch phrase that the libraries stand on a burning platform has been brought forward several times in the discourse and this catchphrase has been used as a kind of rationale for changes. This is of course the consequence of a special or peculiar interpretation of the environment. However, there is no doubt that the ideology of change and the need for change is deeply integrated in the professional identity of public librarians and leaders in the public libraries. It is an interesting question if the interpretation of the environment is in accordance with other indicators of changes in the environment.

USERS AND PREFERENCES

One aspect of organisational effectiveness is a system's ability to cope with users and non-users expectations and needs enabling the system to deliver services appropriate to satisfy needs and expectations. Organisational effectiveness has been one of the ultimate goals and objectives for the performance measurements endeavours for many years. Organisational effectiveness is related to processes, products or services and the customer or the user and it is normally seen as an important element in the quality of a service. The importance or significance for the users of the single services is of course a very important element for the libraries' planning process and assessment of how to proceed.

Libqual is a measurement instrument that is often used for this kind of investigation as it specifies the minimal level of service people would like. However, Libqual has not been employed in these surveys. We have simply asked people to attach the significance or importance for themselves on different services. The end result is a kind of ranking that probably is rather robust. The importance or significance is calculated on a scale from 0 to 100 and it forms the basis of the ranking. The ranking of the importance or the perception of the significance of the public libraries' services follows:

Table. The Users' Perception of the Significance of Different Services in Two Surveys.

	High School	Rank	Aarhus	Rank
A kind and polite service	72	1	90	2
Distance to the library	67	2	91	1
Ambience	64	3	84	3
Collection of non-fiction	62	4	66	5
Quite and peaceful place in the library	59	5	65	6
Collection of fiction	55	6	78	4
Places for relaxation	43	7	51	8
Collection of music	41	8	46	10
Wireless network	40	9	21	14
Collection of film	37	10	47	9
Group work facilities	35	11	15	15
Computers	34	12	28	12
The Library's homepage	34	13	63	7
Study places	33	14	21	14
Exhibitions, lessons	28	15	45	11
N	978		243	

Translated into normal text, one can say that the high school students and the 'traditional public library users' prefer a kind and polite service in nice quite rooms in library with ambience not too far away and filled with books. There are differences between the preferences and significance attached to services among the two groups but rank correlation analysis shows a Spearmans Rho of

0,81 which indicate a very high degree of similarity in ranking the services. The ranking between the two groups are more or less similar, but there appears to be differences in the importance attached to the service.

One explanation for this discrepancy is simple and it is, that the group of high schools students consists of students relying heavily on public libraries and groups or segments that rarely, seldom or never use the public library. This composition of the total group tends to decrease the average figures. In comparison, the respondents from the Aarhus group were all public library users. In the 2006 investigation in Furesoe, we also asked questions about preferences and significance, but we employed a measure-ment tool based on forced pair-wise ranking.

It is impossible to make a direct comparison, but one can look at the trends and compare these with caution. The most striking feature of the answers to this question is the similarity in preferences. The respondents were asked on a forced scale where they had to prioritise alternatives. Overall, the users preferred present openings hours more than longer opening hours with less staff service. The preferred more books in favour of longer opening hours or music.

The preferred more film than more music. They preferred a broader range of literature more than additional copies of the popular books. We did not find any differences in pair-wise preferences in relation fiction versus non–fiction, computers versus more reading places or more reading places versus more places for relaxation or social interaction. The conclusion is that users–even the young age group—want more documents. It is a very clear first priority.

We do see that this priority and preference increase with age, but it is still a very striking result that young people that rely heavily on and use the library's collection of film and music much prioritise books and documents more if they had to choose. The preferences and the prioritising are probably an expression of the perception of what a public library is—and ought to be. It is obvious that the structure of preferences in relation to public libraries is rather traditional. The nationwide study of high school students also showed some interesting features of the significance they attached to the services in relation to different demographic factors.

First of all, there appears to be differences in perceptions of significance and importance dependent on the type of high school. There are 3 types of high schools in the country. The general high school is the classic one. In the table it is called G. There is also a high school oriented towards business topics called B and at last a technical high school called T.

The general picture is that the high school students from the general school place more significance on most of the library services than students from the other two hig schools do. We also notice marked differences between male and female high school students. Female high school students tend to value the collection of fiction an non- fiction much more than the male students. It is also interesting to note that the students through their study process tend to place less significance to the library as a place to be and work in.

Table. The Students' Perceptions of the Importance of Services and Facilities in Relation to Demographics.

Type	High School			Gender		Study Year		
	G	B	T	Female	Male	1	2	3
A kind and polite service	77	69	63	76	66			
Distance to the library	74	61	61	72	61			
Ambience	68	61	59	67	60			
Collection of non-fiction	70	54	52	66	56	56	61	68
Quite and peaceful places in the library	63	55	51					
Collection of fiction	61	49	49	63	44			
Places for relaxation						49	44	36
Collection of music						45	36	38
Wireless network						45	40	35
Collection of film Group work facilities						41	35	28
Computers				32	37			
The Library's homepage	37	28	33			28	36	37
Study places						38	30	29
Exhibitions, lessons								

However, overall the ranking of the single services is not hugely affected by this segmentation, but the segmentation indicates that the different groups have very different preferences and strength of preferences attached to the single services.

MANAGING A LIBRARY

One of the most important aspects of adult learning. It explains that libraries in adult education set-ups have an important role to play in facilitating access to information for learning, education and training. They also play important role in supporting research programmes of adult education set-ups as well as their outreach programmes designed to educate and inform adult user groups on social, economic and educational issues, and problems.

Another role of libraries is to raise awareness about economic opportunities available in the marketplace. Like any other library in academic set-up or research institutions, adult education libraries have also to be planned, organised and managed using standard management principles and standard library procedures and techniques for access and retrieval. These issues and provides PALDIN learners with very useful skills to perform their tasks better. Besides enabling physical access to collections, libraries have to be organised for rendering information services such as instructions in the use of library catalogue and reading materials, reference service, information dissemination, etc.

LIBRARY OBJECTIVES

Strategic planning and development of a library is guided mainly by the goals and objectives of the parent institution of which the library is a part. In any given adult education set-up, you could frame library objectives along the following lines:

- Facilitate access to information for knowledge, education, and learning;
- Support research activities and programmes of the set-up by offering proactive information services;
- Support outreach programmes of the adult education set-up, designed to educate and inform adult user groups on social, economic and educational issues, problems, and opportunities of interest them;
- Offer proactive services for effective use of all types of library materials;
- Store and preserve information of archival nature such as local traditions, customs, and locally generated process documentation reports, etc; and
- Use library as the platform for social, economic, and cultural development of the target communities.

HOW TO MANAGE A LIBRARY

Library management involves functions such as planning, organising, leading, and controlling. Planning is about systematically making decisions about the library goals. Organising is about assembling and coordinating human, financial, physical, informational, and other resources needed to achieve library goals. Leading is about functions that involve efforts on the part of the librarian to stimulate high performance by employees, and controlling about monitoring various library operations and services.

These four management functions are highly integrated, but libraries that excel in organising material resources and in leading their human capital are known to give better performance.

Keeping in view the fact that libraries in adult education set ups are, by design, small budget libraries, confined to one room space, and adult education staff manages them manually on part time basis, these four management functions would occur in varying degree. In such a typical set up, the functions of organising and controlling would receive greater attention compared to other two functions. For managing a library you may take the following step-by-step approach:

- Step 1: Defining library policies for collection development.
- Step 2: Defining library authority and library advisory committee.
- Step 3: Define procedures for library organisation and administration.
- Step 4: Defining library space, equipment and tools for library operations and services.
- Step 5: Defining procedures for maintenance of library collections.

STEP 1: LIBRARY POLICIES FOR COLLECTION DEVELOPMENT

Step 1 includes the following task:

- *Define the Objectives of your Library:* State clearly the purpose of its existence;
- *Define your User Community and their Information Needs:* This requires complete knowledge and understanding about library stakeholders. This may include adult education teams, extension workers and adult education professionals, local community members and those who provide funds for the library. Their information needs can be assessed through library surveys, personal interviews, and informal discussions with all stakeholders;
- *Define Library Policy for Building Collections:* The policy states the guiding principles and procedures under which collection development activities, including the selection, maintenance, and weeding of print, electronic, and media library materials will occur. This would also mean specifying subject areas of interest to library stakeholders, their languages preferences, and formats of published and unpublished material.

  Non-print material could include films, slides, transparencies, photographs, maps posters, charts, etc. The policy must also define the limits in terms of collection size, keeping in view the users strength in a given subject, space available within the library premises, and annual budget earmarked for the purpose. The policy may also specify the subject areas in which the library is going build its archival collection, if any. Such a policy statement on the part of the library ensures continuity and consistency in selection and revision of materials for the library collections;
- *Define what Different Collections are Required to be Developed and Sustained Keeping in View Users' Information Needs:* The possible options include books collection, reports collection, pamphlet collection, multimedia collection, and reference collection (comprising dictionaries, yearbooks, directories, who's who almanacs, general and subject encyclopaedias), etc. The library may decide on developing some of these collections keeping in view the users' information needs.

- *Define your Book Selection Policy:* State the distribution of library budget by subject and by collection. The policy may also state guidelines for acquiring multiple copies of books, guidelines for accepting books from donors, and guidelines for weeding out material.

STEP 2: LIBRARY AUTHORITY AND LIBRARY ADVISORY COMMITTEE

Libraries in adult education setups are, by design, small budget libraries, confined to one room space, and managed manually on part time basis by adult education staff. The person incharge of the library should be the library authority, responsible for organisation and management of the library. He/she should play a dominant role in decision making, should enjoy the authority to communicate freely with groups across the organisation, and enjoy financial and administrative powers for managing library operations and services smoothly.

The financial and administrative limits of the library authority should correspond to staff of equivalent status in the organisational hierarchy. The library authority should be reporting to the top management in the organisation. There is a need to set up a Library Advisory Committee, which would perform the role of advising the library on its growth and development. It will also act as interface between the library management and the top management in the organisation and between the users groups, for ensuring smooth functioning of the library operations and services without compromising on policies set out for library development. The Committee should comprise members mainly drawn from the organisation, and representing various user groups on the Committee.

Its terms of reference could be worked out on the following lines:

- To formulate policy for developing library resources for reading, reference and projects;
- To develop a general programme of library services to suit the interests and requirements of different categories of users;
- To frame, review and approve library rules;
- To recommend suitable budgetary provisions for the library and resource centre;
- To make recommendations for proper functioning of library as knowledge centre.

STEP 3: PROCEDURES FOR LIBRARY ORGANISATION AND ADMINISTRATION

In any larger set up, library organisation tasks involve assembling, forming logical units of works, defining hierarchical structures, identifying staffing requirements, assigning tasks and responsibilities, coordinating human, financial, physical, informational, and other resources needed to achieve library goals. Administration is another activity required to be undertaken for performance and achieving library goals. It is defined as the process of getting things done through men and materials within the organisational framework.

Library organisation and library administration are closely related to each other. The distinction between the two is very subtle. Organisation comes before administration. The latter starts when the organisation ends. One lays down theoretical principles, whilst the other puts those principles into practice. In the adult education set up, wherein libraries by design are small and are going to be managed on part time basis by adult education staff, not much needs to be done in so far as library organisation is concerned.

In such flat hierarchical structures, the staff has no option but to perform multitasking operations such as administration, technical functions, service support, and library maintenance. For effective performance, it is advisable for the library to opt for outsourcing of library maintenance operations such as stack maintenance, catalogue card maintenance, photocopy services, library up keep, stock verification, gate security, etc. It may also consider outsourcing classification and cataloguing operations if circumstances so warrant.

The libraries in adult education set ups need to undertake planning activities such as strategic planning (*i.e.* identifying library goals, objectives, methods, resources needed to carry out methods, responsibilities and dates for completion of tasks), budget planning (for document collections, library equipments, library furniture, library stationery, media library equipments, if planning for a multi-media library), and library promotion planning. These are not perennial activities and are required to be undertaken once in year.

The extent of budget planning activities would depend upon the size of adult education programmes, network linkages, and staff deployed within the organisation, etc. For building a library from the scratch, it must begin with a small annual budget of ₹100,000/-during the first three years. In the subsequent years, budget requirements may be reviewed and decided based on collection already built and actual requirements. It is a good practice to undertake budget planning exercise in consultation with the Library Advisory Committee for developing collections, library equipments, library furniture, media equipments, etc. It is also a good practice to formulate library plans for promoting and popularizing library services.

STEP 4: LIBRARY SPACE, EQUIPMENT AND TOOLS FOR LIBRARY OPERATIONS AND SERVICES

Bureau of Indian Standards provides that a library should have a stack room, a Librarian's room and a Reading Room having seating capacity of 40 to 120 chairs. The stack room should be big enough to accommodate between 6,000 and 10,000 books. The library-in-charge would need to plan actual library size and seating capacity of 'reading room' keeping in view the optimum number of members in an adult education setup, the variety of library services it is planning to offer, and the members of the adult community who would be coming to visit the library for social interactions. The library equipments and tools like furniture, fittings and accessories should of standard pattern and design, so that users feel comfortable in using them.

The following is the list of essential furniture and fittings for an adult education set up:

- Reading tables,
- Chairs for pupils,
- Librarian's table,
- Circulation or charging desk and chair,
- Librarian's shelf list trays,
- Card catalogue trays,
- Card catalogue cabinet,
- Bulletin board and notice board,
- Book supporters,
- New arrivals display case,
- Dictionary stands,
- Periodicals display stand,
- Newspaper display stand,
- Storage cabinet for work room,
- Filing cabinets,
- Atlas stand,
- Wall clock.

Besides, the library may acquire radio and television set, tape recorder/ player, VCR and VCP, slide and film projector, overhead projectors, computers with internet connection, Xerox machine, etc.

STEP 5: PROCEDURES FOR MAINTENANCE OF LIBRARY COLLECTIONS

You will find that the following procedures help in maintenance of library collections.

Preservation of Library Material

Proper care of library collections is necessary with a view to prolong its life. This requires preserving and protecting books against decay and deterioration. As preventive measures, dusting and cleaning of books and shelves must be carried out on regular basis. Books must be exposed to adequate air and sunlight for a short time in case the library room does not get sufficient sunlight. Avoid keeping books is in damp places. Pest control treatment may be got done on periodic basis. Books and other reading material may be got bound from time to time. Besides, book supporters may be used to keep books upright on the shelves. Reference books such as dictionaries, encyclopaedias, directories and picture books are costly and heavy in weight. They must be handled with care.

Organising Reading Materials on Shelves and Their Rectification

Normally, books and other reading display of new books and other reading material received in the library, preparing stack room guides, and shelving volumes returned after use, etc. Library may also perform stock verification on periodical basis, with a view to weed out books, as per its policy, and writing off books, etc.

THE QUALITY OF INFORMATION AS BASIS OF THE LIBRARY MANAGEMENT QUALITY

A great number of scientific, reference, educational, methodical and practical publications is devoted to the quality of library activity in Russia. One of the most characteristic tendencies is the active interest to management, especially quality manage-ment that explains the fact of formation of new management concept in the sphere of library science. Modern management researches show a great significance of rational information processing for achieving strategic and operative aims. The quality of information defines the quality of management because information covers all spheres of management.

Being the most important function of management process, information must meet the following requirements: authenticity, accuracy and completeness, efficiency and regularity, its conformity with management level. Management of documen-tation as function of management is realised in the conditions of decision making process to achieve the aim. That is why documen-tation management is closely connected with the problems of management, organisation structures, the problems of design of information systems management, their implementation and operation, with automation of managerial procedures and processes.

Urgency of the problem consists in support of the processes of documentation information management due to more effective technologies of its processing including analytical components and the connection of management functions with documents, their servicing. The development of new management technologies plans systematic approach to the decision making process on the base of flexible information analytical integrated management system.

DOCUMENTS MANAGEMENT

The organisation of work with documents is a very important part of management processes and taking managerial decisions influencing efficiency and management quality. From the point of view of information technologies documentation information management activity and the management activity itself—as a subsystem of an integrated technological system of library. So, the library management is characterised as technological process that supposes regularity of management. In management activity a document is a tool, means or method of management. The whole documentation is closely connected with the concrete management function for which it is created. It allows, in Larin's opinion with the help of systematic analysis to identify the content of managerial documents and to connect it with the definite management function.

Optimal system of internal legal regulation helps to provide successfully and realise substantially the local legal regulation of general principles of activity, some decisions and concrete aspects of library operation. The complex of internal regulated documents, being formed in each library objectively consists of a package of separate interrelated and mutually complementary blocks. The documents, included, reflect legal organisational and technological sides of professional activity, fix aims, order and conditions of library functioning as informational, educational and cultural institution.

Pilko suggests to classify the complex of documents regulating the activity of the library for convenience according to the following functions: organisational—administrative documen-tation, scientific—methodical documentation, normative documen-tation and technological documentation. At the present stage in the system of library management the whole range of documents concerning different types and kinds of documentation systems and being a part of documentation support of management.

INFORMATION MANAGEMENT SYSTEM

The use of information technologies in the sphere of management gives opportunities of more effective and rational organisation of information processes, increase of their flexibility and dynamics expansion of the range of analysed factors when making decisions. 'Perfect' information system of management must automate all or the majority of protective kinds of activity in the frames of integrated information space and in interrelation of automated functions. It is more optimal to use the system which is the part of the architecture of the system of complex library automation that implies the use of joint technologies of management automation and documents circulation.

The creation of the system of automated management of documents or service database in the library is a very complicated organisational technical task, administrative office automation being the main, basic platform within information library system. Designing database, one should orient on the use of standard management system of data and technology 'client–server' which allows to combine operative work with archiving documents. Automated system in the library:

- Provides coordinated work of all departments;
- Simplifies work with documents, increases its effectiveness;

- Increases labour efficiency due to shortening time for creation, documents processing and search;
- Increases efficiency of access to information;
- Allows to delimit the competence of access of workers to information.

The implementation of such system in the library will optimize the activity of the library in whole, to get analytical information for using and taking important managerial decisions. Without any doubts, the system will influence on effectiveness of library activity as well as on increase of professional personnel training, the culture of the use of modern information technologies.

DATABASE OF REGULATING DOCUMENTATION

For solving intersystem tasks of the library one can suggest the module of service database of regulated documentation as foundation of effective library management. Designing technological project of database we relied on methodical basis and regulations considered by Pilko and Voroisky. The main source when forming database is regulated documents of library.

Database supports the main functions of documents processing on-line which include: documents development and custody; search of documents according to different parameters, input, support and custody of any kind of documents; control over implementation of documents; protection and management of separation of rights for access.

Database includes the complex of functional means realised as a programme modules helping to plan work, to get interim and resort valuation of separate operations, to control and, if necessary, to correct the plan or process. The idea of centralised storage of e-documents is also obvious: integrated database in server keeps documents safely, systematizes them and finds necessary information very quickly. Not the least of the features of the system is unification of the most widespread types and kinds of documents in management, development and use of patterns.

Database is corporate storage of regulating documents of the library. In includes the catalogue of organisational efficient, regulatory–methodical and technological documentation, unified forms of documents, documents archive, office documents of departments or separate workers. Through interface of database, installed in all computers, the workers of the library get access to hierarchy of folders and operations concerning design and search of documents. The search of documents is realised through folders navigation.

Creating a new document a database offers users to identify its belonging to concrete theme by classifier and to use standard sheet, pattern. Information, formed by users in the process of selecting data, is displayed as a reference in matrix format, graphic material, fulltext document or pattern. Different functional and practical tasks are solved by the method of contiguous look of database modules and data selection or seriating. The tasks can be operational analysis of technological processes; valuation of resort support of processes; valuation of work content of library production.

Managers of a library, having full access to all documents, can control the process of creating office documents any time. The analysis of report documents formed in database, gives opportunity to correct the library activity, to improve organisational structure, character and content of implemented works, personnel, provision with financial, material and other resources.

2

Leadership in the Library and Information Network

ANTECEDENTS

The subject of leadership has been described as a very imperative one that can never be over-flogged in management research. More imperative is the relevance of the theme in library and information management profession. While literature abound on the topic in management research, books on the subject as it relates to the library and information services are still terse. Western researchers even affirmed this and noted that not until the recent times that we have journal articles and short communications on the subject in LIS literature. General observation revealed that formal leadership training, if not totally absent in our library and information establishments, is very scarce.

EXIGENCIES

There is concern within the library profession that we are short of leaders. Why is this such a common lament. Those of us who are responsible for recruitment in our organisations often get together to scratch our heads and complain about the apparent lack of colleagues within the profession who will take up leadership roles. Why is this? The quote simply leads us to the first statement of exigency that:

There is a dearth of library and information profession leaders.

Of course, leadership is also hard work – managing, persuading, motivating, inspiring others is not easy, although it can definitely be rewarding. I suspect many people are scared off by what is required. The second statement of exigency is that:

Leadership qualities, skills, and competencies are hard to come by.

One theory is that the typical value set of those who work in libraries are not compatible with managing people or managing physical resources such as budgets, or operating confidently in a political and business environment. Some blame the library qualification providers for not attracting the right people. The third statement of exigency is that:

Even if people are not born leaders, the library and information schools should do better in teaching leadership skills to prospective library and information practitioners.

Librarianship as a profession has entered an area where its workforce is ageing and its leadership is becoming more "graying".

Fifty eight percent of librarians in the U.S. are projected to reach the retirement age of 65 between 2005 and 2019 and forty percent of library directors plan to retire in less than nine years. There is also an international trend of graying.

In Australia, over 52 per cent of librarians are currently more than 45 years old. If they retire, at the age of 60, then about half of the population of Australian librarians are expected to retire within the next 10 to 15 years. The fourth statement of exigency as derived from the above is that:

The library and information system need succession planning – Hence, the need for leaders.

To meet the demands of today's fast-paced and competitive business environment, people at all levels are being asked to step up and assume leadership behaviours... companies are investing millions of dollars annually in leadership development training to meet this challenge. The fifth statement of exigency is that:

The library and information system profession should take a cue from the business and corporate world by having leadership development agenda.

THEORIES OF LEADERSHIP

Students of leadership have produced theories involving traits, situational interaction, function, Behaviour, power, vision and values, charisma, and intelligence among others.

EARLY HISTORY

The search for the characteristics or traits of leaders has been ongoing for centuries. History's greatest philosophical writings from Plato's Republic to Plutarch's Lives have explored the question of "What qualities distinguish an individual as a leader?" Underlying this search was the early recognition of the importance of leadership and the assumption that leadership is rooted in the characteristics that certain individuals possess. This idea that leadership is based on individual attributes is known as the "trait theory of leadership." This view of leadership, the trait theory, was explored at length in a number of works in the previous century. Most notable are the writings of Thomas Carlyle and Francis Galton, whose works have prompted decades of research.

In Heroes and Hero Worship, Carlyle identified the talents, skills, and physical characteristics of men who rose to power. In Galton's Hereditary Genius, he examined leadership qualities in the families of powerful men. After showing that the numbers of eminent relatives dropped off when moving from first degree to second degree relatives, Galton concluded that leadership was inherited. In other words, leaders were born, not developed. Both of these notable works lent great initial support for the notion that leadership is rooted in characteristics of the leader. For decades, this trait-based perspective dominated empirical and theoretical work in leadership.

Using early research techniques, researchers conducted over a hundred studies proposing a number of characteristics that distinguished leaders from non-leaders: intelligence, dominance, adaptability, persistence, integrity, socioeconomic status, and self-confidence just to name a few.

RISE OF ALTERNATIVE THEORIES

In the late 1940s and early 1950s, however, a series of qualitative reviews of these studies prompted researchers to take a drastically different view of the driving forces behind leadership. In reviewing the extant literature, Stogdill and Mann found that while some traits were common across a number of studies, the overall evidence suggested that persons who are leaders in one situation may not necessarily be leaders in other situations. Subsequently, leadership was no longer characterised as an enduring individual trait, as situational approaches posited that individuals can be effective in certain situations, but not others. This approach dominated much of the leadership theory and research for the next few decades.

RE-EMERGENCE OF TRAIT THEORY

New methods and measurements were developed after these influential reviews that would ultimately reestablish the trait theory as a viable approach to the study of leadership. For example, improvements in researchers' use of the round robin research design methodology allowed researchers to see that individuals can and do emerge as leaders across a variety of situations and tasks. Additionally, during the 1980s statistical advances allowed researchers to conduct meta-analyses, in which they could quantitatively analyse and summarise the findings from a wide array of studies. This advent allowed trait theorists to create a comprehensive and parsimonious picture of previous leadership research rather than rely on the qualitative reviews of the past. Equipped with new methods, leadership researchers revealed the following:

- Individuals can and do emerge as leaders across a variety of situations and tasks.
- Significant relationships exist between leadership and such individual traits as:
  - Intelligence.
  - Adjustment.
  - Extraversion.
  - Conscientiousness.

- Openness to experience.
- General self-efficacy.

While the trait theory of leadership has certainly regained popularity, its re-emergence has not been accompanied by a corresponding increase in sophisticated conceptual frameworks. Specifically, scholars noted that trait theories still:

- Focus on a small set of individual attributes such as Big Five personality traits, to the neglect of cognitive abilities, motives, values, social skills, expertise, and problem-solving skills.
- Fail to consider patterns or integrations of multiple attributes.
- Do not distinguish between those leader attributes that are generally not malleable over time and those that are shaped by, and bound to, situational influences.
- Do not consider how stable leader attributes account for the Behavioural diversity necessary for effective leadership.

ATTRIBUTE PATTERN APPROACH

Considering the criticisms of the trait theory, several researchers have begun to adopt a different perspective of leader individual differences - the leader attribute pattern approach. In contrast to the traditional approach, the leader attribute pattern approach is based on theorists' arguments that the influence of individual characteristics on outcomes is best understood by considering the person as an integrated totality rather than a summation of individual variables.

In other words, the leader attribute pattern approach argues that integrated constellations or combinations of individual differences may explain substantial variance in both leader emergence and leader effectiveness beyond that explained by single attributes, or by additive combinations of multiple attributes.

BEHAVIOURAL AND STYLE THEORIES

In response to the early criticisms of the trait approach, theorists began to research leadership as a set of Behaviours, evaluating the Behaviour of 'successful' leaders, determining a Behaviour taxonomy and identifying broad leadership styles. David McClelland, for example, Leadership takes a strong personality with a well developed positive ego. Not so much as a pattern of motives, but a set of traits is crucial.

To lead; self-confidence and a high self-esteem is useful, perhaps even essential. Kurt Lewin, Ronald Lipitt, and Ralph White developed in 1939 the seminal work on the influence of leadership styles and performance. The researchers evaluated the performance of groups of eleven-year-old boys under different types of work climate.

In each, the leader exercised his influence regarding the type of group decision making, praise and criticism and the management of the group tasks according to three styles:

- Authoritarian,
- Democratic and
- Laissez-faire.

Authoritarian climates were characterised by leaders who make decisions alone, demand strict compliance to his orders, and dictate each step taken; future steps were uncertain to a large degree. The leader is not necessarily hostile but is aloof from participation in work and commonly offers personal praise and criticism for the work done. Democratic climates were characterised by collective decision processes, assisted by the leader. Before accomplishing tasks, perspectives are gained from group discussion and technical advice from a leader.

Members are given choices and collectively decide the division of Labour. Praise and criticism in such an environment are objective, fact minded and given by a group member without necessarily having participated extensively in the actual work. *Laissez faire* climates gave freedom to the group for policy determination without any participation from the leader. The leader remains uninvolved in work decisions unless asked, does not participate in the division of Labour, and very infrequently gives praise.

The results seemed to confirm that the democratic climate was preferred. The managerial grid model is also based on a Behavioural theory. The model was developed by Robert Blake and Jane Mouton in 1964 and suggests five different leadership styles, based on the leaders' concern for people and their concern for goal achievement. B.F. Skinner is the father of Behaviour Modification and developed the concept of positive reinforcement. Positive reinforcement occurs when a positive stimulus is presented in response to a Behaviour, increasing the likelihood of that Behaviour in the future. The following is an example of how positive reinforcement can be used in a business setting. Assume praise is a positive reinforcer for a particular employee. This employee does not show up to work on time every day.

The manager of this employee decides to praise the employee for showing up on time every day the employee actually shows up to work on time. As a result, the employee comes to work on time more often because the employee likes to be praised. In this example, praise is a positive reinforcer for this employee because the employee arrives to work on time more frequently after being praised for showing up to work on time.

The use of positive reinforcement is a successful and growing technique used by leaders to motivate and attain desired Behaviours from subordinates. Organisations such as Frito-Lay, 3M, Goodrich, Michigan Bell, and Emery Air Freight have all used reinforcement to increase productivity. Empirical research covering the last 20 years suggests that reinforcement theory has a 17 per cent increase in performance. Additionally, many reinforcement techniques such as the use of praise are inexpensive, providing higher performance for lower costs.

SITUATIONAL AND CONTINGENCY THEORIES

Situational theory also appeared as a reaction to the trait theory of leadership. Social scientists argued that history was more than the result of intervention of great men as Carlyle suggested. Herbert Spencer said that the times produce the person and not the other way around. This theory assumes that different situations call for different characteristics; according to this group of theories, no single optimal psychographic profile of a leader exists. The theory, "what an individual actually does when acting as a leader is in large part dependent upon characteristics of the situation in which he functions." Some theorists started to synthesise the trait and situational approaches. Building upon the research of scholars academics began to normatise the descriptive models of leadership climates, defining three leadership styles and identifying which situations each style works better in. The authoritarian leadership style, for example, is approved in periods of crisis but fails to win the "hearts and minds" of their followers in the day-to-day management; the democratic leadership style is more adequate in situations that require consensus building; finally, the laissez faire leadership style is appreciated by the degree of freedom it provides, but as the leader does not "take charge", he can be perceived as a failure in protracted or thorny organisational problems. Thus, theorists defined the style of leadership as contingent to the situation, which is sometimes classified as contingency theory. Four contingency leadership theories appear more prominently in the recent years: Fiedler contingency model, Vroom-Yetton decision model, the path-goal theory, and the Hersey-Blanchard situational theory.

The Fiedler contingency model bases the leader's effectiveness on what Fred Fiedler called situational contingency. This results from the interaction of leadership style and situational favourableness. The theory defined two types of leader: those who tend to accomplish the task by developing good-relationships with the group and those who have as their prime concern carrying out the task itself. There is no ideal leader. Both task-oriented and relationship-oriented leaders can be effective if their leadership orientation fits the situation. When there is a good leader-member relation, a highly structured task, and high leader position power, the situation is considered a "favourable situation".

Fiedler found that task-oriented leaders are more effective in extremely favourable or unfavourable situations, whereas relationship-oriented leaders perform best in situations with intermediate favourability. Victor Vroom, in collaboration with Phillip Yetton and later with Arthur Jago, developed a taxonomy for describing leadership situations, taxonomy that was used in a normative decision model where leadership styles were connected to situational variables, defining which approach was more suitable to which situation. This approach was novel because it supported the idea that the same manager could rely on different group decision making approaches depending on the attributes of each situation. This model was later referred as situational contingency theory. The path-goal theory of leadership was developed by Robert House and was based on the expectancy theory of Victor Vroom. The essence of the theory is "the meta proposition that leaders, to be effective, engage in Behaviours that complement subordinates' environments and abilities in a manner that compensates for deficiencies and is instrumental to subordinate satisfaction and individual and work unit performance.

The theory identifies four leader Behaviours, achievement-oriented, directive, participative, and supportive, that are contingent to the environment factors and follower characteristics. In contrast to the Fiedler contingency model, the path-goal model states that the four leadership Behaviours are fluid, and that leaders can adopt any of the four depending on what the situation demands. The path-goal model can be classified both as a contingency theory, as it depends on the circumstances, but also as a transactional leadership theory, as the theory emphasises the reciprocity Behaviour between the leader and the followers. The situational leadership model proposed by Hersey and Blanchard suggests four leadership-styles and four levels of follower-development. For effectiveness, the model posits that the leadership-style must match the appropriate level of followership-development. In this model, leadership behaviour becomes a function not only of the characteristics of the leader, but of the characteristics of followers as well.

FUNCTIONAL THEORY

Functional leadership theory is a particularly useful theory for addressing specific leader behaviours expected to contribute to organisational or unit effectiveness. This theory argues that the leader's main job is to see that whatever is necessary to group needs is taken care of; thus, a leader can be said to have done their job well when they have contributed to group effectiveness and cohesion. While functional leadership theory has most often been applied to team leadership, it has also been effectively applied to broader organisational leadership as well.

In summarising literature on functional leadership These functions include:

- Environmental monitoring,
- Organising subordinate activities,
- Teaching and coaching subordinates,
- Motivating others, and
- Intervening actively in the group's work.

A variety of leadership behaviours are expected to facilitate these functions. In initial work identifying leader behaviour, Fleishman observed that subordinates perceived their supervisors' behaviour in terms of two broad categories referred to as consideration and initiating structure. Consideration includes behaviour involved in fostering effective relationships. Examples of such behaviour would include showing concern for a subordinate or acting in a supportive manner towards others. Initiating structure involves the actions of the leader focused specifically on task accomplishment. This could include role clarification, setting performance standards, and holding subordinates accountable to those standards.

TRANSACTIONAL AND TRANSFORMATIONAL THEORIES

Eric Berne first analysed the relations between a group and its leadership in terms of Transactional Analysis. The transactional leader is given power to perform certain tasks and reward or punish for the team's performance. It gives the opportunity to the manager to lead the group and the group agrees to follow his lead to accomplish a predetermined goal in exchange for something else. Power is given to the leader to evaluate, correct and train subordinates when productivity is not up to the desired level and reward effectiveness when expected outcome is reached. The transformational leader motivates its team to be effective and efficient. Communication is the base for goal achievement focusing the group on the final desired outcome or goal attainment. This leader is highly visible and uses chain of command to get the job done. Transformational leaders focus on the big picture, needing to be surrounded by people who take care of the details. The leader is always looking for ideas that move the organisation to reach the company's vision.

EMOTIONS

Leadership can be perceived as a particularly emotion-laden process, with emotions entwined with the social influence process. In an organisation, the leader's mood has some effects on his/her group.

These effects can be described in 3 levels:

- The mood of individual group members. Group members with leaders in a positive mood experience more positive mood than do group members with leaders in a negative mood. The leaders transmit their moods to other group members through the mechanism of emotional contagion. Mood contagion may be one of the psychological mechanisms by which charismatic leaders influence followers.
- The affective tone of the group. Group affective tone represents the consistent or homogeneous affective reactions within a group. Group affective tone is an aggregate of the moods of the individual members of the group and refers to mood at the group level of analysis. Groups with leaders in a positive mood have a more positive affective tone than do groups with leaders in a negative mood.
- Group processes like coordination, effort expenditure, and task strategy. Public expressions of mood impact how group members think and act. When people experience and express mood, they send signals to others. Leaders signal their goals, intentions, and attitudes

through their expressions of moods. For example, expressions of positive moods by leaders signal that leaders deem progress Towards goals to be good.The group members respond to those signals cognitively and Behaviourally in ways that are reflected in the group processes.

In research about client service, it was found that expressions of positive mood by the leader improve the performance of the group, although in other sectors there were other findings. Beyond the leader's mood, her/his behaviour is a source for employee positive and negative emotions at work. The leader creates situations and events that lead to emotional response. Certain leader behaviours displayed during interactions with their employees are the sources of these affective events. Leaders shape workplace affective events. Examples – feedback giving, allocating tasks, resource distribution. Since, employee Behaviour and productivity are directly affected by their emotional states, it is imperative to consider employee emotional responses to organisational leaders. Emotional intelligence, the ability to understand and manage moods and emotions in the self and others, contributes to effective leadership in organisations. Leadership is about being responsible.

NEO-EMERGENT THEORY

The Neo-emergent leadership theory espouses that leadership is created through the emergence of information by the leader or other stakeholders, not through the true actions of the leader himself. In other words, the reproduction of information or stories form the basis of the perception of leadership by the majority. It is well known that the great naval hero Lord Nelson often wrote his own versions of battles he was involved in, so that when he arrived home in England he would receive a true hero's welcome. In modern society, the press, blogs and other sources report their own views of a leader, which may be based on reality, but may also be based on a political command, a payment, or an inherent interest of the author, media or leader. Therefore, it can be contended that the perception of all leaders is created and in fact does not reflect their true leadership qualities at all.

ENVIRONMENTAL LEADERSHIP THEORY

The environmental leadership model describes leadership from a group dynamics perspective incorporating group psychology and self awareness to nurture "Environments" that promote self-sustaining group leadership based on personal emotional gratification from the activities of the group. The Environmental Leader creates the psychological structure by which employees can find and attain this gratification through work or activity.

It stems from the idea that each individual has various environments that bring out different facets from their own Identity, and each facet is driven by emotionally charged perceptions within each environment. The Environmental

Leader creates a platform through education and awareness where individuals fill each others emotional needs and become more conscious of when, and how they affect personal and team emotional gratifications. This is accomplished by knowing why people "react" to their environment instead of act intelligently. "Environmental Leadership is not about changing the mindset of the group or individual, but in the cultivation of an environment that brings out the best and inspires the individuals in that group.

It is not the ability to influence others to do something they are not committed to, but rather to nurture a culture that motivates and even excites individuals to do what is required for the benefit of all.

It is not carrying others to the end result, but setting the surrounding for developing qualities in them to so they may carry each other. The role of an Environmental Leader is to instill passion and direction to a group and the dynamics of that group. This leader implements a psychological support system within a group that fills the emotional and developmental needs of the group.

THE RELATIONSHIP BETWEEN LEADERSHIP AND INFLUENCE

What is the relationship between leadership and influence? Is leadership always influence and is influence always leadership? To say that leadership always entails influence is like saying that all snow is white. It's true but the inference doesn't work the other way. That is, not all white things are snow. Similarly, although all leadership is influence, there are lots of types of influence that don't count as leadership.

Here are a few examples:

- Intimidating or forcing someone to do something.
- Bribing someone to do your bidding.
- Paying for things you want someone to do for you.
- Teaching a student to behave better in a classroom.
- Encouraging your children to eat their vegetables.

The last two examples are not leadership because they have nothing to do with a group striving to achieve a goal. Teaching students and encouraging children to eat vegetables is for their own interest, not for the good of a larger group. Similarly, salespeople may be very influential but their influence is self-interested. The salesperson and the customer do not constitute a group.

FORMAL AUTHORITY AND LEADERSHIP INFLUENCE

Suppose you are the boss and you decide to ramp up production by 50 per cent, requiring everyone to work faster and longer hours without overtime. Is this leadership? No, it may be influence but it is not leadership because the employees had no choice. To say that leadership is informal influence means that followers have a free choice to follow or not. What are some prime examples of true leadership influence? One of the most familiar is Martin Luther King's demonstrations against segregation on buses which led the U.S., Supreme Court to outlaw this practice. King had no formal authority or other power to move the U.S., government.

This is the real meaning of leadership. Another example of genuine leadership influence was the Sony employee who influenced management to adopt his idea for PlayStation despite their feeling that Sony wasn't into making toys. Whenever you convince your colleagues or your boss to adopt a new idea, you have shown them leadership. Or, you might simply set a good example for others and, if they follow, you have shown leadership. Market leading businesses influence their competitors to change course, another example of real leadership. When executives make decisions that take their teams in new directions, they are taking managerial actions, NOT showing leadership because employees have no choice. To count as leadership, influence must be informal and followers must get on board completely of their own free will. Leadership is also a group phenomenon and is aimed at serving some unselfish purpose, something to improve the group's effectiveness. For this reason, even if your children willingly follow your plea to eat their vegetables, you haven't shown leadership because you and your kids are not a group working Towards a common goal.

INFORMAL LEADERSHIP AND INFLUENCE

We often distinguish between formal and informal leadership. The only difference between these concepts is that the informal leader takes charge informally. The formal leader has been given formal authority to govern the group while the informal leader is granted this role by the group itself. The informal leader has personal power - charisma, knowledge or some form of expertise that the group values. It is vital to recognise that the conventional concept of informal leadership is not the same thing as saying that all leadership influence is informal. The conventional concept, formal or informal, is all about being in charge of the group. The claim made here is that real leadership is independent of position, as it was in the case of Martin Luther King. He was not an informal leader in the conventional sense - the Supreme Court didn't recognise him as their informal leader.

As another example, a technical geek might influence his peers to adopt a new piece of software. He has influenced them informally. However, this geek might be so disinclined to manage the group that they might never view him as their informal leader - someone who they would turn to for help in organising their day to day work, who they would look to for advice and the resolution of conflict. The geek's informal leadership is a one-off act, not an ongoing role. His influence is informal but he is not what we normally call an informal leader because he has no interest or ability to take charge of the group in a managerial sense. So what? By reformulating the meaning of leadership, I am saying that the old distinction between formal and informal leadership is outdated. There is really only formal and informal management because all leadership is informal where this term refers to willingly following someone's lead NOT to informally taking charge of the group.

SOCIAL CURRENCIES AND SENIOR LEADERSHIP

One of the innate social exchange algorithms that all people seem to have is the ability to trade favours in order to build social relationships and systems of mutual obligation. In the traditional societies long-studied by anthropologists, this is manifested in gift exchange systems where social obligations are created and repaid through the exchange of gifts. Even without a physical accounting of who owes what to whom, people are very proficient at keeping score, not only in terms of knowing how much is owed, but what is owed—favours, goods, payments, or special privileges.

The exchange of gossip is a very powerful "social glue" and plays a vital role in keeping a group together and informed of the status of its members. Different social groups have different systems of exchange, different kinds of tokens—what we call *social currencies* – for creating affinities, building relationships of mutual advantage, and enabling the valuing and trading of different kinds of skills, privileges, and goods. In other words, people in social and work networks create their own markets around their particular skills and resources and use these transactions to build social cohesion and trust within and across social networks.

Social currencies are typically denominated in the types of skills and resources that define a social network. For example, in some *professional* networks, the prevalent social currencies are knowledge, expertise, and access to important events and people; in other *soical* networks, social status and privilege of membership can be the principle inducement.

In many cases, the social currencies that fuel the many informal networks that make up businesses and formal organisations are often more powerful than other more traditional forms of inducement, such as financial incentives. Indeed, most large organisations are made up of peer networks of constituencies who, by virtue of shared skills and mutual interests, act more on the behalf of their network than for benefit of the overall organisation. Members within these networks realise that their peer relationships have more influence over their future success than the formal organisation or enterprise.

Successful senior leaders, for example, know what the currencies are for such peer networks and they know when and how to cash in their chips to advance their interests and those of their peer networks.

This kind of behaviour is often dismissed as politics, and when undertaken in an opaque, self-serving, and episodic manner, can completely undermine the trust and efficacy of an organisation. non-etheless, it is through such shrewd negotiations that truly effective and credible senior leaders arise, and it is as natural as breathing for most accomplished senior leaders.

These senior leaders, however, tend to combine for a variety of leadership roles, with particular emphasis on connector leadership skills. They tend not to be visionaries or truth-tellers, who by bent of personality can be so committed to their vision and truth telling that they fail to build the requisite social capital with their peers to advance to more senior levels. Examples in the military are Billy Mitchell, George Patton, and John A. Boyd. The leadership roles that emerge under these circumstances are the connector, fixer, and facilitator.

Such leadership roles seem better adapted to reading and responding to complex social signals and building the requisite social capital to assume senior leadership roles. In this camp, one would find Dwight Eisenhower, Omar Bradley, and George Marshall. Only under the rarest of circumstances do you find military leaders who combine visionary roles and skills with those of the connector, exemplar, and fixer: Lord Nelson, the Duke of Wellington, Carl Phillip von Clausewitz, Otto von Bismarck, and George Marshall.

The challenge is not to eradicate such Behaviour, but to harness it by making the coining, exchange, accrual, and cashing in of social currencies wholly transparent and driven by criteria that support the mission and capabilities of the entire organisation. One of the most ubiquitous and natural of social currencies is reputation.

It is not surprising that it is the driving force behind so many different Open Source and peer production networks. Individuals can have multiple reputations and a reputation in one field may not be easily transferable into another, because reputation is highly contextspecific and subject to the conditions of local rules.

Nonetheless, just as trust can be transitive—*e.g.*, I trust whom you trust—especially if it is predicated on strong ties established over long periods of time, so can reputation be transitive even when circumstances may not warrant it.
For example, someone who is a great hockey player may not be a great businessperson, but because of the desire of one group to affiliate with another, reputation points or social currencies garnered in one area are often convertible into another.

Careers can often be built by leveraging a highly visible success in one area of endeavor to a succession of successes in other areas of endeavor such as athletics, business, academia, politics, and public service. The challenge is to trade up and to increase the cumulative value of a personal currency.

Great "cross network players" include George Washington, Benjamin Franklin, Henry Kissinger, Ronald Reagan, Arnold Schwarzenegger, and Rupert Murdock. A remarkable fact is the extent to which high reputation ratings are transferable across domains, especially in the case of "world class" ratings where Nobel Laureates, NBA athletes, film stars, and media commentators can form a common peer group, irrespective of glaringly different competencies.

It would seem that extremely high competency creates a peer network of celebrity and achievement. In terms of building robust social networks that offer the right combination of leadership roles to achieve a larger organisational purpose, what might be good for the individual may not be good for the organisation. Visionaries, for instance, may provide needed innovation and achieve significant personal and organisational success through their visions. Yet if such visions are not challenged by truth-teller leaders and held accountable by enforcers, they may result in "false" successes and inappropriate learnings at the cost of the organisation's success.

Visionary leaders, on the other hand, would have moved on to other organisations and social networks based upon their proclaimed "success". Similarly, an excess of truth telling and enforcement leadership can stifle both innovation and risk taking, just as an excess of connector leadership within private firms can result in acquisitions that are neither strategic nor synergistic. Associate Dean of the Yale School of Management and head of the CEO Institute, companies tend to go through a succession of CEO leadership roles without a coherent understanding of how they relate to either one another or to the interest of the corporation and its shareholders.

ISSUES IN LEADERSHIP IN THE LIBRARY AND INFORMATION ENVIRONMENT: FOCUS ON LIBRARY DIRECTORS

Despite all the theoretical bases for leadership, the leadership role of a leader cannot be divulged from his basic functions in a specific situation. Therefore, for practicability, this portion of this presentation will hang essentially on the propositions of Versosa as depicting the functional/leadership roles of the library leadership. The highlights as submitted in her presentation are given as thus:

- Leadership is just one dimension of the managers work.
- It involves "the exercise of social influence by infusing the parent organisation with purpose and direction in order to achieve its goals.
- Leadership requires that the library director should influence members of the parent institutions to provide resources in order to:
  - Support expansion plans.
  - Accept the goals of the library as valid and deserving support.
- The 3 dimensions used to measure library leadership are:
  - Leader activities.
  - Management of organisational change and
  - Reputational Effectiveness.

Leader Activities:

- Managerial role activities.
- Professional activities and involvement.
- Membership on community committees.
- Strategies for influencing the environment.

The managerial role/activities are further broken into six:

- Which involves directing the work of subordinates; integrating subordinates goals with the librarys goals and objectives; allocating human resources to tasks; evaluating subordinates job performance; resolving conflicts between subordinates and providing new staff with training.
- Involves attending social functions for contacts; attendance at conferences/meetings; maintaining informal communication networks; and relating with people outside.
- Includes initiating new ideas for services and operations; keeping up with professional trends/changes; keeping abreast of technological developments; scanning the environment for new opportunities to improve services/ operations; collecting information about users touring facilities to observe and reading reports of other units.
- Involves planning and implementing changes in the library, initiating change in the library and solving problems by instituting changes in the library.
- Includes serving as an expert or advising people outside the library; keeping others abreast of developments in the library, attending to correspondences, and serving on committees, and representing the library.
- Changes in organisational domain *vis-a-vis* other community/cognate entities; Internal changes

Reputational Effectiveness includes considerations of:

- Years in managerial positions.
- Libraries worked in.
- Continuing education.
- Professional journals scanned/read.
- No. of publications.
- Membership of Association, and
- Services to University/Parent Establishment.

THE LIBRARY/INFORMATION PROFESSIONALS LEADERSHIP AGENDA/STRATEGY

The following initiatives are desirable and could be found rewarding:

- Creation of awareness for need of leadership development skills among professionals.
- Self-development in leadership skills by Librarians and Information Professionals.

- Integration of leadership development into the library/information centre strategic planning.
- Leadership Development Programme to run through the ladder
- Library and Information Schools to integrate Leadership Skills development into their curricula.
- Need for librarians and information professionals to maintain strong network within and without their organisation to enhance development of skills and knowledge.

NEW STANDARD FOR MONOGRAPH AND SERIAL HOLDINGS

Having presented a model for vertical thinking about organisations, and having discussed the general issues of access to materials and personnel administration, I want to discuss next a more particular topic that is closely related to the issues of access and storage. That topic is the extremely important new ANSI standard Z39.71 for the display of holdings of both monographs and serials in all media, physical or electronic, and whether manual or automated means are used to keep records. This new standard was approved unanimously by National Information Standards Organisation (NISO) representatives after very careful consideration by many organisations and it has just been readied for publication. The importance of the standard lies in its direct and positive confrontation of some mistakes of our past and its responsible attitude towards new ways of delivering information.

It reverses the old separation of serial and Non-serial publications, and thus it justly proclaims to have made obsolete the two earlier standards for the display of holdings for those two sorts of publications. It also claims to apply to the display of holdings statements of bibliographic items in any format at either summary or detailed levels, or even a mix of the two for libraries that cannot create fully detailed holdings statements for their older publications.

It is independent of any particular cataloging system or code, and it leaves librarians free to choose among several alternatives to make practice possible under different local needs and possibilities. This is the same spirit of the latest revisions of AACR2 and new documents like the 1994 *ALA Guidelines for Bibliographic Description of Interactive Multimedia*. At last, the participation of all of us in the field, and in particular in technical services, is now continuously requested and appreciated. In this case, the standard was developed in full consultation with many specialists in American libraries. The main goal of standard Z39.71 is to make holdings statements consistent in all sources for such data and therefore make it possible to communicate the data across computer systems.

The standard, however, only addresses the display of holdings, not their communication. The latter is the job of the MARC holdings format, and the acceptance of Z39.71 will require some changes to that format. The recommendation is that catalogers and serials librarians must adopt the directions of Z39.71 as fully as local circumstances allow, and try to use its four levels of specificity intelligently. While single part titles can be satisfactorily recorded at the first level, multipart titles, titles with supplements, indexes, accompanying materials or any other sort of secondary bibliographic units, and serial titles—all still represented by a single bibliographic record—can only be satisfactorily treated at the second, third, or fourth levels of specificity. The second level provides only "general" information about holdings.

The third level provides a compressed summary statement of holdings. The fourth level provides detailed holdings information, either compressed or itemised, which, it seems to me, will deliver completely successful retrieval by computer in every conceivable case, no matter what complexity the record might include. For the purposes of my organisational model, the two older standards were another expression of horizontal thinking, while the new standard makes more sense from the point of view of vertical thinking..

RE-STRUCTURING OF MESH

While the Z39.71 standard is an important new tool for descriptive cataloging, the restructuring of MeSH—*Medical Subject Headings*—the medical vocabulary of the National Library of Medicine (NLM) represents an important advance in subject analysis. The 1999 version of MeSH was prepared by the Cataloging Section of the NLM to exploit the capabilities of their new Voyager library automation system.

The new MeSH proposes to overcome the old difference between cataloging and indexing that has been an impediment for medical librarians and their patrons. NLM will now perform subject analysis in cataloging the same way as it does in indexing. This should result in a new equality in the treatment of all materials relevant in medical information seeking. No longer will there be two parallel systems: one for the analysis of journal articles by indexers and another for the analysis of books, audiovisuals, and computer software by catalogers.

Beginning in 1999, any document in any format will be analysed the same way, with subject headings distributed mostly in terms of descriptors subdivided topically, while earlier form, linguistic, and geographical subheadings will become genre, language, and geographic descriptors. Uptodate automated systems will be able to retrieve and combine such new headings with more powerful and accurate results. In keeping with the same spirit of liberty and participatory responsibility, NLM has opened a dialog with other medical libraries to present them with three choices for the use the new vocabulary structure depending upon local traditions, computer characteristics, and relationships among libraries.

Recognising that many medical libraries are associated with other types of libraries in many university systems, the first choice still allows for the stringing of headings and subheadings done in previous years, a technique which is much closer to the style of LC subject analysis that will continue to appear in most bibliographic records of those universities. The second choice is to comply with NLM's new practice. A third, intermediate choice is a hybrid of the other two that might take advantage of the strengths of both systems. I have taken the position that, if at all possible, medical libraries should follow NLM's lead and convert to its new practice as soon and as fully as possible, given staff retraining considerations, the economics of conversion, etc. The advantages of a unitary system of subject analysis that covers the article databases, the indexes, and the online catalog seem to me enormous.

In terms of my proposed vertical model, the new use of MeSH should represent the revitalisation of the branch of practical knowledge that is cataloging in its relation to the branch we call indexing and to the main trunk of all library work. The pruning of the previous MeSH will be a painful procedure, but it should result in a more rational and vital tool which will serve us well for years to come. An example of the greater intellectual correctness of the new vocabulary is that, at last, the topical subheadings epidemiology and ethnology will be exclusively related to geographic subject headings. On the other hand, in spite of the change a few years ago of the two topical subheadings legislation and statistics to legislation and jurisprudence and statistics and numerical data respectively, catalogers in many medical libraries have still been using them as equivalent to the form subheadings legislation and statistics and in practice applying only or mostly the form subheadings.

This change illustrates the need to reform the structure of the vocabulary. One cannot substitute a form subheading for a more precise topical heading and then expect success in the retrieval of pertinent literature. Discussions of laws are not enough like a collection of the texts of those laws, and the same applies to the second case about statistical data. The classical concatenated string of headings and multiple subheadings is an extreme example of horizontal thinking, with all its advantages and disadvantages. By contrast to LC vocabulary, MeSH has always had a built-in tree structure of concepts related vertically, and now it will be cleaned and polished as horizontal strings are replaced by vertical sets of subjects that apply to a given document. If only we could now go further and also clear up the horizontal relations among the various trees to make MeSH the perfect "forest."

POLICIES FOR CATALOGING COMPUTER FILES ON DISC

Another, and still more specific, example of the need for vertical thinking is in the development of policies for cataloging Non-audio compact discs, *i.e.*, CD-ROMs. We face an interesting situation with compact discs. On one hand, we do not look at them with the same awe of a few years ago, when their novelty and characteristics made them a hit among librarians as well as the public at large. On the other hand, they still are being published and distributed in large quantities and in many fields, from pornography to scholarship and anything in between. If anything, it appears that more and more of our traditional materials are either accompanied by a compact disc or are reissued in this contemporary technology.

The pressing issues for libraries seem to be their preservation and "fair use," which has led to discussions about the necessity or convenience of arranging a new collection of discs at the reserve desk. The bibliographic character of CD-ROMs is also an issue, including traditional questions such as monograph or serial, accompanying material or independent publication. By now, LC has prepared draft interim guidelines for cataloging electronic resources (excluding Internet documents). Their proposals seem quite reasonable and sufficient, and, if followed prudently, they provide the basic elements for a local policy on compact discs.

In practice, the most difficult aspect may be establishing whether the material is a reproduction (whether with the same title of the original or not) or a new publication. After that, it is a question of determining whether the disc stands alone or is part of a larger package. If the disc is truly a separate publication which stands on its own, a new bibliographic record must be prepared, with the MARC fields 007, 300, 516, and 538, which will fully describe its physical characteristics and the hardware required to use it. If the disc is accompanying material for another published item, then its physical description must be subsumed in subfield e of the 300 field for the primary bibliographic unit, and an 006 field should also be included to reflect that relation between the two. One should not conflate these approaches with the excuse that the primary bibliographic unit is not present or that it has not been possible to establish what is the case. It has been said that the difference between the two kinds of discs can be clearly shown by asking whether the publication "is" a disc or "has" a disc.

This also illuminates the added problem of discs that are only forms of advertisement (then the book "has" not a disc), or are part of a multimedia package (then the package "is" not just the disc). The ultimate goal has to be, as always, the full level cataloging of any disc worth adding to the collection, and of course the provision of means to insure proper preservation of the materials. A new factor in the situation with optical discs is that, instead of being used at readers placed around the library, many libraries are now mounting them on local networks to make them available to several patrons simultaneously. Some librarians even want to put them on the Web to make remote access possible, but this appears to be prohibitively expensive. If they are added to the Web, MARC fields like 538 - System Requirements and 856 - Electronic Location and Access would have to be adjusted in order to keep users informed of the physical or electronic availability of each product. LC's guidelines call these two uses of discs "directly accessed" and "remotely accessed" electronic resources and they cover both of them equally.In terms of my model of vertical thinking and management in libraries, it is horizontal thinking when discs are looked at as an intermediate technology between print (*e.g.,* books, indexes, etc.) and remotely accessed electronic resources. Every day we have more discs to catalog, separately or as accompanying material, because publishers avail themselves of this technique of reproduction for many purposes, without having it replace or be replaced by something else. As a successful technology, discs will continue to have their place in library collections, which helps keep healthy the live trunk of the green trees libraries are.

DEVELOPING NETWORK LEADERS

VISIBILITY AND DIGITISATION

As more and more interactions become digitised and observable, opportunities abound for using the naturally occurring data about the volume and the nature of the interactions among members of network organisations. Collaborative technologies, as simple and ubiquitous as e-mail, make it possible to make visible the millions of social interactions among the participants in networked organisations and thereby gain insight and eventual control over how members manage their work relationships. Not only is it possible to capture data about who is interacting with whom, but it is also possible through analytics to identify some of the emergent network leadership roles. Simple modifications to existing collaborative platforms make it possible to identify the network signatures of different types of leadership roles.

By making different members' Behaviours visible to one another, and by developing metrics for rating leadership performance, many of the techniques that are used in peer production systems—Open Source, eBay, and even MMORPGs—can be applied to the self-synchronised management of networked organisation. For example when setting up multifunctional or cross-organisational teams through e-mail, it was possible for all the members to see who communicated with whom about what topics and how frequently. A new kind of self-enforcing accountability could be introduced.

Furthermore, by providing metrics of responsiveness, connectedness, loop closing, and peer ratings, not only would shared awareness be increased but new forms of self-synchronisation would emerge. As more data on the interactions of social networks becomes available, it should not be too long before network leadership roles are identified in much the same way that different roles are identified in online games and peer production systems. It is just a matter of time before network leadership roles become digital, and by virtue of their becoming digital become measurable, teachable, and systematically deployed to maximise network performance.

IDENTIFY PERFORMANCE METRICS FOR NETWORK LEADERS

Social network analysis has identified some of the preliminary network structures associated with different kinds of leadership roles, such as the importance of connectors and hubs in network organisations, or how small world effects can be achieved. With the advent of social software to manage social interactions, form *ad hoc* groups, close decision loops, and enable self-synchronisation Behaviours, leadership qualities that had been unmanageable intangibles for so long can be measured, improved, and taught in a way that was never before possible. With the wide-scale adoption of RFID and mote technologies for tracking physical assets in real time, and the enormous strides in information sharing, improved awareness, collaboration, and self-synchronisation demonstrated by the war in Iraq, the time is not so distant when leadership roles will be measured and tracked digitally and become an integral part in how networked organisations are managed. These cumulative innovations will significantly reduce agency costs and improve the flexibility and productivity of large-scale organisations by orders of magnitude. New metrics will make it possible to measure the degree of trust, reciprocity, successes, failures, social capital, diversity, network value, etc., within an edge organisation. By making all assets—physical, human, content, and interactions— observable and providing for the selective disclosure of information and the dynamic allocation and revocation of security access, it will be possible to have much more secure and robust networked organisations.

CAREER PATHS

In order for new models of network leadership to be adopted and become an integral part of networked organisations, there have to be clear career paths that reward the skills of network leadership as a recognised part of career development. In military organisations where the alpha leadership role is still wedded to certain traditional combat roles, identifying new alpha roles that exemplify important and valued competencies outside those of the traditional military culture could prove challenging. In forms of warfare that are increasingly informational, analytic, sensemaking, and collaborative, communication and interaction skills are becoming increasing important.

New kinds of competencies will be selected and need to be rapidly incorporated into the training of all recruits. By having explicit, real-time measures not only of important leadership traits but also the demand for different types of leadership roles, human resource departments will have an easier time not only in developing credible and practical work performance criteria, but also in anticipating the demand for current and new types of leaders and skills. As suggested earlier, through the real-time content analysis and tagging of messages, primarily e-mail and instant messaging, it would be possible to differentiate visionary leadership roles from truth-tellers. The analysis might reveal a dearth of truth telling interactions and that visionary-type communications dominate the interactions within the social network, leading to bad decisions and failed missions.

Individuals could be evaluated in terms of how well they are able to fulfil different network leadership roles and recommended for the roles that they are best suited for. There are specific metrics associated with different types of leadership roles and these measures could derived from naturally occurring metadata that are the byproduct of e-mail interactions. Given these capabilities in the future, not only could there be a "real-time inventory and stocking system" for leadership skills and roles, but real-time systems for evaluating the performance of human assets and knowing when to replace or upgrade them. Such metrics will also be used to conduct forensic analyses of different missions where there have been leadership successes, failures, or the need for new kinds of leadership roles or combinations of roles. Given the explicitness of the leadership models, lessons learned from one networked organisation can be rapidly applied to another, thereby accelerating organisational learning and innovation adoption.

A NETWORK DEFINITION OF LEADERSHIP

One of the great unknowns in the business and organisational development literature is what accounts for great leadership. It is one of the softest areas of the social sciences, having defied rigorous analysis for decades. Yet, leadership is considered one of the key ingredients for the success of any organisation. The position taken here is that leadership is both born and nurtured. The evidence for the biological and evolutionary basis underlying the personality associated with leadership is compelling and growing. Individuals have innately different leadership capacities in the same way that they have different mental and physical capacities.

These personality traits are some of the genetic variables that evolution periodically and randomly shuffles. But what makes a personality trait—such as the ability to interpret emotional cues, to connect with other people, to detect cheaters, to gossip and trade favours—a property of the social network are the rules that govern how individual members interact and cooperate.

In this sense, leadership is a network effect that can result in highly responsive and effective leaders, or contrarily, degradation into kleptocracy or demagoguery. On the other hand, if networked organisations can be designed that select for certain leadership roles and competencies that can be measured, evaluated, and improved upon, then leadership ceases to be an ineffable quality, but becomes a tangible asset that can be learned, improved upon, and replicated.

Table summarises some of the potential metrics of network leadership that are associated with the eight different leadership roles. These lists are not meant to be definitive, but rather illustrative of how explicit network metrics might be related to both the definition network roles and the self-management of those rules through the appropriate metrics and feedback.

Table. Network Properties of Leadership.

Network Roles	Signature Pattern	Types of Links	Performance Metrics	Social Currencies
Exemplar	star, asymmetric invite, offer,	inform, challenge, assert	independence, trust, reach, completion	expertise, reputation reputation, rate, trust,
			access	Gatekeeper
asymmetric,			transparency	access,
	gateway, hub, weak links, power law	uninvite	independence, completion, reputation	information, reputation
Visionary	star, sparse asymmetric, strong ties, weak links	inform, question, challenge, assert	social capital, reputation, initiation, reach, trust	expertise, information, reputation
Truth-Teller	dense, sub-networks, strong ties,	question, request, inform, assess, challenge	independence, reputation, transparency, trust	reputation, trust
Fixer	strong ties, weak links, hub, power law	request, offer, question, assess, directive	completion rate reputation, reach reputation Connector	access, goods, services, income,
symmetric,	inform, gateway, weak links, small world	density, access, invite, offer, request	access, diversity, redundancy, reach, trust	favours, reputation
Enforcer	strong ties, subnetwork, power law	directives, compliance, request, question	completion rate reputation, transparency, trust	access, favours, reputation
Facilitator	gateway, sparse, GFN	invite, request, offer	completion rate diversity, initiation, reputation	reputation, access, favours

SIGNATURE PATTERN

Much of the research on social networks stresses the fact that an individual's role in a social network is dependent upon their structural position in the network. Individuals who act as go-betweens or connectors are typically seen as having a network signature measured in terms of how many other members are linked to them and the directionality of these links. The field of social network analysis is still in its early phases of development, and there are many different types of network measures: density, power laws, hub-and-spoke, small world effects, reach, strong ties, weak ties, stars, subnetworks, clusters, clumpiness, constraints, redundancy, effective sise, etc., These measures for the most part ignore the type of links and try to derive a description of a network principally from its topology. As Barabasi observed in noting the limitations of his own analysis of scale-free networks and as Watts noted in his critique of small world effects, the types of links are very important, as are the rules governing the addition and removal of links. Hence, a description in terms of structure alone is insufficient.

TYPES OF LINKS: TAGGED

The fact that two parties are only removed by three to six links is no guarantee that one party can access another. It all depends upon the nature of the links. Not everyone can or ever will have access to one another. There are social, cultural, and economic rules that preclude certain forms of interaction. More importantly, for the purposes for understanding network leadership roles, the tagging of the links is associated with the nature of the leadership role. Visionaries' characteristically originate informational links, and, unlike fixers, are not in the business of asking people to commit to completing tasks, whereas gatekeepers are periodically inviting and uninviting people to join a group. The notion of tagged links as discussed here is very similar to Searle's notion of "speech acts," forms of dialogue that people use to get other people to do things. This is a fertile and highly developed field of linguistics—discourse analysis and pragmatics—that offers significant promise for identifying the grammars of interactions among members of a social network. There are rules or social protocols for the addition and removal of combinations of such links, thereby making most complex social networks not scalefree.

PERFORMANCE METRICS

Given the visibility that being a member of a network provides and the opportunity to track and measure interactions, it then becomes possible to provide relatively simple, straightforward, empirically based measures related to the quality of leadership. For example, a leader should not lose track of people, resources, or projects, but have a high completion rate for the number of commitments or "loops" that he has initiated. Measures can tell how many loops remain open, how fast they are being closed, and who is the bottleneck. In a world of such visibility, there can be real accountability. Perhaps the initial metrics are not correct and do not reflect true performance. They then could be modified over time through feedback, and adjusted to drive the desired Behaviours.

As was noted in the earlier analysis of peer-to-peer networks, reputation is a widely shared performance metric and a profound driver of Behaviour. There are more sophisticated measures such as reciprocity and social capital measures, but every performance measure would have to be adjusted for the particular needs and circumstances of the networked organisation. This can be an important measure because each network and leadership role evolves its own social currency, and these currencies are relational measures indicating the status of an individual's relationships with others in the network. The ability to amass significant amounts of social currencies can translate into effective leadership. The ability to convert from one social currency account into another can greatly facilitate a leadership role, such as a connector or a fixer. This is an important dimension of network interactions and needs to be understood in order to direct overall network Behaviours.

NETWORK STRUCTURES AND LEADERSHIP ROLES

Social networks self-organise to acquire and allocate resources such as information, goods, favours, access, privileges, and protection. As discussed earlier, the specialisation of roles in social networks has been demonstrated to have strong long-term survival value, and therefore has been biologically encoded through evolutionary forces as innate psychological or personality traits.

These traits are reflected in how people read social cues, detect cheaters, create and share ideas, and form affinities with strangers. In addition to having innate social exchange competencies, some alpha or exemplar individuals are especially proficient at a skill or exhibit a prised trait that warrants widespread emulation and imitation.

Typically, alpha individuals have a special physical prowess, physical attraction, intelligence, social proficiency, or some combination of these traits. When one considers Cosmides and Tooby's findings on innate social exchange algorithms and Damasio's analysis of the neuro-physiology of social emotions combined with Dunbar's studies on the role of grooming and language in social groups, a compelling argument can be made that these different roles are an evolutionary stable strategy that makes possible the efficient functioning of any self-organising social network.

Few of these network roles have any intrinsic individual value. However, when combined with other roles, they enable the organisation and functioning of complex networks of exchange relationships. Leadership in this context can be regarded as a proficiency in any one or combination of these network roles.

In this sense, some individuals may have greater innate talents than others, but the effectiveness of these gifts is dependent upon the overall qualities of the network and the roles of other members of the network. Network leadership roles assume different levels of importance depending upon the phase of evolution of a networked organisation.

This fact is often not fully appreciated in the business leadership literature where visionary leaders are periodically revered and reviled depending upon the ebb and flow of their company's earnings.

The value of such leadership roles might be more fruitfully understood by attempting to determine the conditions under which a visionary role is adaptive and when it is not, thereby recognising that it is one of many combinations of leadership roles that is required. Likewise, the absence of certain critical leadership roles, such as truth telling, can contribute to the failure of corporate governance or the excesses of overly zealous visionaries.

A further example of the importance of different kinds of network leadership roles can be found in the failure of large organisations to manage relationships across functional and organisational boundaries. Here the high "agency costs" of coordinating across organisational or functional boundaries is largely due to the absence of leaders who are connectors and who know how to interact and affiliate with third parties to build trust. These are what Burton identifies as the *tertiaries*, the brokers between organisational networks. In each of these examples, there are leadership roles whose value and appropriateness depend upon the state of the network.

The effective governance of a networked organisation should therefore involve knowing the status of the organisational network, being able to assess the strengths and weaknesses of different roles, and then allocating the appropriate leadership assets to improve the overall performance of the network.

This is something that Louis Gerstner understood when he first took the job of CEO at IBM. Initially, he was criticised for being insufficiently visionary, to which he responded that the company had become too enamored of its own vision and detached from reality. What was needed, he contended, was a good dose of truth telling, an operational overhaul, and then a new vision. These were different leadership roles that he seemed to switch in and out of comfortably and effectively.

JOINT LEADERSHIP AND META-LEADERSHIP

Just as there are different leadership roles *within* social networks, there are also metaleadership roles that cut *across* networked organisations. When it comes to leading across different organisations, such as coalition partners, partnerships, alliances, joint command, or multi-agency missions, a new set of meta-leadership roles comes into play. These roles are different from those in a hierarchical organisation where subordinates are required to execute orders or follow management directives and are held accountable for doing so.

In joint command efforts, on the other hand, collaboration is peer-based, consensual, and mutual. There are no prior histories for building reciprocity, trust, or transparency. Therefore these have to be created anew over time.

Moreover, as the leadership role is more one of governance than of command, the issue becomes how to cooperatively develop metrics and protocols that respect the integrity of each of the respective organisations.

That being said, creating new meta-networks is much the same as creating any peer networked organisation, except that the units are significantly larger and each has its own distinctive culture.

Certain leadership roles have to be established for all participants—specifically, what Behaviours or traits best exemplify the qualities and standard being sought of the meta-network. Since, leadership in joint efforts typically rotates over time, exemplar leadership roles should be filled by those who have qualities that are not closely identified with any one particular organisation or Service. Rather, an effort should be made to give this networked organisation its own independent identity.

An early visionary can act as the exemplar member and personify the desired qualities, thereby setting a precedent for others to follow. However, there should be an effort to identify other network leadership roles and the associated metrics and protocols that the different representatives of the joint organisations would undertake.

This networked approach to joint leadership differs significantly from the traditional, hierarchical Napoleonic staff codes wherein a small number of fixed staff personnel with limited specialisation perform most of the joint leadership support functions. The networked approach more closely resembles former Marine General Anthony Zinni's proposal for a Modular Commander Center, which stresses specialisation and flexibility. As a former CENTCOM commander, General Zinni recognised that commanders had variable missions requiring combinations of different functions, resources, and partners.

In effect, the command structure had to be agile enough to adapt to the different circumstances of the mission from unilateral humanitarian missions to coalition-based major combat. The combinations of skills for each differed significantly and therefore would entail specialised social network protocols and combinations of different network leadership roles and skills. Under such conditions where it is difficult for one coalition partner to exert authority over another, as many of the organisations are sovereign and independent, the only form of effective control is the selective exclusion of partners or the minimisation of their role.

The qualities of the connector and the facilitator network leadership roles are especially important at this senior level and have their own specialised "social protocols" and skills for setting and coordinating joint missions.

LEADERSHIP AND SCOPE OF CONTROL

In hierarchical and bureaucratic organisations, leadership is often confused with scope of control and authority—power. In such organisations, leaders are given the latitude, even the expectation, to exercise significant control at all levels of the organisation. This is often expressed in budgetary terms: the willingness and the ability to control, cut, or redirect a subordinate's budget.

The power of a superior is virtually absolute in such organisations as they have the authority to project control all the way down the organisation. There are no autonomous layers, and in this sense, decision rights are not protected but revocable and alienable. Usurping local control and autonomy through topdown budgetary restrictions can undermine the efficacy and self-organising capabilities of an organisation and thereby prevent it from effectively learning and adapting.

The integrity of local rules and allocation protocols have to be maintained, and while there can be a decrement in the gross resources available to a subordinate or sub-network, these resources should not be explicitly earmarked or constrained, as such interventions will prevent the network from being self-organising.

This is the same type of issue as the requirement for tactical autonomy in a command system, where the supra-ordinate strategic layer determines the objectives and the assets to be allocated, but the subordinate commander has the authority and the responsibility to make the tactical decisions. In a networked organisational model where there are also independent layers of selforganisation and different types of protocols for interaction, the transecting of layers by a supra-ordinate to a subordinate, in effect, micromanaging and second-guessing, is dangerous for the well-being of the network.

It transforms a collective, networked asset into an episodic individualised asset, thereby undermining trust and accountability. This may happen out of frustration by a senior manager wanting to get things done and going outside official channels.

However, in every case it undermines the collective capability of a networked organisation to self-organise. For this reason, it is very important to move away from the individualised model of leadership and authority and to develop governance mechanisms that build up the overall ongoing assets of the networked organisation. Network leadership roles that are held accountable to the interests of the whole will yield far more efficient, effective, and accountable organisational structures than those that are governed through sporadic and episodic interventions that undermine local authority.

3

Library Organisation

STANDARDS

Most small, private, or classroom library collections do not need a formal system of library organisation as the individual books can be easily located. As the collection becomes larger, access becomes problematic unless some method of grouping is devised. Many different systems address this problem.

For most school libraries, the international standard is the Dewey Decimal Classification (DDC) scheme and either Sears List of Subject Headings or the Library of Congress Subject Headings. Descriptive cataloguing is defined by rules outlined in the Anglo-American Cataloguing Rules (AACR2). Refer to the latest editions of these resources to obtain the most current practices in cataloguing. Every item in the collection must be described using a standard format.

The same basic components are contained in each description. Always cited in the same order, they must employ consistent punctuation. Such standardisation of procedures enhances the local, national, and international exchange of bibliographic data and is essential in computerised systems. To a computer, Hamlet and Shakespeare are just a string of characters.

The machine will fail to recognise one as a title and the other as an author unless it is told where each is located in a descriptive record and how each will be introduced. If schools intend to exchange bibliographic data on a local or provincial basis, they should conform to the standards outlined in this document.

The exchange of bibliographic data or information can occur in a number of ways, one of which is participation in a union catalogue. Historically, union catalogues have progressed from manual card and paper files to on-line shared databases to catalogue records electronically linked via Internet.

Union catalogues form one of the main building blocks of resource sharing or shared services such as interlibrary loan, cooperative cataloguing, cooperative preservation, and cooperative collection development activities. Standards must be used by libraries and library systems to participate in union catalogues.

EDUCATIONAL RATIONALE

For students and staff to make the most effective use of the school's educational resources, the nature, extent, interrelationship, and location of these resources must be clearly identified. School libraries do not exist in an information vacuum but are part of a growing information network. Therefore, they should be provided with access to systems that are compatible with national and international standards. The process of standardised cataloguing and classification results in the creation of a library catalogue.

In a school library, the catalogue is a tool to:

- List, according to a consistent plan, the print and Non-print resources available in the school.
- Describe print and Non-print resources.
- Direct users to similar materials.
- Record purchasing and publishing history.
- Indicate the location of the resources.
- Assist students in obtaining the skills of information retrieval.

The catalogue enable users to:

- Retrieve information efficiently.
- Increase understanding by students and staff of information retrieval systems.
- Plan, order, and check resources efficiently.
- Develop information retrieval skills that are transferable from one school library to other school, public, college, university, and special libraries.

NON-STANDARD SYSTEMS

In-house devised methods of library organisation are to be discouraged. These Non-standards-based solutions result in the following:

- Students and staff requiring training in the specific use of the collection, the knowledge of which is not transferable to other libraries.
- Systems becoming inconsistent over time with changes in Personnel.
- Cataloguing becoming useless when an attempt is made to convert it to a standard machine readable format.

METHODS OF IMPLEMENTING STANDARDS

In applying these standards, school libraries and school divisions/districts which do not have centralised cataloguing have a number of options.

They may:

- Do their own original cataloguing.
- Obtain derived cataloguing.
- Purchase commercially produced cataloguing.
- Use any combination of the above.

Wherever possible, commercially produced cataloguing should be attained. No matter what options are used, consumers of cataloguing should be knowledgeable in terms of what to look and ask for about the standards. This recalls the importance of the training in cataloguing required to ensure consistency and accuracy. School libraries must be familiar with cataloguing standards and should establish local cataloguing policies.

Original Cataloguing

Original cataloguing refers to cataloguing an item by examining certain parts of it to obtain information needed to describe it. While original cataloguing allows for on-site, immediate, and locally applied cataloguing, there are some concerns.

These include:

- Original cataloguing is time-consuming for the cataloguer and the data processor/typist. The teacher-librarian's time can be much better spent working with teachers and students. In addition, library technician and library clerk time in school libraries is usually at a premium.
- Lack of library technician and library clerk time usually results in a backlog of materials which have not been catalogued or processed fully. These materials cannot be used by staff or students.
- Inexperienced cataloguers spend long hours misapplying rules. Thus, the advantages of using a standard system are often negated and re-cataloguing is often necessary at a future date.
- Cataloguing is an expensive process when done by unqualified personnel. If the hours spent by cataloguers and data processors/typists were costed out, it would become apparent that commercial cataloguing is more economical.

Derived Cataloguing

Derived or copy cataloguing refers to the process of cataloguing items by using existing bibliographic records obtained from various sources and altering those records to conform to local cataloguing standards.

Cataloguing information may be found in:

- Cataloguing-in-publication (CIP) data found within the item
- Book catalogues
- Non-book catalogues (*e.g.,* microfiche and CD-ROMs)
- Electronic catalogues (*e.g.,* the Internet). An on-line directory known as Hytelnet provides a well-organised means by which to browse through library catalogues or databases worldwide. Two telnet addresses worthy of mention are: 1) telnet locis.loc.gov (Library of Congress,

mainly books) and 2) telnet dra.com (Library of Congress—Data Research Associates, Inc., mainly films and videos). Two important Uniform Resource Locators (URLs) for web-based searching are: 1) http://lcweb2.loc.gov/ammem/booksquery.html (Library of Congress) and 2) http://library.usask.ca/hywebcat/.

While derived cataloguing does result in definite cataloguing savings, both in terms of cost and time, it should be noted that catalogue cards still must be typed manually or cataloguing records must be entered manually into an automated library system. Furthermore, cataloguing standards and formats may vary from catalogue to catalogue. This will also affect the amount of editing required to meet locally established practices.

Commercial Cataloguing

Commercial cataloguing refers to cataloguing services now being offered by a number of firms. It may take the form of simplified cataloguing records for only certain titles to customised cataloguing for specialised collections. Care should be taken in choosing commercial cataloguing that follows national and local cataloguing standards. The advantages to purchasing commercial cataloguing include:

- Requiring less expertise on the part of the teacher-librarian (the main task for the school library staff may be in filing the cards in a manual environment or loading MARC records in an automated environment)
- Converting a card catalogue to an electronic format enables the school to have it done by a commercial vendor
- Improving consistency
- Centralising cataloguing reduces time spent duplicating the cataloguing for the same titles

Many jobbers or wholesalers routinely offer cataloguing for a nominal fee. Libraries considering automation in the future will want to consider ordering MARC catalogue records along with card sets. This investment in the future allows the school to stockpile MARC data for the automation project. It also greatly reduces the amount of time required to complete the recon, or retrospective conversion of the catalogue.

Combination

Most schools opt for a combination of commercial and original cataloguing, purchasing commercial cataloguing whenever possible, and doing original cataloguing for items in the collection for which commercial cataloguing is not available.

UNION CATALOGUES

Centralised cataloguing in a divisional or district processing centre can result in a union catalogue where the print and audiovisual materials of that network of libraries are known. Union catalogues achieve uniformity throughout the system, avoiding duplication of effort and promoting resource sharing.

ADVANCE INFORMATION APPLIANCES IN DIGITAL LIBRARY

Although digital libraries are intended to support education and knowledge work, current digital library interfaces are narrowly focused on retrieval. Furthermore, they are designed for desktop computers with keyboards, mice, and high-speed network connections. Desktop computers fail to support many key aspects of knowledge work, including active reading, free form ink annotation, fluid movement among document activities, and physical mobility.

This paper proposes portable computers specialized for knowledge work, or *digital library information appliances*, as a new platform for accessing digital libraries. We present a number of ways that knowledge work can be augmented and transformed by the use of such appliances.

These insights are based on our implementation of two research prototype systems: XLibris, an "active reading machine," and Tele- Web, a mobile World Wide Web browser.

Fig. XLibris Prototype in a Reader's lap.

The standard platform for accessing today's digital libraries is a desktop computer with a keyboard, a mouse, information retrieval software, and a network connection. Unfortunately, desktop computers are not suitable for many types of knowledge work.

Studies of people using electronic and paper documents show that desktop systems fail to support four important activities:

- Active reading,
- Free form ink annotation,

- Fluid movement among document activities,
- Physical mobility.

As a result of focusing on the desktop, today's interfaces for accessing digital libraries support retrieval in isolation, without addressing these broader work practices. We propose a new platform for accessing digital libraries: specialized portable computers designed for knowledge work, or *digital library information appliances.*

In this paper, we draw on our experience designing and building two research prototype information appliances— the XLibris "active reading machine" and the TeleWeb mobile Web browser— to show how these devices can support a broad range of activities in the digital library.

FLUID MOVEMENT AMONG DOCUMENT ACTIVITIES

The third key aspect of knowledge work is fluid movement among different styles of reading and different document activities. As an example, consider the process of "information triage" where an analyst skims through a pile of search results and reduces them to a manageable set.

The current practice is to fire off a query to a search engine, retrieve the 100 top-ranked documents, print them out, mark them up with highlighters, and put them into piles. Analysts then read the most relevant passages to answer the original question. Consider an alternative scenario where the analyst owns a digital library information appliance.

After conducting a search, the analyst skims the documents online. The appliance enhances skimming by emphasizing important material. As on paper, the analyst marks up important information as it is found. Instead of reviewing the collected information by thumbing through piles of paper, the analyst views a concise collection of his or her text annotations.

If any of the annotated material is worth reading in greater depth, the analyst can do so comfortably online. If the analyst needs more information, the text that has already been highlighted can be used to generate the next query.

At a high level, this scenario demonstrates fluid movement among document activities. The analyst quickly moves among searching, skimming, annotating, reviewing, and deep reading.

There is no waiting for a printer. Because skimming and deep reading are tightly integrated with retrieval, analysts can determine if the information they are collecting is useful before they invest much effort. This scenario also demonstrates how computation can enhance skimming, reviewing, and searching.

Because the interface is based on a paper document metaphor, the reading and annotation activities remain much the same as on paper. In our design, the "computer" remains in the background and, when requested, rises to the surface to assist the reader with the tasks of skimming, reviewing, and searching. Below we describe how XLibris supports and augments these three activities.

Skimming Mode

Skimming is one way readers gain a quick impression of a text. When skimming, the reader's eyes typically search for and alight on key words or sentences and take in short passages before moving on. Sometimes the reader becomes engaged and shifts into deep reading, or is distracted and moves into quicker skimming or into riffling.

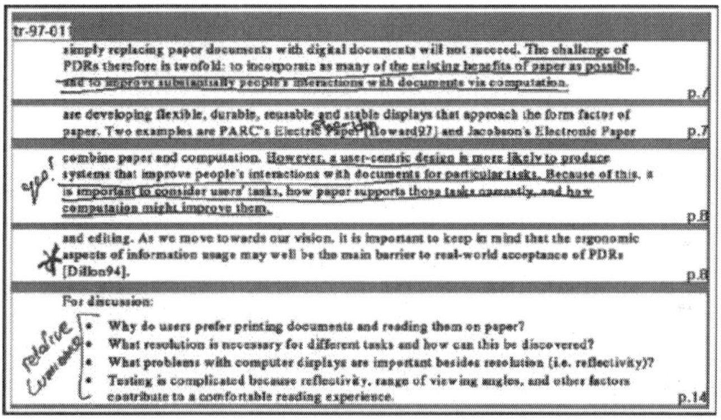

Fig. The Reader's Notebook shows annotated clippings of documents laid end-to-end. Clippings are labeled with document title and page number and are linked to the corresponding pages.

XLibris' "skimming mode" highlights phrases and sentences that are characteristic of the document being skimmed. We call out key phrases because they can be read at a glance and tend to reflect the topic of the nearby text.

This assists with the activity of scanning the text for relevant portions to read. The *Wall Street Journal* and *People Magazine* use a similar technique of boldfacing company names and Hollywood celebrities' name to help readers find information. We also highlight summary sentences to support a speedreading– like activity. Skimming mode uses a commercial text summarizer to identify summary sentences that are emphasized. Skimming through a document of highlighted summary sentences provides a narrative overview that is not available by just reading key phrases.

Both of these highlighting techniques permit a smooth transition from skimming to deep reading: key terms and sentences can help readers decide whether a passage is worth reading and are likely to be appropriate places to transition to deep reading. Skimming mode uses shades from gray to black to indicate term importance. Meaningful terms are identified by heuristics that select noun phrases.

The shade for each term is then based on a statistical information retrieval measure: terms that occur frequently in the document but occur rarely in other documents are coloured black, while terms common to many documents are coloured light gray. For example, the term "digital library information appliance" would be coloured black when it appears in this document. Skimming is a common practice: a study of college students' reading habits reported that skimming occupied 32per cent of their reading time, and that "86per cent of the descriptions of skimming strategies mentioned a selection process based on key words and/or particular sentences and paragraphs in certain text locations".

Although our design requires empirical evaluation to confirm its utility, from our experiences thus far, we are optimistic that computers can improve the skimming activity and that augmented skimming is a useful function for a digital library information appliance.

Reviewing the Reader's Notebook

Reviewing paper documents is facilitated by the marks made during reading: marks not only record information but are also used to organize it for later review. There are three common venues for marking: annotating on the page, taking notes in a notebook, and writing on loose-leaf paper. Annotations on the page highlight key information but tend to be lost in piles of paper. Notebooks are compact and can be reviewed quickly, but taking notes can be tedious and error-prone.

Unbound notes can be reorganized flexibly, but require even more effort by the note taker. XLibris' Reader's Notebook combines the best features of annotating directly on the page, of taking notes in a separate notebook, and of organizing index cards. As with paper documents, readers mark on the page in the context of the document, yet without the laborious and imprecise step of copying.

As with a bound notebook, readers can review concise annotations by time. Finally, as with note cards, flexible filtering and sorting of the view allow readers to reorganize their information as needs change. The Reader's Notebook extracts "clippings" of annotated text and lays them end to end in a separate, multipage view.

Each clipping is linked to the corresponding annotated page, so readers can move fluidly between notes and documents. Each clipping includes some surrounding text, and is labeled with document title and page number to help readers understand the meaning of the marks. In designing clippings, we had to decide how much of the document should be shown for each annotation.

Starting with the bounding rectangle of each ink stroke, we expand it horizontally to the width of the page and vertically to include complete words. Snippets that overlap are merged together resulting in reasonably sized clippings of annotated text. The Reader's Notebook can display, sort, and filter clippings from one document or from all documents. By default, clippings are sorted by document page number, which is analogous to rummaging through a pile of paper, but should be faster because readers do not see the less important (i.e., un-annotated) information. Clippings can also be sorted by time so that new information appears at the end, as in a paper notebook.

Finally, readers can filter the clippings by ink colour to search for different kinds of marks or to group related items together. Many readers already use different pens to mark different types of information. For example, some lawyers highlight "pro" information in green and "con" information in red.

Finding Information Related to Readers' Annotations

Readers often search for related material and move from one text to another. For example, an ecology student studying the effects of acid rain in the Appalachian Mountains decides to search the Internet for information on the economy of West Virginia. A doctor reading up on a drug she has never prescribed decides to follow a reference to a study of its side effects.

Unfortunately, in both online and offline situations, finding related materials and reading are not well integrated. Typical information retrieval interfaces force users to stop reading, to identify related documents, and then to print them.

References found in paper documents are even more timeconsuming to track down. Although hypertext was designed to address some of these problems, authors cannot anticipate the information needs of all readers. Ironically, despite the fact that readers' interests may change rapidly, interfaces for moving from reading to finding and back to reading again are time consuming and disruptive.

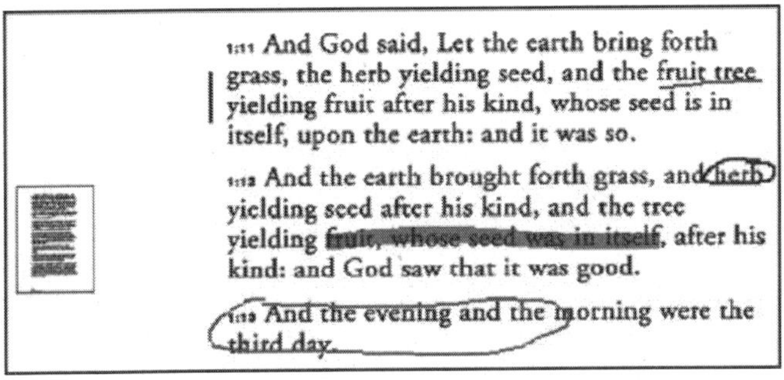

Fig. Examples of Highlighting, Underlining, Circling, and margin Annotations. Each Annotation Generates a Query. If a good match is found, XLibris adds a margin link (Rectangle on the left) that shows the thumbnail of the Destination page.

Clearly this is another example where fluid movement across document activities is desirable. XLibris facilitates fluid transitions among reading, searching and browsing by creating a dynamic hypertext from readers' marks.

The system observes readers' annotations and the text of the underlying document and generates hypertext links (margin links) to related documents:

no additional effort from readers or authors is required. Because XLibris suggests links of interest to particular readers at particular times— based on the passages they are marking— people can discover useful information *serendipitously*. This type of serendipitous retrieval is a benefit of paper libraries: as people walk to the shelf for a particular book, walls of related books surround them, making it possible to find interesting material accidentally.

Although serendipity in the library is often a rewarding experience, it is generally lacking in online systems. XLibris provides two user interfaces that integrate reading, searching, browsing, and serendipity. These are described below.

MARGIN LINKS

Margin links provide serendipitous access to related documents *during* the active reading process. As readers mark up passages, the system finds related documents and presents links unobtrusively in the margin; our intent is to provide a modeless link suggestion mechanism. Because margin links persist, readers can follow links at their leisure.

We use thumbnail images of the target page as anchors. The reader taps on an anchor to move to that page. For the most part, link creation does not disrupt the reading process since the reader is free to disregard the suggestion and to continue reading. In the current design, however, margin links intrude on the reading process more than we would like.

One problem is that XLibris computes a separate query for each stroke (although strokes often do not result in margin links because of a similarity threshold).

We have begun to address this by adding a button to turn links off and by designing ways to manage the frequency with which margin links appear.

READING AND DIGITAL LIBRARIES

The first and most fundamental document activity is reading. “Reading” encompasses a broad range of complex and poorly understood practices involving documents, including skimming, searching, browsing, speed-reading, surfing, reviewing, and rereading. Although we often take it for granted, reading can be hard work. We use the term *active reading* to distinguish this rich collection of activities from simply looking at words on a page.

Desktop computers do not support active reading. Once expected to create a paperless office, computers have instead produced ever-increasing quantities of paper documents. Dataquest predicts printers and copiers will generate over 1012 pages in the U.S. in 1997.

This statistic suggests that people do not use computers to read. The reason for this is obvious: paper supports extended, focused, deep reading practices better. Current research on digital libraries does not address a broad range of reading activities. Instead, as David Levy points out, digital libraries support shallower, more fragmented, and less concentrated reading.

The research focus in this field is on tools for search, selection, and distillation, tools that promote identification and extraction of information fragments. Because digital library interfaces do not support active reading, people search online and then print documents to read them. This "search and print" reality contrasts with the "search and read" ideal held by researchers.

Although a dual online/paper system is not *a priori* undesirable, we will show the many advantages of an online system that enables a variety of reading practices. The XLibris active reading machine supports a broad class of reading activities by employing a "paper document metaphor" (as opposed to the desktop metaphor) that imitates the physical experience of reading and marking on paper.

The paper document metaphor follows lessons learned from a number of studies comparing reading online to reading on paper, summarized below.

TANGIBILITY

Beyond Paper: Supporting Active Reading with Free-form Digital Ink Annotations

Bill N. Schilit, Gene Golovchinsky, Morgan N. Price
FX Palo Alto Laboratory, Inc.

Readers often move paper documents to avoid glare, to speed up handwriting, or to adjust their perspective of a text. In contrast, most computer displays are stationary while in use, so that readers must move themselves—their heads, their bodies, and their arms— rather than their display.

XLibris supports paper document-like tangibility by running on tablet displays. Although XLibris has not been deployed for real use, people say that holding a page-sized display in their lap and being able to easily reposition it changes their online reading experience. The tangibility of paper documents also supports navigation. Turning paper pages seems easy and natural, and the weight and thickness of a paper document convey length and location.

In XLibris, pressure strips on the case of the device provide a tangible interface for page turning: pressing on one side of a sensor moves to the next or previous page, and holding down initiates riffling through pages. The harder you press, the faster you move. A quick animated transition indicates the direction of turning.

Finally, "location guides" of varying thickness drawn in the top cor- ners of each page provide feedback about the length of the document and the reader's current location.

Page Orientation and Fixed Layout

Paper documents are laid out on fixed-size pages. The page layout often communicates the type of the document (*e.g.,* business letter versus technical article) and where to find important information (*e.g.*, a return address). The fixed layout also supports spatial memory and helps readers find old information. In these and other ways, paper pages give readers an excellent "sense of the document." This sense of the document is often lost online.

Most CRT monitors cannot display a full page of text legibly, leading to awkward scrolling and zooming. Word processors and Web browsers commonly re-flow the text on a "page." And hypertext versions of paper documents can lead to disorientation and a sense of being lost. XLibris respects pages by displaying the image of a single page at a time.

Because the LCD panels we use are designed for landscape viewing, XLibris rotates the image 90° to approximate the portrait orientation of a typical printed page. XLibris stores the image of each page and the underlying text; this "image + text" file format is compatible with printed and with scanned documents.

Multiple Displays

People often work with multiple pieces of paper simultaneously, either with several pages from one document or with several documents. Most of today's computers provide multiple virtual displays through use of a windowing system. Unfortunately, the effort of managing window layout and switching among windows can interfere with reading.

Therefore XLibris displays a single page image and does not support windows. Since limiting the digital library information appliance to a single page image is problematic, we have considered a number of ways to address the need for collateral displays.

Presenting two full-page images side by side, as in Book Emulator, makes text unreadable on current tablet displays, but may be feasible as

LCD technology evolves. A form factor with multiple physical displays is another approach.

(Bush's vision of a Memex desk included multiple displays). In our case, to maintain mobility, a book (instead of a tablet or desk) with two opposable LCD panels may be appropriate. Weiser presents an enticing vision of ubiquitous computing with devices so cheap they can be scattered and used as paper.

In the near term, however, a small number of pen computers in conjunction with nearby desktop displays or even paper may provide the most practical solution to the problem of collateral document work. In summary, XLibris employs tangibility, page orientation, and fixed layout to provide an online reading experience comparable, in many ways, to reading from paper.

FREE FORM INK ANNOTATION

"Until we provide support for smooth integration of annotation with reading, it is likely that people will continue to annotate paper materials, even as they read materials in a digital library." – Cathy Marshall The second key document activity is annotation.

Knowledge work involves reading combined with categorizing, speculating, remembering, judging, or, more broadly, critical thinking.

This active reading process is facilitated by underlining, highlighting and making notes on the text or in a separate notebook. Marking on paper helps readers "make the text their own" and is a common practice associated with deep understanding of written information. In a nutshell, readers write.

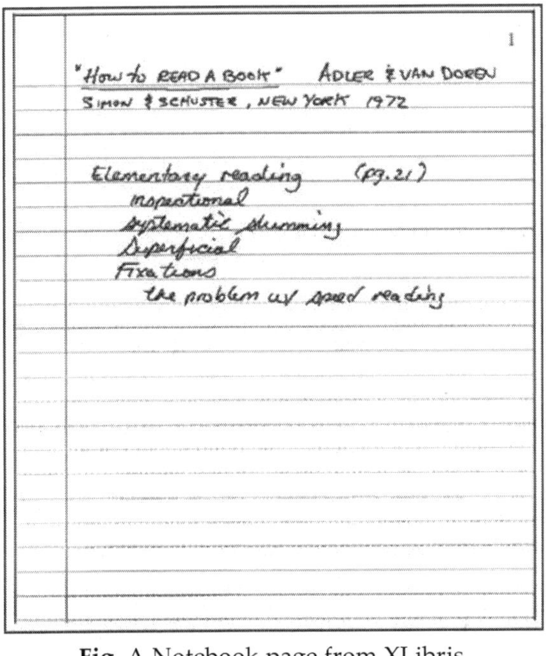

Fig. A Notebook page from XLibris.

Unfortunately, annotation online is quite different from its paper-based cousin. Interfaces for annotating often involve selecting a command, pointing with a mouse, and typing on a keyboard. They generally require much more effort than scribbling with a pen. Text annotations are not as visually distinct as ink marks, and online annotations often cause changes in the layout of the document. We believe that the ability to make unstructured, free-form, idiosyncratic ink marks is a crucial feature of any interface to digital libraries.

Although such marks may not have explicit meaning to the computer, they have rich semantic meaning, supporting visual and episodic memory. An essential aspect of ink on paper is its lack of modality: users can write anything they want, anywhere on the page.

In XLibris, we followed this principle by letting users scribble notes, draw figures, highlight, or annotate text, all without switching modes or applications. Readers highlight and mark-up document page images as they read or flip to a blank page in a lined notebook for more space. XLibris provides several colours of ink, several highlighter pens, and a stroke-based eraser.

ORGANISATIONAL STRUCTURES AND INFORMATION FLOWS

An organisational structure is a means to incorporate various functions in order to pursue some predetermined objectives. Organisational structures also provide the lines along which information flows. Researchers have described two ways to organise libraries. They are:

- Specialisation; and
- Coordination and integration.

Coordination and integration simply means bringing together all individual efforts to achieve particular objectives. Specialisation, however, can be interpreted in two approaches: departmentalisation and hierarchy. Departmentalisation means the organisation is structured horizontally by identifying and grouping similar or related required activities or tasks into departments, for example, function, activities, geography, subjects, form of material, etc.

There are two main approaches to departmentalisation within academic libraries, function and subject, and they are matters of continual debate. The first approach is a structure dominated by administrative function. The subject divisional library is the alternative approach to the strictly functional. The staff are split by subject, with services and processing entirely subordinate.

- The introduction of computers into academic libraries is a major reason why the debate between functionalism and subject organisation has been by-passed.

One consequence of automation has been that:

- Technology has reduced the time necessary to carry out one of the most tedious part's of librarian's work, record creation and manipulation.

The second method of specialisation in organisations is the creation of a vertical hierarchy, with the individuals located on the top of organisation having more authority than those at successively lower levels.

- 'Such structures are often also represented diagrammatically as a family-tree, depicting line management responsibilities above and below. And any given structure can be either functional or subject-orientated.'

The merits of a hierarchical structure have been questioned by researcher; he points out several problems, such as:

- 'Reporting lines tends to be long, and the responsibility of any individual very limited. Many staff rarely come into contact with staff more than one or two grades higher, with the result that communication is often poor and it is hard for staff below a senior level to have any sense of involve-ment in the organisation.'

In place of a hierarchical structure, researcher proposed a 'flat' structure as one possibility for libraries in the near future. In examining the rapid change and different climate that are being encountered by libraries, The 'flat' management structure as having:

- Fewer middle managers, and more reliance on the two extremes—the senior administrators and lower level staff—to make decisions.

It could be speculated that the implications for the development of Management Information Systems (MIS) in libraries with 'flat' management structures may be comparable to the general problems of introducing MIS in small organisations:

- Larger organisations have found greater success with MIS use than smaller ones. Libraries, even the largest, are relatively small organisations and much planning is required to initiate and gain acceptance of MIS. There will be more resistance in small organisations than in very large ones since the likelihood of a lesser degree of bureaucratisation and traditional line and staff authority divisions are in place in such operations. The perception of the MIS as crystallising these divisions may offset their initial acceptance.

DECISION-MAKING, ORGANISATIONAL STRUCTURES, AND INFORMATION NEEDS

Whether organisations are large or small, there is managerial stratification. The tasks of top management are development of the organisation's domain, management of the interface with external environments and establishment of the organisation's administrative climate; middle management develop rules, procedures and policies for day-to-day operations; and technical management sees that services are rendered and policies carried out.

In a conference on Management Information Systems, researcher identified the library staff with each of these management levels as follows:

- Senior/top managers (*e.g.*, deputies and chiefs).
- Middle managers (*e.g.*, heads of major divisions).
- Line/technical managers (*e.g.*, service desk super-intendents).
- 'Some individuals will straddle more than one category. Deputies, for example, will be concerned with middle management and senior management. Furthermore the model is generalised, and it is true that in smaller libraries such stratification may break down since everyone is doing a bit of everything!'

Decision-making has been defined as:

- The formulation of alternative courses of action to meet the situation under consideration and in the choice between these alternatives after an evaluation of the effectiveness in achieving the decision maker's objectives. One of the most important factors is information from which an appreciation of the decision can be made.

There are three stages in decision making:

- Intelligence;
- Design, and
- Choice.

The intelligence stage encompasses collection, classification, processing, and presentation of the data necessary for the later stages of the decision making process. During the design stage, the decision maker outlines alternative solutions, each of which involves a set of actions to be taken. He usually uses quantitative techniques and design tools such as are common in management sciences and system analysis. The data gathered in the previous stage is now examined in statistical and other models to forecast possible outcomes for each alternative. In the choice stage, the decision maker is faced with various alternatives. One alternative must be selected, which becomes the formal decision and consequently generates actions to be taken.

This may seem deceptively easy, but in reality there are many difficulties that usually make choice a complex stage. It becomes clear that decision making is the conversion of information into action. The intended actions are planning, organising, directing and controlling of activities to achieve objectives.

However, decision-making at different managerial levels is not necessarily an identical process, and there are clear implications for the type of management information required.

- The degree of structure is dependent on the degree of predictability of the variables involved in a given decision. Unstructured decisions have few predictable variables; structured ones have many... Unstructured decisions are usually made at the strategic planning level and semi-structured decisions at the operational management level. The most structured decisions are reached at the operational control level.

Library managers might, therefore, be supposed to need access to the information which is appropriate to their level of decision making.

The relationship between the needs for information in all three levels of library management is:

- These levels and their various concerns obviously overlap, and in some cases may be undertaken by the same person, especially in smaller libraries. Nevertheless, the distinction remains a generally valid one, in terms of information need. At operational and some middle levels, formal information, systemati-cally provided in short time comparisons, forms the bulk of what is required. Higher up the pyramid, unstructured information, much of it external, is a more significant consideration; also the more senior librarians will only want snapshot or selective sets of data derived, for example, from operational systems and the university budget.
- There are two kinds of management information, the formal and the informal. Both of them derived from external and internal sources to the academic library but informal management information are mostly found externally such as from the users and the administrators who govern budgets.

THE METHODOLOGY OF ACHIEVING ORGANISATIONAL CHANGES

Recent years were for the libraries a period of faster, greater and more dramatic changes than has ever before been experienced. The omnipresence of the new technologies, the ever-increasing cooperation, the globalization as premises of the evolution towards the *Global Information Society,* the emphasis on quality, the diminution of the financial resources are the main agents imposing the change of libraries. Implementing the necessary changes for the academic libraries is no easy job as it requires a differentiation between changes to ensure the coherence of actions within the available resources.

It is also important to use planning and control methods that contribute to reduce the span of the change process and to optimize the use of resources. Finally, it requires suitable structures, staff training and overcoming the resistance to change. All these respects are subjects of change management—a distinct discipline whose key-aspects-in point of increasing the success and the efficiency of organisational changes—we present. The concept of organisational change, as defined by the management theories, is a significant, extended, important change that affects the entire organisation or parts of it.

Such changes do not occur naturally, they are changes whose implementation is the task of the management team. The methodology of achieving these changes is one of the main issues of change management and it is treated in very different ways by management theoreticians. The best known approach is the one proposed by Kurt Lewin and E. H. Schein that identifies three essential stages in the process of organisational changes, stages somewhat similar to chemical processes: unfreezing—the trial to create the reasons for change; moving/implementing change—identifying solutions adequate to circumstance and applying them; freezing—a new equilibrium is crystallizing.

From the point of view of implementing changes in the university library, the methodology presented by Popescu, M. has the advantage of a pragmatic approach that defines two major stages of the process of starting and implementing change: identifying the need of change and achieving change. Identifying the need of change aims to establish the favourable changes that may add value to the organisation.

In the authors' opinion the important changes must be implemented from a strategic point of view; this means that, when establishing the changes that must be done and their order, the mission and the strategic objectives of the organisation are kept in mind. This way one can avoid the risk of starting complex and expensive processes that can not be financially supported or that have little or no effects upon the performances of the organisation. Several studies discussing changes in libraries develop the above idea.

Thus, Troll, A.D. underlines that the evaluation activity usually carried out in libraries is not enough in order to plan changes: without knowing the external and the internal context and the library's strategy, such an evaluation is of no help in understanding what changes are relevant and can assure the accomplishment of the library's mission. It's necessary to define clearly the strategic objectives and the main lines of change that sustain planning changes in the library. To complete this idea we state that, once the strategy is elaborated it has to be communicated; making public and discussing the mission, the policy and the general objectives of the library are means of communication through which the top management acknowledges everyone concerned its view on the future of the library and obtains their support. Communicating, informing and involving the staff are elements that contribute to overcome the resistance to change which is normal in the case of any major change. The bigger the changes, the greater the resistance to change and ignoring this is the source of many failures as shown in many studies on this topic.

Achieving change, the second stage, is a complex process having clearly stated beginning and ending points and, between, a sequence of three activities:

- The preliminary study or the planning–it's goal is to define change, to evaluate the achieving conditions and the expected results;
- Projecting the change–it refers to defining solutions and including them in specific documents;
- Implementing and checking the results–it is a stage that, paradoxically, often raises difficulties because of the resistance to change.

These three activities are intricately interconnected: change is achieved progressively, but the process is not linear, solutions adopted in one stage are often rectified in a following one. The amount of innovation the solutions bear, the fact that change by definition involves contouring and implementing new solutions—what causes it to seem unique and risky—the important quantity of resources involved, the participation of many specialists and actors from different structures are characteristic elements that render complex and difficult the achieving of organisational changes.

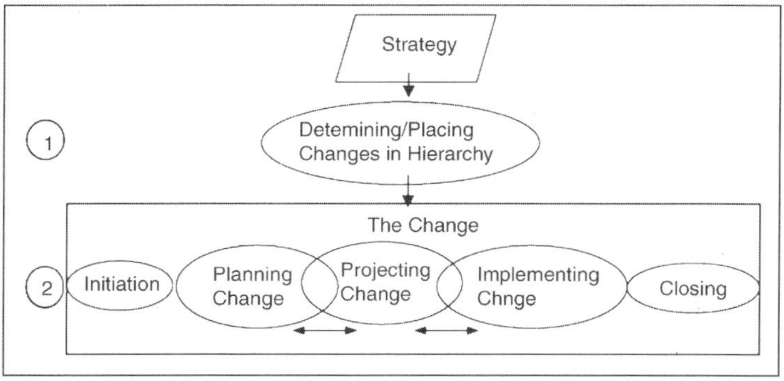

Fig. Stages of the Process of Achievement Organisational Changes.

The solution is to approach them as projects, in the manner proper to project management. The scheme in figure synthesizes the methodology for accomplishing the organisational changes, whose application ensures: on one hand–the coherence of the actions, through relating to the strategy of the organisation, on the other hand, advantages determined by approaching the change as project, by using the project as 'vehicle for the change', which means, implicitly, applying the principles and methods specific to project management.

CASE STUDY: LIBRARY OF TRANSILVANIA UNIVERSITY

The case study realised at the Library of Transilvania University of Brasov sets out to analyse the changes made during the last decade within the university library, from the perspective of the change management, to present the change priorities inscribed in the library strategy along the years to follow and to identify the key factors on whom there depends the success of the change projects. *Transilvania* University of Brasov is an institution of higher education and research, which enjoys high prestige on the local, national and international level.

It is an extended university, with 16 faculties—8 are of technical profile and 8 of university profile, with more than 22.000 students at the university degree, master's degree and doctorate cycles, full time and distance learning. In the context of globalization, of Romania's integration within the EU, the University achieved important changes in all fields of activity and structures, in view of harmonizing with the new requirements and in view of assuring the quality of the services of education and research.

The Library is a structure of *Transilvania* University of Brasov, an entity without its own judicial personality, subordinated to the top management of the university. The mission of the university library is to ensure the documentary and information basis necessary for the education process, to enhance and to communicate them, as well as other services, to the benefit of the information users, facilitating the diversified and rapid access to all categories of sources.

The documentary patrimony of the Library of *Transilvania* University of Brasov includes: books, serial publications, manuscripts, cartographic documents, printed musical documents, audio-visual documents, graphic documents, electronic documents etc. The collections of the Library are constituted and developed through acquisition, transfer, national and international exchange, donations and sponsorship. The endowment is ensured through financing from the university management, as well as through transfers, donations and sponsorship.

The organisation and the functioning of the Library observe the provisions of the specific legislation elaborated on the national level, as well as the internal regulations of the university. The Library has its own strategies and plans of activity whose approval by the Senate of the University ensures the integration in the general strategy of the institution. Like the university it is part of, the library achieved a series of changes in order to improve its performance.Seen from the perspective of the results, the described actions display a series of defaults.

For instance:

- The relocation of the library became a strategic objective during the year 2005 after the finalization of a building with another initial destination. The placement of the Library in this building ensured the concentration of the activities and the amelioration of the working environment, however the adaptation costs were high, without ensuring the perfect compliance with the needs of the library;
- The automation of the processes of document management and communication is likewise questionable under the aspect of the adopted solutions, taking into consideration that the used software requires expensive hardware resources, and the results with respect to the performance of the processes were not up to the expectations;
- The efficacy of the actions undertaken within the library for the access to digital information may be appreciated as reduced, because of the lack of correlation between the equipments in the structure of the informatics system, as well as of the insufficient training with respect to the users' access to these resources. These resources did not benefit from an adequate promotion among the users who, to a too great extent, ignore their informative value and even their existence;

- The modernization of the evaluation system is slowed down by the lack of an adequate evaluation model and also by the generalized delay of the automated means for collecting and processing the data, and the efficiency of the evaluation is also affected by the persistence of the non-trained and disinterested staff in accomplishing this activity.
- The endowment with sufficient, stable and qualified staff is hindered by the still low number of librarians with specialized studies from the geographical area, by the unattractive level of the wages, by the rooting in certain posts of non-efficient employees, refractory to the new.

The outlined deficiencies are, at least in part, determined by the manner in which change management was implemented in the university library, both as regards planning the changes and settling the solutions, and as regards their implementation. It is to be observed especially the neglecting of the social aspects with respect to the staff's training, the resistance to change etc.—as factors which have negatively influenced the efficacy and the efficiency of the change processes.

The university library will continue the process of the qualitative transformations during the following period, but in different ways. The aim is at using efficiently the strategy, as management instrument and at developing mechanisms that should allow the continuous control and improvement of the library performance through systematic actions. To this purpose, in a first stage there was carried out the diagnostic analysis of the management system of the library, whose conclusions are presented as follows, synthesized in strengths and weaknesses.

STRENGTHS

- There is a strategy of the library, harmonized with that of the university. The mission of the library and the system of values are published on the site. The objectives are realistic, measurable; the accent is laid on improving the performance, in order to contribute to ensuring the quality of the educational and research services carried out by the university. There was set as priority axis of research the implementation of a system of quality management, through which there is created the framework for the continuous improvement of the quality.
- The university and library management has the capability to professionally approach the changes, evinces competences as regards the ample perspective and its concretization in valid strategies of development, the settling of the plans for further action and the provision with the resources necessary for accom-plishing the change projects, the optimization of the structure, the implementation of modern methods of management.

- Human resources: the library has 52 employees, among which 32 with higher education and 11 with higher education in the field. The staff benefited from training and of mobility exchanges in the country and abroad.

WEAKNESSES

- *Control of the Performance*: The library achieves the assessment of the performance every year; however the criteria and the indicators which are used do not reflect the qualitative aspects of the activity, the effects of the library services upon the educational and scientific research processes. There is no management system that should measure the costs of the services/activities realised by the library.
- *Control of the Processes:* There has begun to be implemented the management through processes, however the action is in an incipient phase of analysis and description of the key processes through procedures.
- *Human Resources*: Staff's evaluation is done in compliance with the law, however the insufficient resources used in this process make the evaluation not always relevant. The participation of the staff in solving the problems is unequal and the rewarding system is non-stimulating.
- *Organisational Culture:* There is no culture of the quality, there are insufficiently promoted values such as team work, staff's implication, opening towards change.

Taking into account the submitted situation, the priority axes for the development of the capability of the library to continuously improve its performance are the following:

- *People:* The continuation of the process of staff training in quality management, with accent on achieving behavioural changes, on raising the degree of implication in solving the problems and on team work.
- *Users:* Orientation towards the customers, definition of the requirements and evaluation of their satisfaction. This implies in the first place the improvement of the system evaluating the library performance, through the introduction of criteria and indicators that should better reflect the effects upon the quality of the educational and research processes. The control will be also extended upon the costs of the services and of the activities realised by the library.
- *Processes:* Development and implementation of instruments and also of working and control procedures that should ensure the optimization of the processes and their continuous improvement.

The achievement of the change processes will be coordinated by the Management Council of the library. Both the initiation of the projects and their unfolding will be largely promoted in the framework of the library, for obtaining the feedback and for attracting the people in realizing the changes. The financing of the projects will be done from its own funds, but there will be likewise accessed funds from the Operational Programmes.

CONCLUSIONS

The existence during the last decades of the university libraries has been characterized by ample changes, a process that will continue. The achievement of the changes is an issue of the management library, whose results may be considerably improved through a professional approach, based on the methods of the change management. The case study developed by the authors presents the first sequences of the change programme that will be achieved during the years to follow at the library of *Transilvania* University of Brasov, with reference to the methodology of change elaboration and implementation.

BRIEF HISTORY OF THE UNIVERSITY OF TARTU

I will start my presentation with a small overview of the University of Tartu as our library is a part of the university and it is not possible to observe them apart. The University of Tartu is the oldest university in Estonia and one of the oldest in the Northern countries. On 30 June 1632, King Gustav II Adolf of Sweden signed the Foundation Decree of *Academia Dorpatensis*, which marks the beginning of our university's history. We can distinguish five periods when we speak about the history of the University of Tartu:

- The Swedish period 1632-1710
- The Imperial Tartu University 1802-1918
- 1919-1940 Tartu University in the Republic of Estonia
- 1944-1989 Tartu State University
- 1991-Tartu University in the newly independent Republic of Estonia

I only describe three of them as the important ones for my presentation. The first, the so-called 'Swedish period', is important while it turned a small provincial town to the university town. The Town Council was interested in having the university here to restore its former prosperity. Tallinn and Riga were big and important centres and not at all interested in the university and the noisy and hectic young men-students. Sweden in its turn wanted to:

- Strengthen the Lutheran religion in the former Catholic country;
- Strengthen the presence of the Swedish kingdom.

The students were mostly Swedes and Finns. We are proud that our university is so old but in fact the university, established during the Swedish period, was not one of the best reconized universities in Europe. The university in Tartu functioned with the Faculties of Philosophy, Law, Theology, and Medicine, enjoying the privileges similar to those granted to the University of Uppsala.

The University of Tartu was closed in 1710 after the Swedish army had surrendered to the Russian forces after the defeat in the Northern War. The second period of the history of the university was 1802-1918 'reopening of the university'. This period can be characterized as the prosperity of the university. The Baltic Germans needed the university to educate their children. After the French Revolution studying abroad was not allowed. Russia also needed its own university. So in Tartu the European science and the Russian state met. The Germans wanted to have a small Heidelberg or Göttingen and somehow they succeeded in it.

The official language at the university was German and the religion was Lutheran. The 19th century was the period of prosperity of the university, the scientists K. E. von Baer, J. W. Struve and many others show us the level of scientific research in Tartu at that time. The teaching of Germanic languages also goes back to this period and has long traditions. Already in 1865 the Department for German Language at the University of Tartu was established. The first professor at the department was Leo Meyer, a linguist from Göttingen who stayed in Dorpat for 33 years. The number of students increased every day, Rutiku and Kegelmann.

OVERVIEW OF THE FOUNDATION OF GERMAN LIBRARY

I concentrate my attention on the fifth period which begins in 1991 while at that time our library was established. After the collapse of the Soviet Union the situation in our country was changing. We had to build up new society, a new educational system. The example of our library illustrates the developments in Estonia very well. In many areas we had to start from scratch. When learning foreign languages, it is natural that the dictionaries, lexicons and scientific literature are at students' disposal, but in Tartu it was not so.

The first German DAAD—Professor in Tartu—Claus Sommer-hage—started establishing a library. Among the many names the DAAD-Lecturer Claus Sommerhage should be emphasized. In 1992-1997 Dr. Claus Sommerhage was Guest Professor at the Department for German Language and Literature, 1997-1999 Extraordinary Professor. He innovated new curricula in teaching German literature, especially Modern German Literature. Since his coming only the overview courses had been taught. He started with analytical literature seminars, Rutiku and Kegelmann. The most important thing he did for the department was establishing our library.

He knew that without a library teaching literature was impossible. As Sommerhage had said we had a couple of copies of the novel Aula by Hermann Kant on our shelves. He was right. He started looking for funds in Germany and Switzerland, he used his own connections and personal charm. Without intensive support of the German and Swiss funds our library would not exist today.

FINANCING, PROGRAMMES, FUNDS

Our library is unique because until 2003 there was no budget for it. Nevertheless, it was increasing with every day. At the beginning many books were donated to our library. Tartu is an old university town and professors and lecturers had their own very good libraries. Many professors and lecturers decided to give their German books to our library.

The theatre 'Vanemuine' liquidated its library in 1999 and we received all their books in the German language. From there we have our 23-volume complete works of Dostoevsky from 1922 which is considered to be the best Dostoevsky translation since then.

The oldest book in our library dates back to 1780. We also received books from our German friends. More than 15 years Professor Norbert Nail from the University of Marburg equipped us with every kind of books and journals about the German language and linguistics. Since 2001 our library is in the project of Gebert Rüf Fund-the Swiss Baltic Net for the Swiss Libraries and Swiss Literature in the Baltic States.

We can order German Swiss literature every year for 1000 ChFr. The sum is not big but very valuable for our library. The project also coordinates the work of Schweizer Lesezimmer in the Baltic States.

We meet every year in Lithuania, Latvia or Estonia to present our annual work and discuss our problems. These meetings are always useful and interesting. This time the meeting takes place in Vilnius In 2005-2007 our library was involved in the programme 'Menschen und Bücher', an initiative of the Goethe Institute for Central and Eastern Europe.

For our library it was a great privilege to be involved in the programme because our financial resources have always been limited. This time we could order books necessary for us and all our lecturers were involved in the ordering process. So we could efficiently enrich our library and every lecturer could order books for his or her course. The budget was 15,000 EUR and we could also invite a German author to Tartu.

DEPARTMENT LIBRARIES AT THE UNIVERSITY OF TARTU

Since 2003 the University Library has pursued the policy of supporting department libraries. Until then the status of a small department library was obscure. At the Department for German Language and Literature the library policy was always clear. We needed a well equipped library for students and lecturers, we were for the open access.

Since 2002 our books are in the library system INNOPAC, which makes every process with books very easy and transparent. Sometimes the department libraries are in a bad state, the books are available for very few readers but our policy was different from the very beginning. When we do have a book, people must know about it, they must have access to it.

IMPORTANCE TO THE STUDENTS AND LECTURERS

One of the priorities of our library is its closeness to students and lecturers. We are informed of every need very quickly and for the students it is comfortable that everything about one subject is concentrated at one place. Since 1999 the Department for German Language and Literature has its own rooms in the former printing-house in the centre of the town, opposite the university main building. The renovation of the building had been contributed by different foreign embassies. It houses Departments for German, French, Spanish and Scandinavian Languages and is called 'Paabel'.

For our library it gave a possibility to expose all the books better, to create a real library system, to create a room where people like to work. The rooms for the German library in this new building are next to the seminar rooms. The students can use library early in the morning and between the lectures and seminars during the day. Our users are the students of the Department for German Language and Literature, the students of the Language Centre of the University, the Master's course students who study translation and interpretation. Every reader who possesses the university library card is welcome in our library. Closeness also means that we always consider the requests of the students.

In the last years when we received our budget, we have ordered books for the students who need them for writing their Bachelor's or Master's theses. The priority of our library is to be of high scientific quality. This is the direction Claus Sommerhage gave to our library and we still hold on to it. It is sometimes difficult because of our insufficient financing, but we always choose books carefully, ask advice from our German patrons and friends, try to be informed of the newest scientific literature. So we can affirm that our library has been created by professionals and it fulfils its tasks.

One of our main tasks is to support the study process. At the Department for German Language and Literature the main research areas are linguistics, sociolinguistics, contact and text linguistics as well the Swiss literature and the German literature by women writers and the Baltic-German literature. Some subject areas in our library are very well presented, for example German linguistics, literary science, German history, German language history. In the last years the collection of our dictionaries and lexicons is almost ideal. As translation and interpretation are taught at our university, the collection of these books is almost excellent. We also have a good collection of German language textbooks. We have a sufficient number of copies thanks to 'LUKKA'—EU supporting programme. At our department teaching of modern Swiss literature has long traditions. Associated Professor Eve Pormeister has taught it already for 20 years and even wrote her Doctoral thesis on this subject. She has connections with the Embassy of Switzerland, Swiss Funds, Pro Helvetia. Her special interest is the reason why Swiss literature is so well presented in our library.

PLEASANT MEETING PLACE, NICE INTERIOR

Last but not least, in a small department library, the milieu plays a big role. There are people who never go to the main library of the university. They do not like too big bleak rooms without cosy corners, with too many strange people. Our library is a kind of a social gathering place for the students who study the same subject, have the same problems and pleasures. The nice and comfortable interior plays an important role here.

As our rooms have interesting architecture, it is possible to establish exhibitions and that is what we regularly do. The last exhibition is from our student who studies art as her minor. She was happy to have an opportunity to show her paintings to her friends and fellow-students. We all can enjoy her colourful and interesting works.

INTEGRATION INTO THE LIBRARY AND RELATED ORGANIZATIONS

The University of Michigan Digital Library Production Service was *not* intended to operate self-sufficiently, in isolation of the contributing organizations. There are important ties to each of the other organizations, and especially the University Library.

For example, DLPS relies on the Information Technology Division and the Media Union to provide a high level of computing support, which those organizations view as critical and enabling infrastructure. The services are provided in a manner consistent with the mission of the digital library (e.g., uninterrupted support for servers, as well as unique security and operating system configurations), ensuring that DLPS staff are devoted to building and maintaining digital library collections, rather than the hardware on which they reside.

Mainstream Library staff members provide an array of services critical to the operation of the digital library. Public service staff members provide user support for online collections, as well as end-user instruction.

Collection development staff members are responsible for selecting digital collections for local deployment and work with DLPS staff on "E-Teams" to weigh the advantages and disadvantages of alternative means of delivery. Preservation staff, with guidance from DLPS, make determinations of the most appropriate means of digital capture, and then prepare the materials for digital capture (occasionally operating equipment for the actual capture).

Mainstream Cataloging staff members create descriptive metadata for locally-converted materials, and specialized digital metadata specialists in the Cataloging Department help guide DLPS in decision-making for mapping between standards, display of bibliographic elements, and related issues.

Similarly, DLPS maintains important relationships with other areas of the Library, including the Library Systems Office, Acquisitions, and Special

Collections. Although DLPS staff members have responsibilities that touch on all of these areas of library operation, the intention of this design is to ensure that the most qualified staff member performs each task; the intention is *not* to recreate the Library within DLPS. Consequently, DLPS is fully integrated into the entire Library operation.

MISSION

Like its staffing, the goals of the Digital Library Production Service are more specific than the larger organizations within which it exists, including those of the campus-wide Digital Library Initiative.

The campus-wide DLI has responsibility for creating a collaborative organization and a coherent environment for networked information, whether locally-maintained or held remotely. Further, the DLI has a broader mission in its responsibility to explore, for example, economic and policy issues for the campus and beyond.

By contrast DLPS' responsibilities are constrained to information that is held locally (either at the University of Michigan, or at other institutions where we are assisting in implementations). It is responsible for designing, creating, and maintaining the mechanisms needed to deliver library information via networked mechanisms. Where possible, DLPS works to provide coherence to distributed activities on campus, typically by federating collections "owned" by organizations outside the Library.

It is important to note that DLPS respects the autonomy of those collections, offering incentives to join in federation and ensuring (where possible) that those collections can be accessed independently through mechanisms supported by DLPS.

Also part of this larger goal is DLPS' responsibility to articulate an "information architecture" for the campus in ways that position the University to participate in inter-institutional cooperative activities. To this end, for example, DLPS has been active in a number of national and international digital library initiatives.

STAFFING

Staffing in DLPS has grown with its accomplishments. Initial staffing was set at levels necessary to provide a baseline of commitment to all of these areas, with growth expected for new formats and for extending DLPS' commitment to issues such as cross-collection/format integration.

In 1998, the University's Provost made arguments on behalf of the Library's budget request, allowing both a consolidation and an extension of funding for DLPS. Currently, DLPS is approximately twenty full-time equivalent (FTE) staff (with only two FTE in partial and student appointments). As of early 1999, there are four primary areas of DLPS:

- Two areas within DLPS are *format-specific*, with responsibility for complex and specialized decisions surrounding the selection of formats, their application, related online implementation issues, and long-term support for these formats. Currently, these two areas are encoded text (SGML and XML) and continuous tone imaging. Chris Powell, the coordinator of the Humanities Text Initiative, has responsibility for the first of these areas, and has staff and resources to ensure that texts are created in appropriate ways and that collections are mounted effectively. John Weise, the coordinator of Image Services, has responsibility for continuous tone imaging, and similarly has staff and resources for creation and conversion, as well as online systems.
- The third area within DLPS is a relatively large and well-integrated Systems Group. The programmers within this group work in close cooperation with the service coordinators (above) to ensure that systems are created to effectively support online access to collections in these and other areas. All systems are built through a team effort, drawing on staff from across the organization, and especially those within the Systems Group. Many progra-mmers within the Systems Group have areas of specialization, including (for example) SGML and XML. This ensures a high degree of technical *and* format understanding in building the online systems.
- The fourth area within DLPS is an "infrastructure" group, including staff members who provide services that touch on most areas of DLPS operations. For example, a DLPS Interface Specialist is responsible for working with implementation teams to perform a functional "needs assessment" for each system, and then to design and evaluate the interface for that system. Also in this group are staff members who perform data loading and technical support for DLPS staff. This group is led by an assistant head of DLPS, who also has as a major responsibility for DLPS "data" management. This critical area provides an integrative oversight role for data creation and management, giving attention to questions such as what data elements are captured, where are they stored, and how can we ensure effective migration of data.

A fifth area of DLPS is the NEH-funded Middle English Compendium operation. The MEC staff members have responsibility for converting and encoding the monumental *Middle English Dictionary*, and creating the complex and authoritative HyperBibliography of Middle English Prose and Verse. The MEC, online at http://www.hti.umich.edu/mec/represents a major effort in Middle English philology, and intends one day to add a large body of encoded text primary sources from the period.

Although the future of the MEC is still uncertain, we are hopeful that it will generate sufficient revenue to support the ongoing extension of the resources it includes.

COLLECTIONS

Currently, DLPS manages collections in three principal areas: bitonal page images (typically with raw text to facilitate retrieval), encoded text with or without associated bitonal page images, and continuous tone image collections.

Within each of these areas are book and journal collections, and a variety of art, architecture, and artifact images. Including the pages in the PEAK collection (Elsevier journals), DLPS manages approximately eight million pages of books, journals, and reference materials online.

In 1999-2000, we will add to this approximately 2.3 million page images as part of a monograph conversion project using titles in our Buhr Storage facility, as well as several million more pages of journal material. Particularly under the aegis of the Humanities Text Initiative, approximately three million pages managed by DLPS are encoded text.

Most of this material is historical literature (fiction, poetry, philosophy, and other prose), but a significant portion of the SGML/XML material is also reference works such as the *Middle English Dictionary*. Image Services manages a diverse body of materials, ranging from high resolution images of papyri from the University of Michigan Papyrology collection, rare books and manuscripts, archeological objects from the Kelsey Museum of Archeology, and art and architecture images from several campus and off-campus organizations.

In all, it contains approximately 25,000 images, and 100,000 descriptive records for visual resource materials. It is important to note that though these resources are nearly without comparison in the digital library community, the size of these collections-approximately 1,200 journals and 20,000 monographic titles -they pale in comparison to the large research library.

ECONOMIES OF SCALE

The size and array of resources within the University of Michigan Digital Library Production Service creates significant economies of scale, making many processes less expensive and ensuring the availability of resources to systems or activities that might not otherwise have them. We are able to capitalize on investments such as expensive search engines (or "free" search engines that are expensive to support), using them for a variety of projects ranging considerably in size. Some examples of these sorts of economies are:

- *"Persistent" URLs*: The Internet still lacks a dominant and successful model for creating URNs, leaving digital library production organizations with a need to invent and sustain interim methods. At DLPS, these methods (based on CGI-accessible database mechanisms) are elaborated once for each type of system supported by DLPS, and are then used subsequently as collections are added.

- *Internet commerce and authentication*: Investments in methods for authentication and commerce are ultimately necessary for organizations of this sort. At DLPS, we have used several methods for per-item commerce transactions, including credit card transactions, and use Oracle databases for multi-institution authentication in the PEAK system. These mechanisms, along with SSL, are available as part of other systems or collections that DLPS builds.
- *Tools and methods*: Like the resources needed for authentication, many specialized and often expensive tools are needed for digital library support. Search engines and compression/decompression tools for on-the-fly conversion are just two examples. DLPS uses tools such as tif2gif, CPC, and wavelet compression are used in a variety of systems as dictated by need and format.
- *Expertise in complex areas*: Skills in challenging areas such as SGML/XML or support for SQL databases are an important commodity, and building a production organization by "leasing" such expertise is not realistic when the systems of access or management depend so fundamentally on them. DLPS has benefited from these sorts of investments, especially in SGML/XML skills and in imaging (formats, colour, and metadata).

DLPS ARCHETYPES: SYSTEMS, NOT PROJECTS

The University of Michigan Digital Library Production Service is working to define classes of systems, and to put in place mechanisms to support these classes. These systems represent archetypes, and each collection is assessed to determine whether and how it might fit existing systems.

We are careful not to *force* a particular body of material to fit one of the existing systems, but when it is possible, we are able to achieve those previously mentioned economies of scale much more effectively. This approach also results in other significant advantages.

- By approaching support for the digital library in this way, we are able to draw on significant format expertise within DLPS.
- We are able to deploy collections in an environment of ongoing support and planning. Each class represents a model or framework for continuing expansion rather than a standalone system that could be orphaned.
- DLPS staff members are able to participate more effectively in national or regional cooperative efforts, sharing models and expertise. These larger efforts enrich DLPS efforts at the same time that DLPS contributes to the larger digital library community.

As we continue development of these classes, we are frequently able to see opportunities for consolidation or expansion. A powerful example of this refinement process was encountered in 1998.

The HTI, in cooperation with SGML Systems, deployed each new collection in its native SGML encoding, re-using access mechanisms previously developed wherever possible. Although DLPS principles of re-use were in wide evidence, the large number of legacy systems for text collections had become a significant problem when we wanted to add new features.

Each new feature assumed a foundation of code that may or may not be in existence, depending on when the collection was put online. A strategy was articulated for encoding all such collections in a common format, and building a single piece of code to provide all of the functionality needed for all of the text collections.

If the collection was predominantly drama and HTI wished to provide searching on speakers and speeches, this subroutine would be invoked; otherwise, in cases where it was inappropriate to the collection (or speaker and speech were not encoded), speaker/speech searching would not be made available.

The approach was christened GUMS (General Unified Markup System), and early work on moving to implement collections and systems using GUMS has been very successful. There is a clear sense, however, that we must undertake an ongoing activity, parallel to the work of extending the current systems, to refine and document of the current set of classes.

THREE SAMPLE MODELS

The principles elaborated earlier are clearly visible in many of the collections or services within DLPS. Each of the following three examples benefited from previous work within DLPS, and each forms a class, as well as a system to which more content can be added.

Making of America and Encoded Text Systems

The system built for the first University of Michigan Making of America collection was designed to fully support preservation-oriented conversion methods and provide a gateway or even bridge to the high-quality access systems developed for the Humanities Text Initiative.

The history of the UM MOA development effort is documented elsewhere, and a more lengthy treatment of the technology used is also available. The UM MOA system has been extraordinarily successful, both as an architecture within the DLPS digital library efforts, and as a digital library resource for a broad range of users.

Of primary importance in the UM MOA architecture is support for the products of a Library Preservation process. Images in the system are 600 dpi bitonal, TIFF G4 files. No derivatives (*e.g.*, GIF or JPEG images) are created or stored, except at the time of viewing request. When a user requests a page, the system generates a GIF or PDF derivative in real time and without any appreciable delay (typically less than one second).

Four levels of resolution in GIF are made available to users, taking into account the wide range of displays and network connections; a 600dpi PDF version is also made available, primarily for printing. While the number of pages—approximately 3 million by late 2000—is relatively small compared to a typical research library collection, its large size, expected continued growth, and continuing changes in desktop technology (including networking) argue against storing anything but the master images online.

Use patterns also suggest that as long as we are able to generate appropriate derivatives in real time, based on user demand, we will significantly minimize the requirements for management. Of course there are still concerns about the appropriateness of TIFF G4 as a preservation-quality surrogate for pages, but the University of Michigan Library believes that this format provides a high quality surrogate for most printed materials.

Page images from the Preservation conversion process are subsequently treated by automated Optical Character Recognition (OCR), and the OCR is associated with the page image using a simple form of SGML.

The extensibility of the MOA system has in fact been tested through our OCR processes: two generations of OCR have been applied to all of the materials without the need to change the system architecture. Current OCR technology used by DLPS is a voting system, providing the MOA system with a significantly high quality of character representation than typical OCR.

The system exhibits approximately 99.8per cent accuracy for nearly all content-bearing pages (*e.g.*, excluding pages with engravings and textual pages such as the title page and advertisements). The SGML applied to the text is XML-compliant, and provides information such as image location, page type (*e.g.*, table of contents), "confidence" of the OCR, and page number.

The automatically generated SGML in MOA is also largely consistent with the Text Encoding Initiative (TEI) Guidelines, allowing a full integration with DLPS' encoded text efforts. While certain attributes such as those mentioned above (e.g., OCR "confidence") have been added to the MOA SGML Document Type Definition (DTD), it is otherwise entirely consistent with the TEI.

This has allowed DLPS' encoded text operations in HTI to extract individual texts and upgrade them, correcting OCR and applying fuller encoding. Because the MOA system is fundamentally TEI-compliant, it can accommodate both the loosely encoded texts and texts with more detailed encoding.

As resources are available to HTI, materials can be enhanced in MOA, ensuring better retrieval and higher levels of functionality for users.

Extensibility is critical for a system of this size and importance. The UM MOA system has been designed to be augmented in a variety of ways without significant overhaul.

For example, DLPS has regenerated OCR for MOA without interruptions in service, thereby improving retrieval. Texts can be augmented by HTI, as discussed above. New texts can be added as Preservation resources allow, and all indexing and preparation of Web pages is automated.

The underlying body of materials can remain largely unchanged while work on enhanced interfaces takes place—a process that took place between November 1998 and January 1999. We believe that the MOA system is a model of scalability and extensibility.

The success of the MOA archetype has been multifold. It has allowed us to add materials, a process now underway with MOA4 (2.3 million additional pages). It has helped reduce HTI costs, providing a readily accessible surrogate for the encoding process; in 1998-1999, HTI will add 100 more texts to the American Verse Project collection.

HTI works with the MOA system and contract services to keep its overall cost down and ensure future integration of its products with a Preservation surrogate. Perhaps most significant among MOA's successes, however, is the level of use by a broad range of users.

While the printed source materials were largely unused (most had not circulated in more than ten years), in their online format they are searched some 100,000 times each month, and approximately 100,000 page images are displayed. The constant stream of positive user responses comes from genealogists, philologists, and academics alike.

Image Services

The system built by DLPS Image Services provides a high degree of functionality for a variety of images of objects ranging from art and architecture, to artifacts, to manuscripts. It is also a model for federating diverse collections, respecting the autonomy and heterogeneity of the source collection while creating a union collection for mainstream users. Image Services uses a mapping strategy for its metadata, keeping the native field names and data but simultaneously "tagging" each field with a corresponding value in a sort of Dublin Core scheme. This allows Image Services to provide collections in two ways: first, as a highly functional version of the database maintained by the contributing organization (*e.g.*, the University of Michigan Museum of Art); and second, with generic field labels common to all of the images in the system. Thus, for example, the Museum of Art might use the field label "Artist," while the History of Art Department might use the field label "Source." Having selected only the Museum of Art data online, the user would be presented with search options for "Artist," and data would be displayed accordingly.

However, if the user search across the entire collection, the Dublin Core value "Creator" is presented to the user as a search option and in the display of records. This, along with features for tailoring display and functionality ensures that a contributing organization such as the Museum of Art will enjoy the benefits of a powerful and highly functional system for their data.

Trying to bring together a wide variety of administratively separate collections on campus is challenging, but we believe that the incentive of a cost-effective, inexpensive, highly functional host service (rather than, for example, administrative mandates) has been very effective in creating a unified database managed by DLPS.

DLPS Image Services uses a unified database to ensure a high level of performance and flexibility. Indeed, many of the collection providers maintain local management systems that could be brought online successfully.

The diversity of systems, including Oracle, FileMaker, Embark, and others, would present a serious challenge to creating a distributed search feature. Instead, data are extracted from each of these systems on a periodic basis, and are then ported into the DLPS Image Services system.

Using the methods described above, Image Services is still able to provide access to each collection as if it were an isolated, separately managed collection; the federating approach does not force a lowest common denominator effect.

Instead, the significant resources of DLPS can be leveraged to provide faster search mechanisms, low-cost RAID, and around-the-clock maintenance of the database. These too are effective incentives to organizations when considering whether to mount their data through a central campus agency such as DLPS.

The Image Services system is very rich in functionality. Primarily to satisfy the variety of needs created by the diverse collections, Image Services has built its system using a template system. By specifying (and possibly even creating) a different template, one can make the system appear radically differently.

For example, the primary interface presented to users is a search interface, with results appearing as a collection of thumbnails with associated descriptive information. Each thumbnail and descriptive label is, of course, a link to a fuller resolution view and more descriptive data.

However, by invoking another template such as that for "slide shows," the system can be made to appear as a set of larger images in a pre-selected and set sequence. Another templates provides an interfaces for comparison of multiple images, critical for use of art and architectural images. Each high-resolution image is ultimately displayed with a pan-and-zoom interface.

Users can take advantage of low network speed connections or low-end displays by sending relatively small segments of high resolution images across the network, and panning directionally to view more of the image. This feature has been extremely useful to a wide variety of users, including our Papyrologists, who use the system to work with extremely high resolution images of papyri, and are rarely equipped with computing resources to be able to bring up the full resolution image.

The approach taken by Image Services is extremely scalable. Adding other collections incurs only small, marginal costs (*e.g.*, RAID and time to process the new collection) rather than requiring us to build a new system for each.

We are also able to add new functionality easily, adding "modules" or subroutines to the current middleware rather than re-writing the programmes each time. At the same time, the system provides a high degree of functionality for a wide variety of users, including those who own and maintain the collections represented.

Peak

The PEAK system is, in the simplest terms, a mechanism for delivering the entire body of Elsevier Science's journals to a dozen institutions, with varying levels of access within and across institutions.

It is, however, an excellent example of the value of a production organization in an academic research institution. The University of Michigan was able to use DLPS to leverage production technologies in support of the research mission of the University.

Although alternatives were available to using a locally-developed system, those alternatives would not have allowed us to use the Elsevier materials to learn about the economic decisions of users and institutions when using current journals.

Critical to our being able to support the research mission was our ability to use known technologies to bring the journals online. The University of Michigan had prior experience with the Effect Specifications (*i.e.*, Elsevier's format for delivering image, OCR, and metadata) during the TULIP experiment, and as mentioned earlier, UM developed several significant tools to make the TULIP journals available.

Notably, Ken Alexander had developed the search engine, FTL, which was subsequently used and refined in JSTOR, and Doug Orr had developed tif2gif to enable real-time generation of GIF derivatives from the TIFF G4 images. The use of these tools in previous environments (*e.g.*, TULIP and the early days of JSTOR development at UM) allowed us to look past these critical hurdles and instead to focus on supporting the research model.

The availability of the known technologies also allowed us to invest energies in putting in place database mechanisms for authentication and for subscription/purchase control information, as well as new methods for compression to handle the large amounts of material. Material began to arrive in late summer, 1997. Within a few months, the system was ready for use at the University of Michigan, and by the beginning of 1998, it was released to the subscribing institutions. With Elsevier's cooperation, Michigan contracted with eleven other institutions to deliver the 1,200 journals with some very unique subscription models. Using a model dictated by Prof. Jeff Mackie-Mason, four types of access were put in place:

- *Free*: Older materials (*i.e.*, pre-1997) were made freely available to all project participants. All project participants were also permitted free access to bibliographic and full-text searches, with no charges levied for viewing citations or abstracts.
- *Traditional subscription*: As its name suggests, this model corresponds directly to the familiar subscription by journal title. A traditional subscription to a journal title permits unlimited access to the articles within that journal for the subscriber or subscribing institution.
- *Per-article purchase*: When access to an article is purchased by a user, the user has unlimited access to that article. While at one level, this is a fairly unremarkable feature, Mackie-Mason's additional stipulation that this access should not be time-bound added the burden of using a database to associate a user identity with an article identity. This ensured that that the user who purchased access to an article would continue to have unrestricted access to the online article for the duration of the project.
- *Generalized subscription:* The generalized subscription is the most novel and most challenging addition to PEAK. A generalized subscription consists of a number of "tokens" that can be spent on articles. An institution would purchase "bundles" of tokens, or generalized subscriptions. When tokens are available, they are spent on behalf of users for articles not covered by other subscription models. For example, if a user attempted to read an article from a journal not in an institution's traditional subscr-iptions, a generalized subscription token would be spent on that article. The article would then be available, without restrictions, to all other users at the institution. Again, the PEAK system must collect information about individual article access permissions, and associate them with users from each institution.

The research model further complicates these methods for access, where all methods for access are not available to all institutions, and not all institutions choose to take advantage of all methods available to them. This creates a complex matrix of users and materials, a matrix that must be available and reliable for the system to function properly. Please note that publications analyzing the results of this research will follow. We have already learned important lessons, however, and are working to share data on use with the participating institutions.

In implementing PEAK, our production technologies *and especially our production organization* allowed us to extend the digital library more fully into the University's mission of research and teaching. Independence from Elsevier was critical in order for us to be able to test these models, and the body of Elsevier materials was equally important to ensure that users would have a valuable body of materials that would draw them into the research environment.

The ultimate control and flexibility of the local production environment allowed the University of Michigan to perform research that would probably not have otherwise been possible, or could not have been performed in ways that the researcher stipulated.

MODELS-CONCLUSION

These model systems help us to understand the value of a production organization in building the digital library. They also amply demonstrate each of the principles or ideals proposed as critical for the functioning of a digital library production organization.

- None of these systems would be possible without the full integration of DLPS into the Library, and indeed the University itself. Politically and procedurally, the fact that DLPS is a part of the University Library ensures a range of outcomes, including effective preservation-oriented conversion and deployment (in the case of Making of America), online strategies guided by information professionals (in all of the systems), and integration of online resources with subscription and acquisition procedures (especially in the case of PEAK).
- Each of these systems is or represents a "class" of information, with consistent characteristics and support. Each is easily extensible through the addition of features or migration of code, and each continues to grow (in size) without revision of the underlying mechanisms. The imperatives of DLPS have ensured that we have invested in these models and long-term value, rather than hastily deploying "stovepipes" of separate and inconsistent systems without integration.
- The investments made in the systems (and support for them) reflect a high level of investment consistent with the institutional mission. The quality of the underlying resources, for example, is extraordinarily high, just as the underlying metadata are extraordinarily rich. The staff resources (20 FTE) are primarily base budget resources, and staff skills are very high.
- All of the systems were constructed so that they could be supported in an open-ended fashion (*i.e.*, as much as it is possible to say this, in perpetuity). Capture formats are all standards-based and high fidelity; in fact, most are suitable for creating replacement copies of original

publications. In nearly all cases, the "archival" version of the digital surrogate is also the online version.

These models are all cost-effective and sustainable, and represent model systems for DLPS, with a significant emphasis placed on long-term support and extension.

The progress of digital libraries will depend increasingly on the creation of production organizations, particularly within libraries.

The digital library cannot thrive on a proliferation of experimental projects, projects that will tend to undermine the viability of collections and work against cooperative architectures. In order for the digital library to thrive, we must begin to see a shift from "projects" to "archetypes." A focus on archetypes rather than projects is only possible in a production organization because of the need for continuity and re-use of resources in a coordinated, planned way.

The effective digital library production organization must be fully integrated into campus' academic mission, and especially into the mission and functions of the library. This can only be done by situating the digital library production organization *in* the library.

Too many of the processes and resources needed to support the digital library are a part of libraries; the principles for information organization and management are an essential part of librarianship.

Success in creating digital library production organizations like those I describe here will also lead to an increased probability that we will successfully federate digital library resources. The holistic approach creates not only economies of scale, but also important opportunities for integration.

At Michigan, this approach is leading to the elaboration of an architecture where every digital object is managed in highly functional ways that ensure the long-term maintenance of that object. This architecture also brings these resources together in ways that are transparent to the user, but which ensures tight integration of multimedia resources. A focus on overall architecture is essential, and again can only ensue from testing hypotheses in production organizations.

Finally, sustainability is one of the key issues of the digital library, and an issue that also argues for the presence of the production operation. Certainly, as an ideal, many of us can readily embrace the notion that decisions must be made with regard for long-term value of the digital object.

It is only through a permanent production organization—an organization with funding in a base budget, with open-ended appointments for staff, and with long-term responsibility for maintenance and migration—that this ideal can be supported.

4

Importance of the Planning Process in Library

A plan can play a vital role in helping to avoid mistakes or recognise hidden opportunities. Preparing a satisfactory plan of the organisation is essential. The planning know the business and that they have thought through its development in terms of products, management, finances, and most importantly, markets and competition. Planning helps in forecasting the future, makes the future visible to some extent. It bridges between where we are and where we want to go. Planning is looking ahead.

FEATURES IN LIBRARY

On the basis of the definition of planning, its following features can be identified:

- Planning is a process rather than behaviour at a given point of time. This process determines the future course of action.
- Planning is future oriented It is primarily concerned with looking into future. It requires forecasting of future situation in which the organisation has to function. Therefore, correct forecasting of future situation leads to correct decisions about future course of actions.
- Planning involves selection of suitable course of action. This means that there are several alternatives for achieving a particular objective or set of objectives. However, all of them are not equally feasible and suitable for the organisation.
- Planning is undertaken at all levels of the organisation because all levels of management are concerned with the determination of future course of action. However, its role increases at successively higher levels of management. Moreover, planning at different levels may be different in the context that at the top management level, managers are concerned about the totality of the organisation and tries to relate it with the environment white-managers at lower levels may be involved in internal planning.
- Planning is flexible as commitment is based on future conditions,

which are always dynamic. As such, an adjustment is needed between the various factors and planning.

- Planning is a pervasive and continuous managerial function involving complex processes of perception, analysis, conceptual thought, communication, decision, and action. The very pervasiveness of these planning elements makes it difficult to identify and observe them in detail.

IMPORTANCE OF LIBRARY

The importance of the planning function should have be clear to you. We can outline the importance of planning function as follows:

- Planning provides a clear sense of direction to the activities of the organisation and to the job Behaviour of managers and others. It strengthens their confidence in understanding where the organisation is heading and what for, how best to make the organisation move along the chosen path, and when should they take what measures to achieve the goals of the organisation.
- Another source of importance of planning is that it permits managers to examine and analyse alternative course of action with a better understanding of their likely consequences. If managers have an enhanced awareness of the possible future effects of alternative courses of action, for making a decision or for taking any action, they will be able to exercise Judgement and proceed cautiously to choose the most feasible and favourable course of action.
- Planning forces managers to shake off their inertia and insular outlook; it induces them to look beyond those noses, beyond today and tomorrow, and beyond immediate concerns. It encourages them to probe and cut through complexities and uncertainties of the environment and to gain control over the elements of change.
- Planning tends to minimise the incidence of impulsive and arbitrary decisions and *ad hoc* actions; it obviates exclusive dependence on the mercies of luck and chance elements; it reduces the probability of major errors and failures in managerial actions. It injects a measure of discipline in managerial thinking and organisational action. It improves the capability of the organisation to assume calculated risks. It increases the freedom and flexibility of managers withing well-defined limits.
- As stated earlier, planning is a prime managerial function which provides the basis for the other managerial functions. The organisational structure of task and authority roles is built around organisational plans. The functions of motivation, supervision, leadership and communication are addressed to implementation of plans and achievement of

organisational objectives. Managerial control is meaningless without managerial planning. Thus, planning is the king-pin function around which other functions are designed.

- Planning is means of judicious allocation of strategic and scarce resources of the organisation in the best possible manner for achieving strategic goals of the organisation. The strategic resources include funds, highly competent executives, technological talent, good contacts with government, exclusive dealer network and so on. If the organisation enjoys a distinct advantage in possession of such resources, a careful planning is essential to allocate them into those lines which would strengthen the overall competitive position of the organisation.
- For an ongoing organisation, planning contributes towards a more efficient functioning of the various work units. There is better utilisation of the organisation's existing assets, resources and capabilities. It prompts managers to close gaps, to plug loopholes, to rectify deficiencies, to reduce wastage and leakages of funds, materials, human efforts and skills so as to bring about an overall improvement in resource use efficiency.
- Planning tends to improve the ability of the organisation to effectively adapt and adjust its activities and directions in response to the changes taking place in the external environment. An adaptive Behaviour on the part of the organisation is essential for its survival as an independent entity. For a business organisation, for example, adaptive Behaviour is critical in technology, markets, products and so on.
- While adaptation is a Behaviour in reaction and response to some changes in the outside world, it is not enough in some situations. In recognition of this fact, planning stimulates management to act, to take hold initiatives, to anticipate crises and threats and to ward them off, to perceive and seise opportunities ahead of other competitions, and to gain a competitive lead over others. For the purpose, some enterprises establish environmental scanning mechanism as part of their planning systems. Thereby such enterprises are able to direct and control change, instead of being directed and controlled by the pervasive external forces of change.
- Planning is an important process to bring about effective integration of the diverse decisions and activities of the managers not only at a point of time but also over a period of time. It is by reference to the framework provided by planning that managers make major decisions on organisational activities, in an internally consistent manner.

CONCEPT OF LIBRARY PLANNING

Planning in organisations and public policy is both the organisational process of creating and maintaining a plan; and the psychological process of thinking about the activities required to create a desired goal on some scale. As such, it is a fundamental property of intelligent Behaviour. This thought process is essential to the creation and refinement of a plan, or integration of it with other plans, that is, it combines forecasting of developments with the preparation of scenarios of how to react to them.

An important, albeit often ignored aspect of planning, is the relationship it holds with forecasting. Forecasting can be described as predicting what the future will look like, whereas planning predicts what the future should look like. The term is also used for describing the formal procedures used in such an endeavor, such as the creation of documents, diagrams, or meetings to discuss the important issues to be addressed, the objectives to be met, and the strategy to be followed. Beyond this, planning has a different meaning depending on the political or economic context in which it is used.

Two attitudes to planning need to be held in tension: on the one hand we need to be prepared for what may lie ahead, which may mean contingencies and flexible processes. On the other hand, our future is shaped by consequences of our own planning and actions. The counterpart to planning is spontaneous order. Planning is a process for accomplishing purposes. It is a blue print of business growth and a road map of development. It helps in deciding objectives both in quantitative and qualitative terms. It is setting of goals on the basis of objectives and keeping in the resources.

WHAT SHOULD A PLAN BE?

A plan should be a realistic view of the expectations. Depending upon the activities, a plan can be long range, intermediate range or short range. It is the framework within which it must operate. For management seeking external support, the plan is the most important document and key to growth. Preparation of a comprehensive plan will not guarantee success, but lack of a sound plan will almost certainly ensure failure. Planning can be summarised in 3 easy steps:

- Choosing a destination,
- Evaluating alternative routes, and
- Deciding the specific course of your plan.

PURPOSE OF A PLAN

Just as no two organisations are alike, so also their plans. It is therefore important to prepare a plan keeping in view the necessities of the enterprise. A plan is an important aspect of business. It serves the following three critical functions:

- Helps management to clarify, focus, and research their business's or project's development and prospects.
- Provides a considered and logical framework within which a business can develop and pursue business strategies over the next three to five years.

- Offers a benchmark against which actual performance can be measured and reviewed.

ROLE OF INFORMATION IN PLANNING

WHAT IS PLANNING?

Planning is a simple process used every day. In the process, one decides where he is, where he wants to be, and how he gets there. Getting to work every day, grocery shopping, preparing for a vacation or trip, and saving for retirement are examples of events that require planning. More formally, planning is an organizational process of envisioning a desired future and developing the necessary infrastructure to achieve it.

WHY PLAN

Overall, the purpose of planning is to achieve excellence in public library service. Some specific benefits:

- Planning provides information to use in decision-making.
- Planning provides a blueprint for future library development.
- Planning guides decision-makers in setting necessary priorities about who receives what service with what efficiency.
- Planning provides information to use in the allocation of resources, particularly when they are scarce.
- Planning leads to structured positive change resulting in improved library service.
- Planning makes crises less critical.
- Planning encourages staff creativity and cooperation.
- Planning encourages accountability.
- Planning provides a basis for evaluating the library's performance.
- Planning can improve communication and give everyone who works with the library a sense of common purpose.
- Planning pays off—organizations that plan out-perform those that do not.

WHAT ARE THE STEPS IN THE PROCESS

There are many approaches to planning. Significantly, the Public Library Association published a new approach to public library planning; *Planning and Role Setting for Public Libraries: A Manual of Options and Procedures* is designed to meet the special needs of this community. The following is a summary of the eight major steps recommended.

PLANNING TO PLAN

- Organizes the planning process,
- Shapes the planning process to the library's needs and resources,
- Coordinates planning with other management activities,

- Defines the responsibilities of major planning participants, and
- Organizes and trains the Planning Committee.

LOOKING-AROUND

- Identifies information needed for planning,
- Collects information about the library and the comm-unity it serves, and
- Analyses information gathered for planning decisions.

DEVELOPING ROLES AND MISSION

- Describes eight distinct roles, or service profiles, that public libraries may emphasize in providing services to their comm-unities;
- Describes a method of determining which roles are to receive a major commitment in the library and which are to be supported only minimally;
- Guides planners in writing a mission statement as a concise expression of the roles chosen for emphasis;
- Helps the library communicate its service focus to the public, elected officials, and staff.

WRITING GOALS AND OBJECTIVES

- Translates the library's role choices and mission into statements of desired ends or targets,
- Defines goals as long-range and representing a vision of excellence in library service,
- Defines objectives as specific, time limited, and measurable or verifiable, and
- Provides a framework for implementation and evaluation.

TAKING ACTION

- Produces tangible evidence of the library's planning,
- Identifies possible activities to implement the goals and objectives,
- Selects activities best suited to the library's circum-stances and resources, and
- Leads to cycle of annual objective setting and updating of five-year plan.

WRITING THE PLANNING DOCUMENT

- Describes creation of a formal report of the library's planning activities, and
- Provides an opportunity for communication with the public, the library staff, and governing officials.

REVIEWING RESULTS

- Reviews the plan and its implementation activities after a period of time,
- Reviews extent to which objectives were accom-plished, and
- Starts the planning cycle again.

"LEVELS OF EFFORT" AS A PLANNING TOOL

Planning and Role Setting for Public Libraries introduces the concept of "levels of effort," an approach that allows library planners to adapt the process to a particular library's needs, purposes, and resources. There are three levels of effort — basic, moderate, and extensive. Any of these will result in acceptable plans. Each library's level-of-effort choice reflects the interplay of several different factors.

- *Participants:* The more individuals and groups represented, the higher the library's level of effort for planning will be.
- *Resources:* Higher levels of effort call for a propor-tionally greater commitment of the library staff's time and larger expenditures from the library's budget.
- *Library Context:* Libraries serving a community with rapid growth or change, a complex and diverse population, shifting economic conditions, or libraries facing a major change in funding may need to plan at a higher level of effort.
- *Planning Purposes:* What the library expects the planning process to accomplish may affect the level of effort chosen for some planning phases.
- *Planning Structure:* Libraries planning at a basic level of effort may approach many planning activities informally; but as library complexity increases, the planning structure becomes more formal, thus increasing the level of effort.
- *Planning Schedule:* Some libraries may complete their first objectives cycle over a very short time period; higher levels of effort may require twelve to eighteen months to complete.

ROLE SETTING AS A PLANNING TOOL

Another unique feature of the planning process developed by the Public Library Association and introduced in *Planning and Role Setting for Public Libraries* is the concept of public library roles.

Public library roles are library service profiles that describe a combination of factors in planning and include:

- What the library is trying to do?
- Whom the library is trying to serve? and
- What resources the library needs to achieve these ends?

IMPORTANT FUNCTION OF LIBRARY MANAGEMENT

Planning is an important function of management. However, the planning may fail if the following limitations:

- Planning relates to future and future is always uncertain and so prediction about future is so much difficult. Moreover, planning are based on data/information relating to past and as such planning based on any wrong information may not be useful to the organisation.
- Formulation of plans involves too much cost which are in the form of time spend, money spent, etc., but some times there is little benefit from in plan and than it becomes a burden for the institution. If the plan is not useful than the amount or time spent on its formulation is a waste.
- Some plans are rigid and a manager faces difficulty while making any changes where as there may be continuous change in environment where as the quick decision is required as per the changed environment.
- Planning requires some time for thinking, analysing the situation and designing the final plan and so in case emergency decision is required it will take time and business will lose its opportunity. Moreover, delay in decision will further delay the action.
- People in organisation have to work strictly according to plan where as they may be able to give better performance in a way decided by themselves. Secondly they do not think beside the plan and performs their activities like a machine without using their psychology.
- There may be some changes in planning only up to some extent because measure changes in plan will further attract the changes in supporting plans also and as such the whole system is disturbed moreover changes in plans time and again will prove a wastage of time and money spent on previous plan.
- Planning are the results of thinking of human being. Information on the basis of which plan is formulated may not be free form bias or there may be some other errors which will further Reebok the better plan.
- Planning is too much theoretical and have a less practical use planning is more suitable when environment is suitable but due to unsuitability of environment business has to take various quick steps/decision time and again and as such the importance of other resources which are used according to changing environment, is more than that of planning.
- Planning/target set at the lower side than the capability of or resources and target on over side than the capacity of the resources both are termed as improper planning because lower target will be easily

achieved and as suggested, feel false sense of security. On the other hand over planned target beyond resources cannot be achieved even all effort both are the situation of improper plan.

- This may delay action if certain cases. But it is also true that, if sufficient time is not given to the planning process, the plans so produced may prove to be unrealistic. Similarly, planning involves costs of gathering and analysing information and evaluation of various alternatives. If the management is not willing to spend on planning, the result may not be good.
- The planner must possess the required initiative. He should be an active planner and should take adequate follow up measures to see that plans are understood and implemented properly.
- It is commonly experienced phenomenon in many organisations. Sometimes, planners themselves do like change and on other occasion, they do not think it desirable to bring change, as it will create resistance on the part of the workers. This attitude makes the planning process ineffective.
- This may deter the managers from taking initiative and doing innovative thinking. So, the planners must have sufficient discretion and flexibility in the enterprise. They should not always be required to follow the procedures rigidly.
- Some people consider present as more important than future because present is less uncertain. Such persons are psychologically opposed to planning.

  But it should not be forgotten that dynamic managers always look ahead. Long-term well being of the enterprise cannot be achieved unless proper planning is done for future.
- Because of external factors, which are beyond the control of the planners. External stringencies are very difficult to predict. Sudden breakout of war, government controls, natural havocs and may other factors are beyond the control of management. They make the execution of plans very difficult.

THE PLANNING PROCESS IN LIBRARY SCIENCE

Normally, the emergency manager serves as the "planning coordinator" responsible for leading the jurisdiction's effort to develop an EOP.

This chapter offers the emergency manager suggestions for the process of developing an EOP.

This process may be more important and useful to the jurisdiction's emergency management community than the final product itself. The suggestions can be easily tailored to the specific needs of a jurisdiction.

PRINCIPLES

Developing an all-hazard plan for protecting lives and property in the jurisdiction may appear to be an extremely difficult challenge. It need not be if following principles are applied:

Don't Reinvent the Whee

Emergency operations planning need not start from scratch. Planners should take advantage of others' experience.

The State is a valuable resource for the local jurisdiction. States typically publish their own planning guides, conduct workshops and training courses, and assign their planners to work with local planners. FEMA supports State training efforts through its Emergency Management Institute (EMI), and offers courses. FEMA also publishes many documents relating to planning for specific functions and hazards.

If the jurisdiction has an EOP or other contingency plans, they are the place to start. Existing plans can point the planning coordinator to applicable authorities, perceptions of risk in the community, members of the jurisdiction's emergency response organisation, mutual aid agreements with other jurisdictions, and more. The planning coordinator should review the existing EOP for questionable assumptions, inaccuracies, inconsistencies, omissions, and vagueness. Critiques of recent emergency operations and exercises in the jurisdiction will help the planning coordinator develop a sense of what needs to be done.

Don't Go It Alone

The planning coordinator's is only one view. If a coordinated emergency response depends on teamwork, planning for response should involve the jurisdiction's emergency "team." Documentary research should be supplemented by interviews with key officials of the jurisdiction's response organisation: They may have information and insights that the planning coordinator lacks, as well as ideas that can spark creative solutions to problems. Key officials also determine what staff will be made available for planning meetings and what priority emergency planning issues will have in day-to-day work, so it is important to secure their commitment to the planning process.

FEMA recommends a team approach to planning for these reasons:

- The EOP is more likely to be used and followed if the tasked organisations have a sense of ownership, *i.e.*, their views were considered and incorporated.
- More knowledge and expertise are brought to bear on the planning effort.
- Closer professional relationships among response and recovery organisations in the planning process should translate into better coordination and teamwork in emergencies.

The planning team should be drawn from various groups that have a role or stake in emergency response. The list is not all-inclusive.

The important thing is for the planning coordinator to ensure that the planning team membership represents a good cross section of the organisations involved in the jurisdiction's emergency response effort:

- The Office of the Chief Executive.
- Law enforcement, fire/rescue, and emergency medical services (including dispatchers/911 at the local level), public health and safety, etc.
- Existing planning agencies (*e.g.*, community development, economic development, city planning commissions/municipal planners).
- Hazard mitigation planner/coordinator.
- Local Emergency Planning Committees (LEPC), for hazardous materials (HAZMAT) information.
- Public works agencies and utility companies.
- Social service agencies and volunteer organisations (*e.g.*, American Red Cross (ARC), Salvation Army, etc.,).
- Area hospitals, emergency medical service agencies, medical examiner, coroner, mortician, and other appropriate members of the medical community.
- Educational administrators.
- Public Information Officer (PIO).
- Local media.
- Industrial and military installations in the area.
- State aviation authority and/or others connected with provision of air support.
- Port authorities, U.S., Coast Guard station.
- The jurisdiction's Chief Financial Officer, auditor, and heads of any centralised procurement and resource support agencies.
- Jurisdiction's legal counsel.
- Labour and professional organisations.
- Organisations in the animal care and control community, including veterinary services.
- Amateur radio/CB groups, such as Radio Amateur Civil Emergency Service (RACES), Radio Emergency Associated Communications Teams (REACT), etc.,
- Emergency managers and agency representatives from neighbouring jurisdictions, to coordinate mutual aid needs.
- State and/or Federal representatives, as appropriate.

Don't Forget the Chief Executive Official (CEO)

Potential planning team members have many day-to-day concerns. For the team to come together, potential members must be convinced that emergency planning has a higher priority—and the person to convince them is the jurisdiction's chief executive. The emergency manager has to enlist the chief executive's support for and involvement in the planning effort. To do so, the emergency manager must show the chief executive what is at stake in emergency planning: share the hazard analysis for the jurisdiction, describe what government and especially the chief executive will have to do, Colour presentations with images from disasters like those that could befall the jurisdiction, discuss readiness assessments and exercise critiques, and remind the chief executive that planning ultimately facilitates his or her job in an emergency. Any backing available from the chief executive's office will help the emergency manager to obtain the respectful cooperation of other agency heads.

STEPS

Following are the basics for development and continual refinement of an EOP. They may be adapted to the needs of a jurisdiction.

Research

The first step is research. This consists of reviewing the jurisdiction's planning framework, analysing the hazards faced by the jurisdiction, determining the resource base, and noting characteristics of the jurisdiction that could affect emergency operations.

Review local and/or State laws, rules, regulations, executive orders, etc., that may be considered enabling legislation. Review Federal regulatory requirements. Review guidance, existing plans for the jurisdiction, and the plans of neighbouring jurisdictions. Review agreements with neighbouring jurisdictions, military installations, private sector organisations, etc., Become familiar with the plans of higher levels of government that may be called on to provide assistance.

Hazard analysis is the basis for both mitigation efforts and EOPs. From an emergency operations planning perspective, hazard analysis helps a planning team decide what hazards merit special attention, what actions must be planned for, and what resources are likely to be needed. Comprehensive hazard analysis merits its own document-length discussion.

However, for purposes of emergency operations planning, basic considerations of process, methods, and sources include the following:

- Process and Methods: Hazard analysis requires the planning team to:
  - Identify hazards, to know what kinds of emergencies have occurred or could occur in the jurisdiction.
    i. Begin with a list of hazards that concern emergency management in your jurisdiction. Laws, previous plans, and elected officials can help define the universe of hazards which

the planning team should address in the all-hazard EOP. A list of "traditional" emergency management concerns might include: airplane crash, avalanche, dam failure, drought, earthquake, epidemic, flood, HAZMAT release (in transport or from a fixed facility), hurricane, landslide, mudslide, power failure (sustained), radiological release (in transport or from a fixed facility), subsidence, terrorism, tornado, train derailment, tsunami, urban conflagration, volcanic eruption, wildfire, and winter storm.

ii. For each of these potential emergencies, determine whether it has happened or could happen in the jurisdiction. Some can be eliminated by common sense (*e.g.*, where mountains do no exist, volcanic eruption is not likely). For the rest, there are three lines of investigation: history (including statistical compilations), expert opinion, and maps—which summarise results of the first two.

- Profile hazards and their potential consequences, to have the information necessary for the next two steps (and to set the stage for other applications of the hazard analysis). The categories of information and the precision of the data will depend on several factors. One is the kinds of decisions the analysis is meant to support. For example, to decide that one hazard poses more of a threat than another may require only a qualitative estimate (*e.g.*, "High" vs. "Medium")—but to plan for health and medical needs the planning team would want to have an estimate for likely fatalities and injuries. Another factor is the availability of information and time. It may be necessary to take a long view of hazard analysis, and have each version build on the preceding one as part of a "research agenda" for emergency management.
- Develop information on each of the hazards identified for the community. Of particular interest are the hazard's frequency of occurrence (both historical and predicted or probable, as available), magnitude and intensity, location (if the hazard is associated with a facility or landscape feature) and spatial extent (either around the known location of the hazard or as an estimate for non-localised hazards like tornado), duration, seasonal pattern (based on month by month historical occurrence), speed of onset, and availability of warning.

i. Develop information on the potential consequences of the hazard. This depends on identifying a vulnerable zone (if the hazard is localised) or relating the estimated spatial extent of the hazard to the jurisdiction (by a simple ratio of the hazard's extent to the jurisdiction's area, to get gross estimates of lives and property at risk, or by "overlaying" the estimated spatial extent of the hazard on a portion of the jurisdiction and determining what would be affected). Several kinds of consequences can be investigated; response planning would be concerned with effects on people (total affected, likely deaths and injuries), critical facilities and community functions, property, and sites of potential secondary hazards (*e.g.*, dams, chemical processing plants). The planning team can use both historical information and modeling to arrive at estimates for planning. In modeling, the general process is to consider what is exposed to a given intensity of the hazard, how susceptible it is to a type of damage or consequence (*e.g.*, death, for people; destruction, for property; days of service loss or repair time for critical facilities), and some measure of loss (*e.g.*, dollars, for property). Over time, collection of this information can be made easier by sectoring the jurisdiction (optimally, in sectors that will also be used for damage assessment) and developing a profile of each sector: *e.g.*, rough number of structures falling into different classes of construction, number of different kinds of critical facilities, rough number of people in different age groups or having special needs, etc.,

- Compare and prioritise risks, to determine which hazards merit special attention in planning (and other emergency management efforts). The planning team must consider frequency of the hazard and the likely or potential severity of its consequences, to develop a single indicator of the threat: This allows comparison and setting of priorities. While a mathematical approach is possible, it is easier to manipulate qualitative ratings (*e.g.*, "High", "Medium", "Low") or index numbers (*e.g.*, reducing quantitative information to a 1 to 3, 1 to 5, or 1 to 10 scale, based on defined thresholds) for different categories of information used in the ranking scheme. Some approaches involve consideration only of frequency and consequences, and treat the two categories as equally important. In other approaches, potential consequences receive more weight than frequency.
- Create and apply scenarios, to brainstorm needed hazardspecific planning provisions and estimate hazard-specific resource requirements. While it is important to have a sense of magnitudes involved (whether the single indicator used to rank hazards, or estimated numbers of people affected), these are static. Planning

is concerned with actions that take place in time. For the top-ranked hazards, or hazards that rate above a certain threshold, the planning team should consider scenarios. Using information from the profile, the planning team should think about how the hazard occurrence would develop in the jurisdiction. Starting with a given intensity of the hazard, the team can imagine the hazard's development from initial warning (if available) to its impact on a specific part of the jurisdiction (as identified through analysis) and its generation of specific consequences (*e.g.*, collapsed buildings; loss of critical services and infrastructure; death, injury, or displacement). Through this initial brainstorming—which can be refined in formal tabletop exercises—the team will decide what actions and resources will become necessary. It will also become conscious of the planning assumptions to be used in functional annexes and hazard-specific appendices to the EOP.

– Sources of maps for hazards would include compilations of hazard information made by FEMA and State emergency management agencies, the U.S., Geological Survey (USGS) and State geological surveys, and the National Weather Service (NWS) and its local offices. For more localised hazards, maps from the Federal Insurance Administration (FIA), maps of 10- and 50-mile Emergency Planning Zones (EPZ) around nuclear power plants, and any maps of HAZMAT sites prepared by the LEPC would be useful. For historical investigation, many potential sources exist. Consult Federal or State hazard analyses, as appropriate, to see if the historical occurrence of the hazard is tabulated by jurisdiction. Also interview representatives from organisations on the planning team about their experience. Check local ARC disaster records. Check police, fire, and other responder records. Research area newspapers at the library. Check with utilities and businesses/facilities that have operated in the area for some time. Involve the local or State historical society, and perhaps area universities (*e.g.*, departments of history, sociology, geography, engineering). Professional or business associations (*e.g.*, of insurers, engineers and builders, etc.,) may have useful information. Long-time community residents can even contribute. For expert opinion on hazard potential, the sources are similar. Federal, State, and local agencies; academic, industrial, and public interest group researchers (or private consultants specialising in hazard analysis); and professional associations concerned with the hazards on your list should be able to help, either through interviews or publications. Sources for information on the community and possible consequences to it vary. Ideally, work already will have been done regarding potential consequences of certain facility-based hazards—and it is a matter of checking with the facility and the agency (local, State, regional, or federal) that regulates that kind of facility. For demographics, Census data are available, as are off-the-shelf computer products that organise such data by ZIP code. The planning team also should make extensive use of the information about the jurisdiction that is constantly developed within the jurisdiction. The local planning and zoning commission or department, for example, probably has extensive data on demographics, on land use, on numbers and types and—with the tax assessor and/or local realtors' association—value of buildings, and on the structural integrity of buildings (or at least on the code to which they were to be built, and what that code was and was not designed to do regarding hazard effects). The local public works (or civil engineering) department and utilities are the obvious sources for information on potential damage to and restoration time for the critical infrastructure threatened by hazard effects. The Chamber of Commerce may offer a perspective on damage to business and general economic loss. Other sources of information mentioned previously—emergency service logs and reports, universities, professional associations, etc., — also apply.

Agency heads and other potential members of the planning team should know what kinds of resources they can bring to emergency response and recovery. The problem is to quantify and list them, and compare the resources available to the resources needed for an effective emergency response. Shortfalls may require negotiating agreements with private suppliers or other jurisdictions. Determination of the resource base also should include a consideration of what facilities are vital to emergency operations and how they might be affected by hazards: Problems that cannot be mitigated should be taken into account in the EOP, not assumed away. The planning team should note geographic and topographic features that may affect operations—for example, dependence on a single main transportation artery in and out of the jurisdiction. Planners also should identify special needs groups (non-English speakers, the aged, the disabled) and where they are concentrated (especially institutions such as nursing homes). Finally, the planning team should be alert to demographic and other trends in the jurisdiction that affect assumptions.

Development

- Develop a rough draft of the basic plan, functional annexes, and hazard-specific appendices to serve as a point of departure for the planning team.

- Develop agendas and invitation lists for first cycle of planning meetings; perhaps deliver invitations in person and conduct preliminary interviews with key officials.
- Brief the "CEO" and perhaps invite him or her as a keynote speaker.
- Conduct a presentation meeting, establish committees for parts of the EOP, appoint committee chairs, and schedule a follow-up meeting.
- Work with committees on successive drafts.
- Prepare necessary graphics (*e.g.*, maps, organisational charts).
- Produce a final draft and circulate the draft to the planning team for review and comment.
- Hold a meeting to incorporate final changes, discuss an implementation strategy and necessary distribution, and obtain (informal) commitments to provide information that could necessitate revision.
- Obtain concurrence from organisations with identified responsibilities for implementing the EOP.
- Present the EOP to local elected officials and obtain official promulgation of the EOP (advise the local media in advance).
- Print and distribute the EOP, with a copy (or press release) to local media. Maintain a record of the organisations and persons that received a copy (or copies) of the plan.

Validation

The written EOP should be checked for its conformity to applicable regulatory requirements and the standards of Federal or State agencies (as appropriate)—and for its usefulness in practice.

Further, conduct of a "table top" exercise involving the key representatives of each tasked organisation may serve as a practical and useful means to help validate the plan.

Consult the next level of government about its EOP review cycle. Plan reviews allow responsible agencies to suggest improvements in an EOP based on their accumulated experience. States may review local EOPs; FEMA Regional offices may assist States in the review of EOPs, upon request. Hazard-specific Federal Programmes (such as the REP Programme) require periodic review of certain sections of the all-hazard EOP, and may require review of associated SOPs. To evaluate new or revised EOP, use functional and full scale emergency management exercises. Exercises offer the best way, short of emergencies, to determine if an EOP is understood and "works".

Maintenance

The EOP is a living document. Problems emerge, situations change, gaps become apparent, Federal requirements are altered—and the EOP must be adapted to remain useful and up to date.

A remedial action process can help a planning team identify, illuminate, and correct problems with the jurisdiction's EOP. A remedial action process captures information from exercises, post-disaster critiques, self-assessments, audits, administrative reviews, and the like, which may indicate that deficiencies exist. It then brings members of the planning team together to discuss the problem, and to consider and assign responsibility for remedies. Remedial actions may involve revising planning assumptions and operational concepts, changing organisational tasks, or modifying organisational implementing instructions (SOPs). They also may involve refresher training on performance of tasks assigned by the EOP to an organisation's personnel. The final component of a remedial action process is a means to track and follow up the assigned actions. Establish a process for review and revision of the EOP. Review should be a recurring activity, accomplished on at least an annual basis. As appropriate, significant issues and problems identified through a remedial action process and/or the annual review should provide the information needed to allow the planning team to make the necessary revision(s) to the plan.

Ensure that each tasked organisation or individual develops the SOPs necessary to facilitate the accomplishment of assigned tasks. The EOP does not anticipate every detail of the tasks it describes—but the details are important to its implementation.

TYPES OF PLANS

Based on what the plans seeks to achieve and the method which the plan would like to adopt, plans can be classified as different types: Objectives, Strategy, Policy, Procedure, Method, Rule, Programme, Budget.

OBJECTIVES

The first step in planning is setting objectives. Objectives, therefore, can be said to be the desired future position that the management would like to reach. Objectives are very basic to the organisation and they are defined as ends which the management seeks to achieve by its operations. Therefore, an objective simply stated is what you would like to achieve, *i.e.*, the end result of activities. For example, an organisation may have an objective of increasing sales by 10 per cent or earning a reasonable rate of return on investment, earn a 20 per cent profit from business. They represent the end point of planning. All other managerial activities are also directed towards achieving these objectives.

They are usually set by top management of the organisation and focus on broad, general issues. They define the future state of affairs which the organisation strives to realise. They serve as a guide for overall business planning. Different departments or units in the organ-isation may have their own objectives. Objectives need to be expressed in specific terms, *i.e.*, they should be measurable in quantitative terms, in the form of a written statement of desired results to be achieved within a given time period.

STRATEGY

A strategy provides the broad contours of an organisation's business. It will also refer to future decisions defining the organisations direction and scope in the long run. Thus, we can say a strategy is a comprehensive plan for accomplishing an organisation objectives. This comprehensive plan will include three dimensions:

- Determining long term objectives,
- Adopting a particular course of action, and
- Allocating resources necessary to achieve the objective.

Whenever a strategy is formulated, the business environment needs to be taken into consideration. The changes in the economic, political, social, legal and technological environment will affect an organisations strategy. Strategies usually take the course of forming the organisations identity in the business environment. Major strategic decisions will include decisions like whether the organisation will continue to be in the same line of business, or combine new lines of activity with the existing business or seek to acquire a dominant position in the same market. For example, a company's marketing strategy has to address certain questions, *i.e.*, who are the customers?, what is the demand for the product?, which channel of distribution to use?, what is the pricing policy? and how do we advertise the product. These and many more issues need to be resolved while formulating a marketing strategy for any organisation.

POLICY

Policies are general statements that guide thinking or channellise energies towards a particular direction. Policies provide a basis for interpreting strategy which is usually stated in general terms. They are guides to managerial action and decisions in the implementation of strategy. For example, the company may have a recruitment policy, pricing policy within which objectives are set and decisions are made. If there is an established policy, it becomes easier to resolve problems or issues. As such, a policy is the general response to a particular problem or situation. There are policies for all levels and departments in the organisation ranging from major company policies to minor policies. Major company policies are for all to know, *i.e.*, customers, clients, competitors, etc., whereas minor polices are applicable to insiders and contain minute details of information vital to the employees of an organisation. But there has to be some basis for divulging information to others. Policies define the broad parameters within which a manager may function.

The manager may use his/her discretion to interpret and apply a policy. For example, the decisions taken under a Purchase Policy would be in the nature of manufacturing or buying decisions. Should a company make or buy its requirements of packages, transport services, printing of stationery, water and power supply and other items? How should vendors be selected for procuring supplies? How many suppliers should a company make purchases from? What is the criteria for choosing suppliers. All these answers would be addressed by the Purchase Policy.

PROCEDURE

Procedures are routine steps on how to carry out activities. They detail the exact manner in which any work is to be performed. They are specified in a chronological order. For example, there may be a procedure for requisitioning supplies before production. Procedures are specified steps to be followed in particular circumstances. They are generally meant for insiders to follow. The sequence of steps or actions to be taken are generally to enforce a policy and to attain pre-determined objectives. Policies and procedures are interlinked with each other. Procedures are steps to be carried out within a broad policy framework.

METHOD

Methods provide the prescribed ways or manner in which a task has to be performed considering the objective. It deals with a task comprising one step of a procedure and specifies how this step is to be performed. The Methods may vary from task to task. Selection of proper method saves time, money and effort and increases efficiency. For imparting training to employees at various level from top management to supervisory, different methods can be adopted. For example for higher level management orientation programmes, lectures and seminars can be organised whereas at the supervisory level, on the job training methods and work-oriented methods are appropriate.

RULE

Rules are specific statements that inform what is to be done. They do not allow for any flexibility or discretion. It reflects a managerial decision that a certain action must or must not be taken. They are usually the simplest type of plans because there is no compromise or change unless a policy decision is taken.

BUDGET

A budget is a statement of expected results expressed in numerical terms. It is a plan which quantifies future facts and figures. For example, a sales budget may forecast the sales of different products in each area for a particular month. A budget may also be prepared to show the number of workers required in the factory at peak production times. Since, budget represents all items in numbers, it becomes easier to compare actual figures with expected figures and take corrective action subsequently. Thus, a budget is also a control device from which deviations can be taken care of. But making a budget involves forecasting, therefore, it clearly comes under planning.

It is a fundamental planning instrument in many organisations. Let us take an example of Cash Budget. The cash budget is a basic tool in the management of cash. It is a device to help the management to plan and control the use of cash. It is a statement showing the estimated cash inflows and cash outflows over a given period. Cash inflows would generally come from cash sales and the cash outflows would generally be the costs and expenses associated with the operations of the business. The net cash position is determined by the cash budget, *i.e.*, inflows minus (–) outflows = surplus or deficiency. The management has to hold adequate cash balances for various purposes. But at the same time, it should avoid excess balance of cash Since, it gives little or no return. The business has to assess and plan its need for cash with a degree of caution.

PROGRAMME

Programmes are detailed statements about a project which outlines the objectives, policies, procedures, rules, tasks, human and physical resources required and the budget to implement any course of action. Programmes will include the entire gamut of activities as well as the organisation's policy and how it will contribute to the overall business plan. The minutest details are worked out, *i.e.*, procedures, rules, budgets, within the broad policy framework.

PLANNING AND IMPLEMENTING KNOWLEDGE ORGANIZATION SYSTEMS IN DIGITAL LIBRARIES

This section provides general guidelines that may be useful for an organization that wants to use knowledge organization systems to organize a digital library. The framework described is applicable for KOSs of any type or subject.

PLANNING KNOWLEDGE ORGANIZATION SYSTEMS

Analysing User Needs

Of primary importance to any digital library project is an analysis of its users' needs, in terms of content and functionality. Many volumes have already been written about needs assessment, and providing detailed guidance on this subject is beyond the scope of this paper. However, when analysing how a KOS might be used with a particular digital library, it is essential to thoroughly understand the environment of the user.

One must look not only at the needs for organizing the digital library materials but also at possible links between content within and outside the digital library walls. This is particularly important for KOSs that are acting as intermediate authority files, because in such cases the links may not be readily apparent. It is important to consider other views that might be valuable for users and peripheral communities that might benefit from the digital library's content were it accessible to them through a KOS.

Locating Knowledge Organization Systems

Once the user's needs have been analysed, it is necessary to locate KOSs to meet the need. While an alternate system can be built locally, it is preferable to find an existing KOS for several reasons. First, it is costly and time-consuming to build a KOS. Second, KOSs often benefit by having been built over time. Many of the systems described in this report have been built over decades; some existed in paper before digitization. The value of a KOS comes from its acceptance by the user community; sources built by noted authorities such as learned societies, trade associations, or standards groups will be viewed as more trustworthy than those built internally.

Finally, the networked environment has resulted in both an explosion of primary materials, including documents, electronic journals, and Web-based databases, and in an equivalent explosion of KOSs on the Web. There are several ways to identify KOSs that may be of interest. Many users are already aware of KOSs on the Web within their discipline. Developers may also turn to directories, librarians in the field, and reference sources, or they may perform a general search of the Internet.

Planning the Infrastructure

It is necessary to make decisions about the architecture of the KOS in the context of the digital library setting. The physical location of the KOS is important. Will the system be held externally or internally? There are pros and cons to either approach. If the system is available on the Web, it is possible to consider linking to the KOS as an external system. This architecture requires a script or some search query to locate the resource. One must then launch a query against the resource to obtain the piece of information that will serve as the key between the two files. This key could be a *universal resource locator* (URL) or input to another search query.

A query may be necessary if the KOS is stored in a database. The script may transfer log-on information from the digital library system to the external KOS, in order to provide access to the Web-enabled database. In the case of a more direct link, the access may be by URL. However, the use of a URL as the link has the same problem with persistence as does direct access via a URL from a browser. The organization may move the KOS, thereby changing the

URL that is being used as the key. It is important to determine how often the URLs in the KOS change, whether there is a means of notification of these changes, and whether it is possible to consider an alternative that would be more persistent.

Schemes such as the Digital Object Identifier and the Persistent URL have been devised to enable resources to be physically moved among servers without having their names changed. Another alternative is the use of other Uniform Resource Identification (URI) schemes and the *Uniform Resource Name* (URN), which can be sent from the newer Web browsers. The benefit of linking to a remote resource is that the resource will always be upto-date. The maintenance of the KOS is in the hands of the owner, not the digital librarian. It may also be more apparent to users that the KOS is not owned by the digital library.

Linking to a remote KOS also has disadvantages. Persistence and unexpected changes in the organization and content of the system may cause problems. The software or telecommunications route between the digital library server and the KOS may be unreliable. In systems requiring fast response time or large amounts of data transfer, and, therefore, high bandwidth, the fact that a connection must be made between the digital library and the external KOS may make the system unacceptable to the user. Alter-natively, the KOS may be obtained from the owner and loaded locally.

In many cases, this requires licensing that may not be required when the KOS is accessed remotely, because a copy of the whole resource is being provided to the digital library. Loading a KOS locally also requires that one consider issues such as maintenance, local system administration, and disk storage. If the KOS uses special software, such as a database management system, loading the KOS locally will require a copy of that software, which may require additional purchase or licensing. Other considerations are the need for firewalls and interface design.

On the positive side, the KOS is under more local control. Therefore, it may be possible to improve the response time by not accessing the KOS over the Internet. If the KOS is to be used behind the scenes, concerns of speed and integration become more important. If additional modifications need to be made to the KOS to integrate it with the digital library, it will also be necessary to load the KOS locally. If the digital library intends to incorporate numerous secondary KOSs, it is important to consider the degree to which the architecture is scaleable.

The National Library of Medicine's UMLS incorporates more than 40 different sources. While its main purpose has been to develop a metathesaurus for moving among these vocabularies, the management of the systems, regardless of the mapping issues, has been a major consideration. Ingest has been a major concern, with the need to develop a system that can handle a variety of input formats-from ASCII text files to highly structured database output.

The architecture must also accommodate the character sets of the incoming sources. This is particularly important if a mark-up language has been used to represent special characters and diacritical marks. Systems that have been developed in Unicode, which extends ASCII to accommodate diacritical marks and non-Roman character sets, cannot be handled by systems that deal only with ASCII or extended ASCII sets. Since many digital library systems are being built as extensions or applications of existing *integrated library systems* (ILS), it is important to consider how the KOSs will integrate with the library system.

Unfortunately, many ILS vendors have not considered links to external files or databases in their system designs. In some cases, the vendor may require that the information be stored in the proprietary format of the ILS. The system may require that the files be on the same directory or server as the accessing ILS. The fields that can be linked to the Web or searched may be limited. Outside communi-cations may require Z39.50 client-server connections. With relatively closed systems, ILSs may be a difficult environ-ment in which to implement alternative and non-traditional KOSs.

Digital libraries that are interested in using KOSs should consider this integration when developing requirements for the procurement of a system to support them. Vendors should be encouraged to support relatively open architectures and to consider the extension of traditional library systems to support broader digital library functionality.

In addition to these immediate concerns, it is important to consider the incorporation of future KOSs. Initial success may spur the desire for integration of additional KOSs or enhanced functionality for the existing KOS. Success may breed additional requirements and increase the strain on hardware, software, and network architectures.

Maintaining the Knowledge Organization System

For a digital library, an outdated KOS can be more of a hindrance than a benefit. Maintenance, both of content and of the system, should be considered when planning a KOS. This is particularly important if the digital library is to be self-supporting or revenue generating. Version control of the KOS is extremely important. Reloading a new version from the system provider is one way to accommodate changes; however, this may not be acceptable if the locally held version differs substantially from that held by the system's provider. If there has been significant transformation or processing of the original KOS, it may be difficult, or impossible, to reload the original and recreate the changes that have been made.

A transaction-based approach, whereby only changes are transferred between the KOS provider and the library, is also possible; however, this requires that the system provider have the infrastructure, both machine and human, to produce these transactions. It also requires that the changes to the original KOS be identifiable in order to create change transactions. For example, Stuart Nelson of the NLM's UMLS Project recently reported that many systems can create annual transaction records to inform the UMLS about the changes that have occurred to the original system.

However, the changes are often not indicated with enough detail to support automatic change transactions in the UMLS. If a change date, for example, is recorded only at the level of the concept record, it is impossible to tell whether the term has changed or if the relationship between this concept and another concept has changed. Since the UMLS splits the incoming terminology and its relationships into a variety of files, it is often difficult to tell how the UMLS files must be change based on the changes made during the maintenance of the original KOS.

Presenting the Knowledge Organization System to the User

In addition to deciding which KOS should be used and what functions it should serve, the digital library will need to determine how to present the KOS to its users. A KOS may be exposed to the user or made relatively transparent. The KOS can be exposed to the user in different ways. Material can be grouped into KOS-related themes or categories on the digital library's Web site.

The KOS may be used at a higher level to identify specific portals for different uses or users. If the content of the digital library includes metadata records, the KOS may be displayed as index terms on the records or in its entirety as a navigation aid to searching. In other cases, the KOS may be transparent. For example, a thesaurus can be used behind the scenes to extend the user's search to include synonyms, to connect the digital library's resources to other information and resources, or to filter or rank the information obtained.

IMPLEMENTING KNOWLEDGE ORGANIZATION SYSTEMS

Acquisition and Intellectual Property Issues

It is critical to properly handle the acquisition of knowledge organization systems. The first question is whether the KOS is under copyright. If so, the copyright holder should be contacted concerning the KOS. It is important to ensure that the apparent contact is the official one. Many references have been reprinted or put on the Web without proper acknowled-gment of the real owner. Once the contact has been made, there are several points for discussion:

- If the provider maintains the KOS, how will the digital library find out about any changes that may be made in it? Is there a notification mechanism in place? How frequently must the information be updated to be of benefit to the digital library's users? Will the maintenance be self-evident, or must the agreement include notification requirements? What will the owner do if the maintenance can no longer be performed?

- What will happen if the provider discontinues the product or sells or transfers it to someone else?
- What uses can the digital library make of the KOS under the proposed agreement? As with other licensing, it is advisable to aim for the broadest permissions and the longest term possible. At a minimum, the library should be able to renegotiate the terms of the agreement relatively easily.
- In a networked environment, it is beneficial to develop mechanisms for linking to online versions rather than to maintain a local copy of the resource. This ensures that what is presented is up-todate, and acknowledges more clearly the ownership of the KOS. However, there are numerous factors to consider. Will the KOS be used on an intranet or behind a firewall, where access to the outside or information coming into the organization might be prohibited? Does the KOS service use "cookies" or require knowledge of the user's Internet provider address? Does it require a user ID and password?
- If the KOS is to be accessed remotely, are there service issues? Is it likely to be accessed with bandwidth, model, and computer speeds that are adequate for outside connections of this type? Is the use of such a critical nature that unreliable service on the part of the KOS or the Internet connection will cause the digital library itself to be viewed as less useful? Does the KOS require a specialized search engine or search query formulation? Can the digital library system properly display the results, or would the results be better displayed through the KOS system? Will the resulting information be used in its native form or must it be extracted or transformed? If the KOS is to be loaded locally, in what formats can the content be received?
- If the KOS is not available electronically, can it be digitized? Is the owner interested in a cooperative venture, and are the human and financial resources for such an effort available?

Making the Link

There are two parts to establishing the link between the digital library and the KOS. The first is locating the key anchor information in the digital library's resource. The second involves the look up against the target file. The creation of this link may be more or less automatic, depending on the particular situation. The characterization of this activity is meant to be general and to allow both "on-thefly" links and embedded links. Regardless of what function the KOS is going to serve in the digital library, the essential information contained in the digital library resource from which the link is to be made must be identified. The mechanism for doing this depends on the type of object from which the link is being made and on the information that is expected to be identified in the digital library's resource. The first step is to review any metadata related to the digital library resource. Do the metadata carry the term that is needed to make the link? If this information is included, the level at which the metadata are assigned should be reviewed.

If the metadata indicate the subject matter of the specific resource in which the user will be interested, the metadata can be used to make the links. However, in some cases, the terms that appear in the title or description at the resource level may not be indicative of the subject at the individual item level. Automatically making a link on the basis of the content description for an entire book may misrepresent the content of a chapter. Whether or not the metadata can be used will depend on the amount and type of information given in the metadata and the level at which the metadata are assigned.

If a text resource in the digital library provides no appropriate metadata, the procedure for identifying the key information may involve text analysis. A programme to perform simple string searching or a search engine that can preserve hit locations can be used if the text string has distinguishing characteristics, such as a database acronym, or a specific structure, such as a latitude and longitude coordinate. If the text string has no such cues, text mining or more complex textanalysis tools may be necessary. These tools use a variety of semantic and syntactic algorithms to locate key information.

There have been significant advances in commercially available text-mining tools, such as IBM's Intelligent Agent, which includes specific algorithms for identification of names of places and persons. The second step of the linking activity is to make the connection to the KOS. The methods for doing this vary, depending on whether the system is being loaded locally or is referenced remotely. If the system is loaded locally, it is possible to perform a significant amount of processing to match the two files, assuming that computer resources of this type are available to the digital library organization. If the system is only available remotely over the Web, the interaction will require knowledge of scripting and various Web-based access techniques.

Scripting should be considered in both local and remote approaches, since the more integrated the linking is with the resource, the more maintenance may be required if there are changes in either the resource or the KOS. Regardless of the approach that is taken, making the link requires an analysis of both the information in the original digital library material and the corresponding information in the KOS. If the KOS is being used as an intermediate file to bridge between the digital library's resource and another resource, it is also important to understand the data and the process whereby the search is performed and information returned from the target resource. If the KOS must return a value to the original digital library resource, the data and process must be evaluated in a bidirectional sense.

Choosing the linking mechanism is equally important. The link may be fixed or "on-the-fly." In the case of a fixed link, a specific URL is embedded at the link point in the digital library material. However, as stated before, problems of persistence are inherent in this approach. Alternatively, a URN can be used. The URN requires the creation of a namespace on the point of the target file, and the search is to this namespace rather than to a specific URL. Persistent locators and *digital object identifiers* (DOIs) can also solve this problem. These schemes are sufficient if the material is an HTML document. Content in databases is more difficult to retrieve.

The National Library of Medicine now supports the searching of a variety of its databases through its *Internet Grateful Med* (IGM) URL function. IGM users can create URLs that will actually perform searches against the databases. Information on the syntax for creating such a URL is provided on the NLM Web site. While the intent is that the search URL will be bookmarked by an individual user, the same concept can be used for creating an active link at the anchor point for the link. With additional scripting, the creation of the term *pneumonia* can be automatically replaced with an active link that picks up the term where the link has been made.

5

Motivating Employees in Academic Libraries

INTRODUCTION

Organisational effectiveness is largely determined by the quality of the employees and how the organisation develops them. Therefore, it is natural that high performing organisations try to recruit and retain the right people and provide them with training and professional development opportunities. However, abilities, skills, personality, and organisational support alone might not lead to individual job performance that contributes to overall organisational effectiveness if people are not motivated. It is possible that some employees choose not to perform even if they have the right qualifications.

Managers face tough motivational challenges especially in economic downturns and it seems helpful to know key organisational Behaviour studies' findings related to human motivation. However, the goal is not manipulating and making people do what managers want them to do, but making people reach their highest job performance potential and getting them excited to do so. The author's literature review revealed that motivation analyses in libraries as workplaces are limited and have been focused on content theories or what motivates people. This chapter attempts to build on the former analyses and explain applications of motivation theories that describe the motivation factors, motivation processes, effective job design, and conditions for sustaining motivation in the academic library workplace.

CONTENT THEORIES: WHAT MOTIVATES PEOPLE

The motivation theories that deal with the content of what motivates people are referred to as content theories or static-content theories as they look at only one point in time and do not predict Behaviour. The most well-known theories in this area include Maslow's hierarchy of needs, Alderfer's ERG theory, McClelland's theory of socially acquired needs, and Herzberg's motivator- hygiene theory. Maslow organised the needs underlying human motivation in a hierarchy on five levels: physiological needs, security needs, social needs, ego or self-esteem needs, and self-actualisation needs.

He further proposed that lower-level needs such as physiological needs and security needs must be satisfied before the individual can address higher-level needs. Although there is little evidence to support the concept of hierarchical progression and all individuals cannot be motivated in the same way, managers can attempt to influence their performance by satisfying employees' needs. Table shows some possible applications in academic library work environment.

Alderfer's ERG Theory, on the other hand, provides an alternative to Maslow's theory and is based on a 3-fold conceptualisation of human needs: existence, relatedness, and growth. It does not assume lowerlevel satisfaction as a prerequisite for the emergence of higher-level needs. To test his theory, Alderfer surveyed 110 bank employees at several job levels.

Table. Maslow's Hierarchy of Needs and Applications in Academic Libraries.

Level	Needs	Examples in the Academic Library Workplace
1	Physiological	* Clean Air * Enough work space * Ergonomically-designed workstations * Appropriate lighting * Appropriate temperature * Convenient and reasonable foodservice facilities
*	Water fountains	
2	Security	* Safe workplace * Stable wages and salaries * Job security * Health insurance * Retirement benefits
3	Social Affiliation	* Employee social activities * Teamwork * Friendship * Sense of belonging * Affection
4	Self-esteem	* Recognition * Awards * Prestige * Autonomy
5	Self-actualisation	* Well-being of others * Accepting self * Meaningful work

Although the results indicated stronger support for the ERG theory than Maslow's theory, both theories are similar in that people shape their actions to satisfy unfulfilled needs. McClelland identified three basic needs that people develop in the society: the need for achievement, power, and affiliation. He argued that each individual is likely to have developed a dominant orientation Towards one of these needs based on our life experiences. An obvious implication for managers might be to draw out those employees with a high need for achievement.

However, McClelland suggested that motivation is changeable and that people can be taught to have certain needs through training Programmes. Herzberg's motivator-hygiene theory is different from other content theories as it suggested that motivation is composed of two dimensions:

- Hygiene Factors or the conditions surrounding the job and can prevent dissatisfaction; and
- Motivators, or the factors associated with the work itself and influence employees to grow and develop.

The hygiene factors include such things as salary, supervision, policies, working conditions, relationship, and job securities. The motivators include promotion, growth opportunities, responsibility, recognition, and achievement. The main implication of this theory is that for employees to be truly satisfied and perform above minimum standards, motivators had to be built into the job.

CONCEPT OF MOTIVATION FOCUSES IN LIBRARY

NATURE OF MOTIVATION

The concept of motivation focuses on explaining what "moves" behaviour. In fact, the term motivation is derived from the Latin word 'movere', referring to movement of activity. Most of our everyday explanation of behaviour is given in terms of motives. Why do you come to the school or college? There may be any number of reasons for this behaviour, such as you want to learn or to make friends, you need a diploma or degree to get a good job, you want to make your parents happy, and so on. Some combination of these reasons and/or others would explain why you choose to go in for higher education. Motives also help in making predictions about behaviour. A person will work hard in school, in sports, in business, in music, and in many other situations, if s/he has a very strong need for achievement. Hence, motives are the general states that enable us to make predictions about behaviour in many different situations. In other words, motivation is one of the determinants of behaviour. Instincts, drives, needs, goals, and incentives come under the broad cluster of motivation.

The Motivational Cycle

Psychologists now use the concept of need to describe the motivational properties of behaviour. A need is lack or deficit of some necessity. The condition of need leads to drive. A drive is a state of tension or arousal produced by a need. It energises random activity. When one of the random activities leads to a goal, it reduces the drive, and the organism stops being active. The organism returns to a balanced state. Thus, the cycle of motivational events can be presented as shown in Figure.

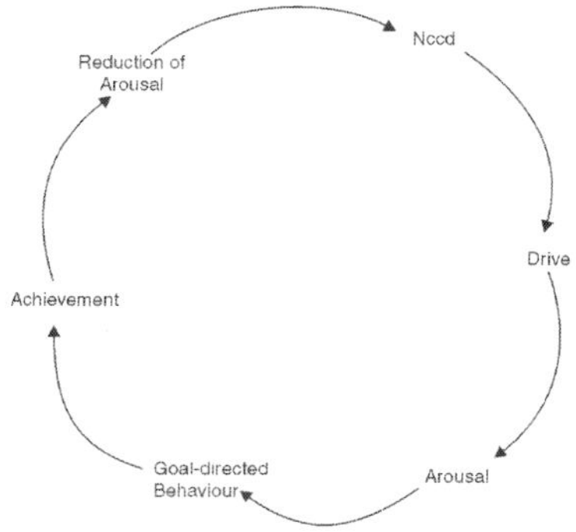

Fig. The Motivational Cycle.

BIOLOGICAL MOTIVES

The biological or physiological approach to explain motivation is the earliest attempt to understand causes of behaviour. Most of the theories, which developed later, carry traces of the influence of the biological approach. The approach adhering to the concept of adaptive act holds that organisms have needs that produce drive, which stimulates behaviour leading to certain actions towards achieving certain goals, which reduce the drive.

The earliest explanations of motivation relied on the concept of instinct. The term instinct denotes inborn patterns of behaviour that are biologically determined rather than learned. Some common human instincts include curiosity, flight, repulsion, reproduction, parental care, etc. Instincts are innate tendencies found in all members of a species that direct behaviour in predictable ways. The term instinct most approximately refers to an urge to do something. Instinct has an "impetus" which drives the organism to do something to reduce that impetus. Some of the basic biological needs explained by this approach are hunger, thirst, and sex, which are essential for the sustenance of the individual.

Hunger

When someone is hungry, the need for food dominates everything else. It motivates people to obtain and consume food. Of course we must eat to live. But, what makes you feel hungry? Studies have indicated that many events inside and outside the body may trigger hunger or inhibit it. The stimuli for hunger include stomach contractions, which signify that the stomach is empty, a low concentration of glucose in the blood, a low level of protein and the amount of fats stored in the body. The liver also responds to the lack of bodily fuel by sending nerve impulses to the brain.

The aroma, taste or appearance of food may also result in a desire to eat. It may be noted that none of these alone gives you the feeling that you are hungry. All in combination act with external factors to help you understand that you are hungry.

Thus, it can be said that our food intake is regulated by a complex feedingsatiety system located in the hypothalamus, liver, and other parts of the body as well as the external cues available in the environment. Some physiologists hold that changes in the metabolic functions of the liver result in a feeling of hunger.

The liver sends a signal to a part of the brain called hypothalamus. The two regions of hypothalamus involved in hunger are - the lateral hypothalamus and the ventro-medial hypothalamus. LH is considered to be the excitatory area. Animals eat when this area is stimulated.

When it is damaged, animals stop eating and die of starvation. The VMH is located in the middle of the hypothalamus, which is otherwise known as hunger-controlling area which inhibits the hunger drive. Now can you guess about people who overeat and become obese, and people who eat very little or who are on a diet?

Thirst

What would happen to you, if you were deprived of water for a long time? What makes you feel thirsty? When we are deprived of water for a period of several hours, the mouth and throat become dry, which leads to dehydration of body tissues.

Drinking water is necessary to wet a dry mouth. But a dry mouth does not always result in water drinking behaviour.

In fact processes within the body itself control thirst and drinking of water. Water must get into the tissues sufficiently to remove the dryness of mouth and throat. Motivation to drink water is mainly triggered by the conditions of the body: loss of water from cells and reduction of blood volume. When water is lost by bodily fluids, water leaves the interior of the cells. The anterior hypothalamus contains nerve cells called 'osmoreceptors', which generate nerve impulses in case of cell dehydration.

These nerve impulses act as a signal for thirst and drinking; when thirst is regulated by loss of water from the osmoreceptors, it is called cellular-dehydration thirst. But what mechanisms stop the drinking of water? Some researchers assume that the mechanism which explains the intake of water is also responsible for stopping the intake of water.

Others have pointed out that the role of stimuli resulting from the intake of water in the stomach must have something to do with stopping of drinking water. However, the precise physiological mechanisms underlying the thirst drive are yet to be understood.

Sex

One of the most powerful drives in both animals and human beings is the sex drive. Motivation to engage in sexual activity is a very strong factor influencing human behaviour. However, sex is far more than a biological motive. It is different from other primary motives in many ways like:

- Sexual activity is not necessary for an individual's survival;
- Homeostasis (the tendency of the organism as a whole to maintain constancy or to attempt to restore equilibrium if constancy is disturbed) is not the goal of sexual activity; and
- Sex drive develops with age, etc.

In case of lower animals, it depends on many physiological conditions; in case of human beings, the sex drive is very closely regulated biologically, sometimes it is very difficult to classify sex purely as a biological drive. Physiologists suggest that intensity of the sexual urge is dependent upon chemical substances circulating in the blood, known as sex hormones. Studies on animals as well as human beings have mentioned that sex hormones secreted by gonads, *i.e.*, testes in males and the ovaries in females are responsible for sexual motivation. Sexual motivation is also influenced by other endocrine glands, such as adrenal and pituitary glands. Sexual drive in human beings is primarily stimulated by external stimuli and its expression depends upon cultural learning.

SOCIAL MOTIVES

Social motives are when people do or give things because they feel they have a sense of responsibility to their community. People with social motives may have endured racial discrimination, poverty or may want to live in a selfless way:

- Social motives manifest themselves in different ways. There are people who work in soup kitchens because they were homeless at one time. Another person may focus on citisen advocacy because he experienced unfair treatment from law enforcement.
- Having a social motive for doing or giving is beneficial because it allows a person to be less self-centered and more focused on the needs of others. For example, if one grew up with a bias towards single mothers, social motives can gradually turn the bias into compassion.
- Some famous people are well-known for their social motives to help to the less fortunate in society. For example, Oprah Winfrey built a school for disadvantaged girls in South Africa so they can have quality education. Michael Jackson was a philanthropist throughout his career.
- If you're a person that seeks to advance the causes of the less fortunate, you can contribute even in small ways. Some ideas include donating items to the local food bank, visiting a battered women's

shelter, bringing school supplies to a foster home or assisting the unemployed in a job search.

- A lot of good has been done in the U.S., because of people with social motives. For example, abolitionists crusaded for the end of slavery and female suffragists made it possible for women to vote.

PSYCHOSOCIAL MOTIVES

Social motives are mostly learned or acquired. Social groups such as family, neighbourhood, friends, and relatives do contribute a lot in acquiring social motives. These are complex forms of motives mainly resulting from the individual's interaction with her/his social environment.

Curiosity and Exploration

Often people engage in activities without a clear goal or purpose but they derive some kind of pleasure out of it. It is a motivational tendency to act without any specific identifiable goal. The tendency to seek for a novel experience, gain pleasure by obtaining information, etc., are signs of curiosity. Hence, curiosity describes behaviour whose primary motive appears to remain in the activities themselves. What will happen if the sky falls on us? Questions of this kind stimulate intellectuals to find answers. Studies show that this curiosity behaviour is not only limited to human beings, animals too show the same kind of behaviour. We are driven to explore the environment by our curiosity and our need for sensory stimulation. The need for varied types of sensory stimulations is closely related to curiosity. It is the basic motive, and exploration and curiosity are the expressions of it.

Our ignorance about a number of things around us becomes a powerful motivator to explore the world. We get easily bored with repetitive experiences. So we look for something new. In the case of infants and small children, this motive is very dominant. They get satisfaction from being allowed to explore, which is reflected in their smiling and babbling. Children become easily distressed, when the motive to explore is discouraged.

MASLOW'S HIERARCHY OF NEEDS

Maslow's hierarchy of needs is a theory in psychology, proposed by Abraham Maslow in his 1943 paper 'A Theory of Human Motivation'. Maslow subsequently extended the idea to include his observations of humans' innate curiosity. His theories parallel many other theories of human developmental psychology, all of which focus on describing the stages of growth in humans.

Maslow studied what he called exemplary people such as Albert Einstein, Jane Addams, Eleanor Roosevelt, and Frederick Douglass rather than mentally ill or neurotic people, writing that "the study of crippled, stunted, immature, and unhealthy specimens can yield only a cripple psychology and a cripple philosophy." Maslow studied the healthiest 1 per cent of the college student population. Maslow's theory was fully expressed in his 1954 book *Motivation and Personality*.

HIERARCHY

Maslow's hierarchy of needs is often portrayed in the shape of a pyramid, with the largest and most fundamental levels of needs at the bottom, and the need for self-actualisation at the top. The most fundamental and basic four layers of the pyramid contain what Maslow called "deficiency needs" or "d-needs": esteem, friendship and love, security, and physical needs.

With the exception of the most fundamental needs, if these "deficiency needs" are not met, the body gives no physical indication but the individual feels anxious and tense. Maslow's theory suggests that the most basic level of needs must be met before the individual will strongly desire the secondary or higher level needs. Maslow also coined the term Metamotivation to describe the motivation of people who go beyond the scope of the basic needs and strive for constant betterment. Metamotivated people are driven by B-needs, instead of deficiency needs.

Self-Actualisation

"What a man can be, he must be?" This forms the basis of the perceived need for self-actualisation. This level of need pertains to what a person's full potential is and realising that potential. Maslow describes this desire as the desire to become more and more what one is, to become everything that one is capable of becoming. This is a broad definition of the need for self-actualisation, but when applied to individuals the need is specific. For example one individual may have the strong desire to become an ideal parent, in another it may be expressed athletically, and in another it may be expressed in painting, or inventions.

In order to reach a clear understanding of this level of need one must first not only achieve the previous needs, physiological, safety, love, and esteem, but master these needs. Maslow's descriptions of a self-actualised person's different needs and personality traits. Maslow also states that even though these are examples of how the quest for knowledge is separate from basic needs he warns that these "two hierarchies are interrelated rather than sharply separated". This means that this level of need, as well as the next and highest level, are not strict, separate levels but closely related to others, and this is possibly the reason that these two levels of need are left out of most textbooks.

Esteem

All humans have a need to be respected and to have self-esteem and self-respect. Also known as the belonging need, esteem presents the normal human desire to be accepted and valued by others. People need to engage themselves to gain recognition and have an activity or activities that give the person a sense of contribution, to feel accepted and self-valued, be it in a profession or hobby. Imbalances at this level can result in low self-esteem or an inferiority complex. People with low self-esteem need respect from others. They may seek fame or glory, which again depends on others.

Note, however, that many people with low self-esteem will not be able to improve their view of themselves simply by receiving fame, respect, and glory externally, but must first accept themselves internally. Psychological imbalances such as depression can also prevent one from obtaining self-esteem on both levels. Most people have a need for a stable self-respect and self-esteem.

Maslow noted two versions of esteem needs, a lower one and a higher one. The lower one is the need for the respect of others, the need for status, recognition, fame, prestige, and attention.

The higher one is the need for self-respect, the need for strength, competence, mastery, self-confidence, independence and freedom. The latter one ranks higher because it rests more on inner competence won through experience. Deprivation of these needs can lead to an inferiority complex, weakness and helplessness.

Love and Belonging

After physiological and safety needs are fulfilled, the third layer of human needs are social and involve feelings of belongingness. This aspect of Maslow's hierarchy involves emotionally based relationships in general, such as:

- Friendship.
- Intimacy.
- Family.

Humans need to feel a sense of belonging and acceptance, whether it comes from a large social group, such as clubs, office culture, religious groups, professional organisations, sports teams, gangs, or small social connections. They need to love and be loved by others. In the absence of these elements, many people become susceptible to loneliness, social anxiety, and clinical depression. This need for belonging can often overcome the physiological and security needs, depending on the strength of the peer pressure; an anorexic, for example, may ignore the need to eat and the security of health for a feeling of control and belonging.

Safety Needs

With their physical needs relatively satisfied, the individual's safety needs take precedence and dominate Behaviour. These needs have to do with people's yearning for a predictable orderly world in which perceived unfairness and inconsistency are under control, the familiar frequent and the unfamiliar rare.

In the world of work, these safety needs manifest themselves in such things as a preference for job security, grievance procedures for protecting the individual from unilateral authority, savings accounts, insurance policies, reasonable disability accommodations, and the like. Safety and Security needs include:

- Personal security.
- Financial security.
- Health and well-being.
- Safety net against accidents/illness and their adverse impacts.

Physiological Needs

For the most part, physiological needs are obvious — they are the literal requirements for human survival. If these requirements are not met, the human body simply cannot continue to function. Physiological needs include:

- Breathing,
- Nutrition,
- Water,
- Sex,
- Sleep,
- Homeostasis,
- Excretion.

Air, water, and food are metabolic requirements for survival in all animals, including humans. Clothing and shelter provide necessary protection from the elements. The intensity of the human sexual instinct is shaped more by sexual competition than maintaining a birth rate adequate to survival of the species.

ACHIEVEMENT

You might have observed some students work very hard and compete with others for good marks/grades in the examination, as good marks/grades will create opportunities for higher studies and better job prospects. It is the achievement motivation, which refers to the desire of a person to meet standards of excellence. Need for achievement, also known as n-Ach, energises and directs behaviour as well as influences the perception of situations. During the formative years of social development, children acquire achievement motivation. The sources from which they learn it, include parents, other role models, and socio-cultural influences. Persons high in achievement motivation tend to prefer tasks that are moderately difficult and challenging. They have stronger-than-average desire for feedback on their performance, that is to know how they are doing, so that they can adjust their goals to meet the challenge.

AFFILIATION

Most of us need company or friend or want to maintain some form of relationship with others. Nobody likes to remain alone all the time. As soon as people see some kinds of similarities among themselves or they like each other, they form a group. Formation of group or collectivity is an important feature of human life. Often people try desperately to get close to other people, to seek their help, and to become members of their group. Seeking other human beings and wanting to be close to them both physically and psychologically is called affiliation. It involves motivation for social contact. Need for affiliation is aroused when individuals feel threatened or helpless and also when they are happy. People high on this need are motivated to seek the company of others and to maintain friendly relationships with other people.

POWER

Need for power is an ability of a person to produce intended effects on the behaviour and emotions of another person. The various goals of power motivation are to influence, control, persuade, lead, and charm others and most importantly to enhance one's own reputation in the eyes of other people. David McClelland described four general ways of expression of the power motive. First, people do things to gain feeling of power and strength from sources outside themselves by reading stories about sports stars or attaching themselves to a popular figure. Second, power can also be felt from sources within us and may be expressed by building up the body and mastering urges and impulses. Third, people do things as individuals to have an impact on others. For example, a person argues, or competes with another individual in order to have an impact or influence on that person. Fourth, people do things as members of organisations to have an impact on others as in the case of the leader of a political party; the individual may use the party apparatus to influence others. However, for any individual, one of these ways of expressing power motivation may dominate, but with age and life experiences, it varies.

CRITICISMS

In their extensive review of research based on Maslow's theory, Wahba and Bridgewell found little evidence for the ranking of needs Maslow described, or even for the existence of a definite hierarchy at all. Chilean economist and philosopher Manfred Max-Neef has also argued fundamental human needs are non-hierarchical, and are ontologically universal and invariant in nature—part of the condition of being human; poverty, he argues, may result from any one of these needs being frustrated, denied or unfulfilled. The order in which the hierarchy is arranged has been criticised as being ethnocentric by Geert Hofstede.

Hofstede's criticism of Maslow's pyramid as ethnocentric may stem from the fact that Maslow's hierarchy of needs neglects to illustrate and expand upon the difference between the social and intellectual needs of those raised in individualistic societies and those raised in collectivist societies.

Maslow created his hierarchy of needs from an individualistic perspective, being that he was from the United States, a highly individualistic nation. The needs and drives of those in individualistic societies tend to be more self-centred than those in collectivist societies, focusing on improvement of the self, with self-actualisation being the apex of self-improvement. Since, the hierarchy was written from the perspective of an individualist, the order of needs in the hierarchy with self-actualisation at the top is not representative of the needs of those in collectivist cultures. In collectivist societies, the needs of acceptance and community will outweigh the needs for freedom and individuality. Maslow's hierarchy has also been criticised as being individualistic because of the position and value of sex on the pyramid.

Maslow's pyramid puts sex on the bottom rung of physiological needs, along with breathing and food. It views sex from an individualistic and not collectivist perspective: *i.e.*, as an individualistic physiological need that must be satisfied before one moves on to higher pursuits. This view of sex neglects the emotional, familial and evolutionary implications of sex within the community.

PROCESS THEORIES: HOW DOES MOTIVATION OPERATE

Although the static-content theories can provide a basic understanding of what energises people, they are not sufficient to explain the complex nature of human motivation as people respond differently to their needs. Factors other than unfulfilled needs also influence motivation, and various process theories were developed to explain how motivation operates.

Expectancy theory, which is also known as VIE theory, assumes that motivation is a function of three components; for an individual to be motivated:

- The reward must be valued by the person;
- The person must believe that higher performance will result in greater rewards (instrumentality); and
- That additional effort will lead to higher performance (expectancy).

For example, if an employee perceives that high performance might not be achieved even after hours of effort due to lack of skills or self-efficacy, even if he or she desires promotion, the person might not feel motivated enough to achieve the goal. Therefore, providing appropriate training, clarifying expectations, and providing guidance are important to strengthen this effort-performance link. Another example might be that if an individual believes that rewards might be given to people with higher seniority regardless of their performance, getting the reward might be perceived as unlikely for junior staff, thus undermining the person's motivation to perform.

Finally, if an employee can perform well but does not value the reward provided, *e.g.*, a gift certificate to a restaurant that the person does not care for, the person is likely to be less motivated. Goal-setting theory is another process theory and suggests the idea that setting goals can be a cause of high performance.

Locke argued that a person's conscious intentions (goals) are the primary determinants of task-related motivation. Managers should:

- Set specific goals;
- Make goals sufficiently difficult (but not too difficult);
- Involve employees in goal setting to ensure commitment;
- Provide feedback; and
- Link goal accomplishment with rewards that are valued by the employee.

This theory can be applied in various library tasks. For example, instead of asking employees to do their best in enhancing information fluency, the goal might be "implementing information fluency Programmes in at least 10 courses next semester." To gain goal commitment, it will be important for managers to provide clear direction and guidance to employees in addition to building their self-efficacy. Organisational justice theories suggest that people's perception of fairness within the organisation regarding how and what decisions are made about the distribution of outcomes affects motivation.

Justice theories are important given the current economy where many organisations have been forced to lay off people. Questions such as "Are we restructuring our organisation in a fair manner?" and "Were the layoffs perceived as fair by employees?" are important for managers. The outcomes of justice perceptions can have an economic impact on the organisation such as absenteeism, withdrawal, theft, sabotage, or even lawsuits against employers. Justice theories consider both procedural justice and distributive justice. Distributive justice theory is also referred to as equity theory and suggests that people compare the ratio of their inputs (effort) and outcomes (rewards) to the input-outcome ratios of other comparable individuals.

The research on equity theory is also more definitive on the reactions of people who perceive that they are under-rewarded. If an individual views a relationship as unequal, an attempt will be made to restore equality either by trying to gain greater rewards or by putting forth less effort. For example, if an employee feels that everyone gets promoted at the same rate regardless of their amount of inputs, he or she who feels under-rewarded might reduce the amount of the effort. At the same time, the employee will not think it is unfair if another employee who contributes more to the organisation receives more reward.

Colquitt *et al.* conducted a meta-analysis of justice theories and concluded that there was a strong negative correlation ($r = -.51$) between distributive justice and withdrawal, suggesting that if an employee views a relationship as unequal, he or she is likely to lose interest in the work or leave the organisation. They also concluded that there was a strong positive correlation ($r = .56$) between procedural justice and performance, suggesting that employees are likely to perform better if procedures are perceived as fair.

Other business literature also suggests that procedural justice increases performance significantly as managers gain trust, commitment, and voluntary cooperation from their employees. It is possible that some managers might be fair in terms of distributing rewards such as recognition, promotion, pay raise, authority, responsibility, and resources, but not so in terms of process. Fair process involves engaging employees, providing opportunities for them to speak up, explaining why final decisions are made as they are, and clarifying expectations.

Fair process is lost when information is filtered and managers retain power by withholding what they know to themselves. It is important for employees to be treated with sincerity and respect, and adequate explanation needs to be provided. When the process is perceived to be fair, most people will realise that compromises are occasionally necessary and accept outcomes that might not be in their favour.

JOB CHARACTERISTICS THEORY: HOW CAN WE MAKE JOBS INTERESTING

Job design and job enrichment also affect human motivation and it will be helpful to know the characteristics that make jobs interesting. The job characteristics model developed by Hackman and Oldham identified five core job dimensions that should be enriched when jobs are re-designed:

- *Skill variety*—the degree to which a job requires a variety of activities that draw on different skills and talents of the employee.
- *Task identity*—the degree to which the job requires completion of a task, from beginning to end.
- *Task significance*—the degree to which the job has a significant impact on the lives of other people.
- *Autonomy*—the degree to which the job provides substantial freedom, independence, and discretion to the individual in scheduling work and determining the procedures to be used.
- *Feedback*—the degree to which workers are provided with direct and clear information about their performance.

As the core dimensions are enhanced, the job characteristics model posits that they influence three critical psychological states:

- Experienced meaningfulness of work, which is increased by skill variety, task identity, and task significance;
- Experienced responsibility for work outcomes, which is enhanced by autonomy; and
- Knowledge of results, which is provided by effective feedback mechanisms.

For example, providing credits to individuals rather than to the department when preparing path-finders, instruction handouts, or other documents will provide opportunities for those employees involved to receive direct feedback from library users and establish client relationships with them. In addition, open lines of communication between employees and managers need to be incorporated into the workplace culture. The more people know how well they are doing, the better equipped they are to take appropriate corrective action. In terms of increasing autonomy, the first step will be to hire people who can do their jobs properly without close supervision.

Second, the individuals will need to be trained to do their jobs effectively. Finally, it should be clear that high-quality performance is expected. Loading jobs vertically by giving employees greater responsibility for their jobs and allowing them to make their own decisions, instead of micro-managing, increase the level of autonomy and sense of accountability that results in higher motivation. At the same time, employees should not be given a great deal of autonomy in any organisations where marginal work tends to be accepted without question.

Autonomy will work only when everyone involved buys into the importance of performing at a high level. One approach in increasing autonomy might be to ask employees what goals they want to accomplish and what resources or support is needed as self-setting goals are naturally self-committed. It is important to note that the job characteristics model recognises the limitation that not everyone wants and benefits from enriched jobs and that people with a high need for personal growth benefit the most. In that sense, it will be essential for managers to hire people who are interested in growing professionally in the work instead of people who are attracted to the work because of work conditions or benefits.

ENVIRONMENTALLY-BASED THEORIES: HOW CAN WE REINFORCE AND MAINTAIN MOTIVATION

Let's now think about some of the ways in which motivation can be sustained. If we are rewarded for behaving in a certain way, we begin to make the connection between the Behaviour and the reward and continue to engage in the Behaviour. As B.F. Skinner's operant conditioning theory explains, Behaviours with positive consequences are strengthened and acquired, and Behaviours with negative consequences are eliminated.

The positive consequences, such as recognition and reward, need to be tied directly to desired Behaviours and be given immediately and continuously so that the connection between the Behaviour and reinforcer is established. For example, staff recognition needs to be provided with an explanation of desirable Behaviour. It should also be repeated if the staff continues to improve the work instead of choosing different employees to be rewarded when in fact the same employee performed the best. Additionally, rewards need to be distributed consistently so that recognition of good work will become part of the organisational culture. It is also important to know what you are rewarding. For example, if you reward someone because she or he answered the largest number of reference questions, the employee and possibly others might try to enhance the number of reference questions instead of focusing on the quality of the service and other ways that reference service can be improved. As social learning theory suggests, people acquire new Behaviours by observing the rewards and punishments given to others.

If you want to increase teamwork but continue distributing rewards according to individual performance only, your desired outcome, *i.e.*, teamwork will not be reinforced. In addition, if an individual performs fine in one area but not so in another, the explanation for the reward needs to be very clear so that the desirable Behaviour is strengthened while the undesirable Behaviour is not. When providing rewards, it will be helpful to know the difference between extrinsic and intrinsic rewards. Extrinsic rewards are contrived and some of them incur direct cost.

They include such things as promotion, monetary reward, gifts, and bonuses. Intrinsic rewards involve no direct cost, and the examples include compliments, public recognition, opportunities, and a smile. Thus, intrinsic rewards are closely related to the work itself and are motivators in the context of Herzberg's motivator. Therefore, intrinsic motivation is synonymous with a desire to work hard solely for the pleasure of task accomplishment. On the other hand, extrinsic motivation encourages us to complete the task to receive the reward.

In other words, rewards motivate people to get rewards. Scholars research implies that the feedback and social reinforcers, such as recognition and attention, may have as strong an impact on performance as pay. Their research also indicates that extrinsic rewards can undermine an individual's intrinsic motivation. However, this is not to suggest that extrinsic incentives are unimportant. Good pay, benefits, and good working condition are often significant factors to attract and retain best people and cannot be ignored.

MEANING OF ENTREPRENEURIAL MOTIVATION IN LIBRARY

It is often said that a person cannot win a game that they do not play. In the context of entrepreneurship, this statement suggests that success depends on people's willingness to become entrepreneurs. Moreover, because the pursuit of entrepreneurial opportunity is an evolutionary process in which people select out at many steps along the way, decisions made after the discovery of opportunities—to positively evaluate opportunities, to pursue resources, and to design the mechanisms of exploitation—also depend on the willingness of people to "play" the game. In this paper, we argue that human motivations influence these decisions, and that variance across people in these motivations will influence who pursues entrepreneurial opportunities, who assembles resources, and how people undertake the entrepreneurial process. In recent years, entrepreneurship research has focused largely on the environmental characteristics influencing firm foundings and the characteristics of entrepreneurial opportunities. Although this focus has greatly enhanced our understanding of the entrepreneurial phenomenon, it ignores the role of human agency. Entrepreneurship depends on the decisions that people make about how to undertake that process. We argue that the attributes of people making decisions about the entrepreneurial process influence the decisions that they make.

Although previous researchers have rightly criticised much of the existing empirical research on the role of human motivation in entrepreneurship, we argue that inadequate empirical work does not negate the importance of understanding the role of human motivation in the entrepreneurial process. In fact, even sociologists who have argued strongly against the usefulness of trait-based research in entrepreneurship implicitly acknowledge that motivation must matter to this process. Scholars write, entrepreneurial activity "can be conceptualised as a function of opportunity structures and motivated entrepreneurs with access to resources". We also believe that these criticisms have resulted in insufficient consideration of the role of the human motivation in the entrepreneurial process in recent entrepreneurship research.

Consequently, we are left with theories of entrepre-neurship that do not consider variation in the motivations of different people. We believe that such an omission is problematic because, as Baumol eloquently argued, the study of entrepreneurship that does not explicitly consider entrepreneurs is like the analysis of Shakespeare in which "the Prince of Denmark has been expunged from the discussion of Hamlet." We identify several human motivations that influence the entrepreneurial process.

In our arguments, we explicitly assume that all human action is the result of both motivational and cognitive factors, the latter including ability, intelligence, and skills. We also assume that entrepreneurship is not solely the result of human action; external factors also play a role. However, environmental factors being held constant, we argue that human motivation plays a critical role in the entrepreneurial process. To this end, we suggest ways that researchers could develop more realistic explanations for how human motivation influences the entrepreneurial process than is the norm in the literature to date. We believe that this approach could overcome many of the criticisms of prior research on person-centric explanations for entrepreneurship. Finally, we offer suggestions on how empirical researchers should test these arguments in ways that overcome many of the criticisms of extant research on this topic.

We define entrepreneurship and present several arguments for why the study of entrepreneurship in general and consideration of the role of human motivation in the process in particular are important. We discuss opposing views of how opportunities may affect the relationship between motivation and entrepreneurship. We summarise the major mechanisms by which previous researchers believe motivation influences entrepreneurship. We identify what we believe are the major problems with prior research on motivation and entrepreneurship. We provide some recommendations for researchers conducting empirical research in this area. We offer some tentative conclusions about motivation and entrepreneurship.

ENTREPRENEURSHIP AND WHY STUDY IT FROM THE POINT OF VIEW OF HUMAN MOTIVATION

We believe that the study of the entrepreneurial process is important for several reasons. First, entrepreneurship drives innovation and technical change, and therefore generates economic growth. Second, as the Austrian economists have explained, entrepreneurial action is the process through which supply and demand are equilibrated. Third, entrepreneurship is an important process by which new knowledge is converted into products and services.

Fourth, entrepreneurship has become an important vocation and we need to understand its role in the development of human and intellectual capital. We adopt Shane and Venkataraman's definition of entrepreneurship as the process by which "opportunities to create future goods and services are discovered, evaluated, and exploited." As these authors have explained, this definition does not require viewing entrepreneurs as the founders of new organisations. An options trader can be an entrepreneur, as can a corporate salesman who discovers and pursues opportunities for the creation of new products. Moreover, this definition shows that entrepreneurship is a creative process. By rearranging resources in a new way, entrepreneurs engage in creative activity.

However, the degree of creativity involved in entrepre-neurship varies across the types of resource recombination that occurs. For example, the creation of business to undertake space tourism may be more creative than the creation of a new restaurant in a strip mall. Entrepreneurship involves human agency. The entrepreneurial process occurs because people act to pursue opportunities. People differ in their willingness and abilities to act on these opportunities because they are different from each other. We argue that the variation among people in their willingness and ability to act has important effects on the entrepreneurial process.

Recent research has been relatively accepting of arguments that people vary in their willingness and ability to engage in the entrepreneurial process because of non-motivational individual differences. Researchers have shown that the willingness of people to pursue entrepreneurial opportunities depends on such things as their opportunity cost, their stocks of financial capital, their social ties to investors, and their career experience. We argue that motivational differences also influence the entrepreneurial process. For example, such things as variation across people in their perceptions of risk and opportunity influence entrepreneurial decisions.

People vary in how they view the risk of expending resources before knowing the distribution of outcomes. Similarly, the probability of success at the entrepreneurial process is low, and those people who are willing to proceed despite these odds might be more optimistic or higher in self-efficacy than people deterred by these odds. We consider the incorporation of this individual-level variation in motivation to be important to the entrepreneurial process. To isolate the effects of entrepreneurial motivation, other factors that could have a causal effect on the process and outcome of entrepreneurship need to be controlled. One category of control variables is the external environment. These would include such things as:

- Political factors (*e.g.*, legal restrictions, quality of law enforcement, political stability, and currency stability);
- Market forces (*e.g.*, structure of the industry, technology regime, potential barriers to entry, market sise, and population demographics); and
- Resources (*e.g.*, availability of investment capital, Labour market including skill availability, transportation infrastructure, and complementary technology).

Most researchers either explicitly or implicitly agree that these categories of factors influence the entrepreneurial process and need to be controlled to measure the effect of motivations on the entrepreneurial process. While it is clear why the above factors need to be controlled if we are to fully understand how motivation is related to entrepreneurship, it is less clear how opportunities affect this relationship. Because the first two authors were unable to agree on the concept of opportunities, we present two versions of the relationship between opportunities and motivation. First, as suggested, present the view shared by Shane and Collins, then as suggested, present Locke's view.

ENTREPRENEURS, OPPORTUNITIES, AND THE EFFECTS OF MOTIVATION

Opportunities are aspects of the environment that represent potentialities for profit making. We follow Shane and Venkataraman to define entrepreneurial opportunities as "situations in which new goods, services, raw materials, and organising methods can be introduced and sold at greater than the cost of their production." Since, potentialities are not yet actual, measuring them objectively and prospectively at the level of an individual entrepreneur poses daunting challenges. Entrepreneurs can pursue opportunities in any industry at any time.

For example, some entrepreneurs build successful new companies by contributing to the founding of a new industry, such as Robert Swanson in biotechnology. Other entrepreneurs build new companies in old and mature industries such as Sam Walton in retailing. Aggregate statistics show us that the general category of opportunities to which Sam Walton and Bob Swanson responded was not equal. The average value of new businesses created in retail is lower than the average value of new businesses created in biotechnology. Because human motivations are likely widely distributed across industry categories at the aggregate level, statistically significant differences in the mean value of businesses created in different industry categories suggest that the value of opportunities varies across industry.

This does not mean that entrepreneurs cannot successfully pursue opportunities in lowopportunity industries. Rather it means that the opportunities in these industries are simply less attractive to the average person. The value of opportunities also varies within industries. Because the opportunities that entrepreneurs identify and pursue have different economic value, the opportunities themselves influence entrepreneurial Behaviour. We believe that it is important for Behaviourally oriented entrepreneurship researchers to consider and measure the economic value of these opportunities in research about the motivations of entrepreneurs.

For example, in the early 1970s, Butler Lampson and Chuck Thacker, researchers at Xerox Parc, invented the Alto—the first personal computer. However, their design would have cost over US$10,000 to build. When Steve Jobs and Steve Wozniak came up with the design for the Apple computer, their design cost less than US$3000 to build. Because the number of people who would pay more than US$10,000 for a PC was much smaller than number of people who would pay US$3000, the financial value of the Jobs and Wozniak opportunity was greater than the value of the Xerox opportunity. One would expect that differences in the estimates of the value of the PC opportunity that resulted from the different solutions influenced the decisions of the different parties about their opportunities. Of course, although it is possible that Jobs and Wozniak possessed more of the relevant motives to pursue entrepreneurial opportunities than did Lampson and Thacker, researchers can only estimate the effect of these motives if they account for the differences in the two opportunities.

Although we argue that opportunities influence entrepreneurial behaviour, we do not argue that opportunities fully determine the process. Entrepreneurs are people and may make different decisions when confronted with similar opportunities. In addition to being influenced by the opportunity that Steve Jobs pursued at the time of founding, the development of Apple was likely influenced by Steve Jobs' motivations. Empirically, the objective and subjective parts of opportunity are difficult to separate. The mechanism for actualising an opportunity often initially exists mainly in the entrepreneur's mind, making the entrepreneur's idea for how to exploit the opportunity a personal interpretation of the opportunity.

This idea is basically what we would call vision. Such judgements may be mistaken; entrepreneurs sometimes believe that they have identified valuable opportunities when, in fact, no valuable opportunities actually existed, at least in the form in which they were conceptualised. Also, entrepreneurs may differ in how they interpret opportunities. For example, the development of the Internet has allowed entrepreneurs to develop new organising methods, such as "e-tailing", that were never before possible. Although a wide variety of entrepreneurs have responded to the opportunities to develop new organising methods that the Internet has generated, these entrepreneurs have developed approaches of different value in response to this organising opportunity. Some entrepreneurs have developed opportunities to compete with established retailers through e-tailing, while others have sought only to design web sites. Even though the way that opportunities are manifested in the entrepreneur's plans for exploitation are personal, the variance in their estimated value likely influences the decisions that people make in the entrepreneurial process and can confound attempts to measure the effects of motivation on this process. This is true even if the value is partially a function of the other decisions that the entrepreneur has made and partially a function of external forces.

IMPORTANT MOTIVATIONAL CONCEPTS FROM PRIOR QUANTITATIVE RESEARCH

Previous research has explored several motivations and their effects on entrepreneurship. We discuss several of these concepts. However, we do not provide a complete review of prior empirical research for two reasons. First, the definitions of entrepreneurship used in previous empirical research on motivation and entrepreneurship are inconsistent with our definition, making it impossible to draw direct implications of prior work for research using our definition. Second, prior research has suffered from significant methodological problems that we discuss, making prior findings suggestive rather than conclusive, even for research that employs the same definition of entrepreneurship as was used in those studies. Therefore, we discuss previous empirical research only to illustrate the ways in which motivation can influence different aspects of the entrepreneurial process.

Need for Achievement

Within the research domain of personality traits and entrepreneurship, the concept of need for achievement has received much attention. McClelland argued that individuals who are high in nAch are more likely than those who are low in nAch to engage in activities or tasks that have a high degree of individual responsibility for outcomes, require individual skill and effort, have a moderate degree of risk, and include clear feedback on performance. Further, McClelland argued that entrepreneurial roles are characterised as having a greater degree of these task attributes than other careers; thus, it is likely that people high in nAch will be more likely to pursue entrepreneurial jobs than other types of roles. Johnson conducted a traditional review of various studies, which varied regarding samples, measurement of nAch, and definitions of entrepreneurship.

Based on this group of studies, Johnson concluded that there is a relationship between nAch and entrepreneurial activity—in this case, nAch distinguished firm founders from other members of society. In a similar review of studies, Fineman concluded that both projective and questionnaire measures of nAch significantly predict firm founding. Collins, Locke, and Hanges conducted the first and only meta-analysis of nAch and entrepreneurship studies, examining 63 nAch and entrepreneurship studies. The overall finding of the meta-analysis is that nAch is significantly related to founding a company.

The nAch both differentiated between entrepreneurs and others and predicted the performance of the founders' firms. Further, they found no significant differences in the predictive validity of three different measures of nAch. Moreover, Collins found that the relationship between nAch and entrepreneurial activity was moderated by several factors. First, nAch was a more robust predictor of group-level effects (*e.g.*, mean differences between firm founders and another profession, mean differences between high-performing and low-performing founders) than individuallevel effects (*e.g.*, predicting the performance of individuals). Second, they found that while nAch is a strong differentiator between firm founders and non-managerial employees, it is not a strong differentiator between firm founders and managers. Based on these results, Collins concluded that nAch is an effective tool for differentiating between firm founders and the general population but less so for differentiating between firm founders and managers. Further, they concluded that nAch might be particularly effective at differentiating between successful and unsuccessful groups of firm founders. Thus, nAch could play a very useful role in explaining entrepreneurial activity.

Risk Taking

Risk-taking propensity is another motivation of interest, which emerged from McClelland's original research on entrepreneurs. McClelland claimed that individuals with high achievement needs would have moderate propensities to take risk. This claim by McClelland is especially interesting for entrepreneurship research because the entrepreneurial process involves acting in the face of uncertainty. Liles argued that entrepreneurs often must accept uncertainty with respect to financial well-being, psychic well-being, career security, and family relations. Moreover, several theories of entrepreneurship view the entrepreneur as bearing residual uncertainty. Scholar argued that individuals who have higher achievement motivation should prefer activities of intermediate risk because these types of activities will provide a challenge, yet appear to be attainable. On the other hand, individuals who score high on the motive to avoid failure will avoid intermediate risks. Instead, they will prefer easy and safe undertakings or extremely difficult and risky ones. Following the lead of Atkinson, risk-taking propensity has been defined in the entrepreneurship literature as the willingness to take moderate risks.

Despite these theoretical claims, previous research suggests that firm owners do not differ significantly from managers or even the general population in risk taking. For example, Litsinger failed to find any difference between motel owners and motel managers on risk preference. Kogan and Wallach found that firm founders clustered around the mean risk-taking score of the general population. In comparisons of firm founders and managers, neither Babb and Babb nor Palich and Bagby found significant differences between the two groups in terms of risk-taking propensity. However, none of the studies identified if firm founders were low, moderate, or high risk-takers.

Only Brockhaus tested for the actual level of risk taking, and he found that firm founders did prefer moderate risk but did not differ from managers in this regard. Only one study found a difference between firm founders and managers in this motivation. In a study of 239 New England business executives, Begley found that risk-taking propensity was the only trait on which founders and non-founders differed. Begley failed to identify whether the level of entrepreneurial risk taking was low, moderate, or high. While these empirical findings suggest that risk taking may or may not be an entrepreneurial motivation, self-efficacy may be confounding the findings.

Several recent evaluative studies using interviews and expert evaluations showed that firm founders objectively have a higher propensity for risk than do members of the general population, but that firm founders do not perceive their actions as risky. Similarly, Sarasvathy, Simon, and Lave found that when expert firm founders were asked to evaluate the same entrepreneurial simulations as bankers, the firm founders saw opportunities in information that the bankers thought indicated risk. Thus, the measurement of risk-taking propensity may be confounded with high self-efficacy.

Tolerance for Ambiguity

Schere argued that tolerance for ambiguity is an important trait for entrepreneurs because the challenges and potential for success associated with business start-ups are by nature unpredictable. Budner defined tolerance for ambiguity as the propensity to view situations without clear outcomes as attractive rather than threatening. Because entrepreneurs continually face more uncertainty in their everyday environment than do managers of established organisations, entrepreneurs who remain in their jobs are likely to score high on tests for this trait than would managers. There is mixed support for this prediction. Begley and Boyd found that firm founders scored significantly higher in tolerance for ambiguity than did managers, defined as non-founders working in business.

In smaller sample studies, both Schere and Miller and Drodge found that firm founders were significantly higher in tolerance for ambiguity than were managers. Finally, based on a review of four additional studies, Sexton and Bowman identified tolerance for ambiguity as a distinguishing psychological characteristic between firm founders and managers. However, several studies did not match these findings.

Babb and Babb found no significant difference in tolerance for ambiguity between founders and non-founders of rural businesses in Northern Florida. Similarly, Begley found no significant differences between New England firm founders and managers on their tolerance for ambiguity. This inconsistency in findings and potential methodological problems in the research that provides support for the tolerance of ambiguity proposition suggests that we do not yet know if tolerance of ambiguity is a motivation that affects any part of the entrepreneurial process.

Locus of Control

Another motivational trait that has received attention is locus of control—the belief in the extent to which individuals believe that their actions or personal characteristics affect outcomes. Individuals who have an external locus of control believe that the outcome of an extent is out of their control, whereas individuals with an internal locus of control believe that their personal actions directly affect the outcome of an event. As McClelland discussed earlier, individuals who are high in nAch prefer situations in which they feel that they have direct control over outcomes or in which they feel that they can directly see how their effort affects outcomes of a given event. This point was extended by Rotter who argued that individuals with an internal locus of control would be likely to seek entrepreneurial roles because they desire positions in which their actions have a direct impact on results. The research on locus of control suggests that firm founders differ from the general population in terms of locus of control. Shapero found that firm founders from Texas and Italy were more "internal" than other groups of professions reported by Rotter.

This same pattern holds with female firm founders versus the general female population and with Black firm founders versus the general Black population. While locus of control orientation differs between firm founders and the general public, most studies have not found a difference between firm founders and managers on locus of control, a result similar to the situation with studies on nAch. For example, Babb and Babb found no differences in locus of control between founders and managers in small businesses in Northern Florida. Similarly, Brockhaus found that managers and owners of new businesses did not differ on locus of control. In a longitudinal study of students, Hull, Bosley, and Udell found that locus of control did not differentiate between students who went on to work in managerial positions and those who started their own business.

Finally, in the studies of New England entrepreneurs, Begley and Begley and Boyd found that locus of control did not distinguish between founders and managers. We suspect that one reason for the difference between firm founder and the general population, but not between founders and managers, is the similarity between founding a company and managing. Defining entrepreneurial situations as starting a company rather than working for others might not capture the real differences between entrepreneurial and non-entrepreneurial situations. For example, serving as a manager in a rapidly growing high-technology company might demand greater entrepreneurial motivations than starting a corner grocery store.

Self-Efficacy

Self-efficacy is the belief in one's ability to muster and implement the necessary personal resources, skills, and competencies to attain a certain level of achievement on a given task. In other words, self-efficacy can be seen as task-specific self-confidence. Self-efficacy for a specific task has been shown to be a robust predictor of an individual's performance in that task and helps to explain why people of equal ability can perform differently. An individual with high self-efficacy for a given task will exert more effort for a greater length of time, persist through set backs, set and accept higher goals, and develop better plans and strategies for the task. A person with high self-efficacy will also take negative feedback in a more positive manner and use that feedback to improve their performance.

These attributes of self-efficacy may be important to the entrepreneurial process because these situations are often ambiguous ones in which effort, persistence, and planning are important. One study directly assessed the effect of self-efficacy on some dimension of the entrepreneurial process. Baum assessed firm founders in the architectural woodworking industry on a number of variables including general traits and motives, specific skills and competencies, situation-specific motivation, vision, and strategic action. In a LISREL model, Baum found that self-efficacy had a strong positive relationship with realised growth. In fact, it was the single best predictor in the entire array of variables.

Goal Setting

Tracy, Locke, and Renard conducted a study of the owners of small printing firms. Both concurrent and longitudinal measures of four aspects of performance were obtained: financial performance, growth, and innovation.

The quantitative goals the entrepreneurs had for each outcome were significantly related to their corresponding outcomes, both concurrently and longitudinally. Baum, Locke, and Smith also found that growth goals were significantly related to the subsequent growth of architectural woodworking firms. Although there have been other studies of entrepreneurial goals, to our knowledge, only these two have related quantitative measures of goal difficulty to performance.

OBJECTIVES AND ACHIEVEMENTS OF MOTIVATION IN LIBRARY

MAIN OBJECTIVES OF MOTIVATION

Self-preservation, whether this is pointed directly to survivial or towards our image of ourselves painted by our beliefs and ideals. What I mean by this is that we have in our mind a view point of who we are and we trive to accomplish this in either advancement or a continuation of our currant state. This personal view point might look down upon theft, and so seeing a theft we might feel "motivated" to call police, in order to up keep our currant view of what kind of person we see ourselves as.

ACHIEVEMENT

Over the years, behavioural scientists have noticed that some people have an intense desire to achieve something, while others may not seem that concerned about their achievements. This phenomenon has attracted a lot of discussions and debates. Scientists have observed that people with a high level of achievement motivation exhibit certain characteristics. Achievement motivation is the tendency to endeavor for success and to choose goal oriented success or failure activities.

Achievement motivation forms to be the basic for a good life. People who are oriented towards achievement, in general, enjoy life and feel in control. Being motivated keeps people dynamic and gives them self-respect. They set moderately difficult but easily achievable targets, which help them, achieve their objectives. They do not set up extremely difficult or extremely easy targets. By doing this they ensure that they only undertake tasks that can be achieved by them. Achievement motivated people prefer to work on a problem rather than leaving the outcome to chance.

It is also seen that achievement motivated people seem to be more concerned with their personal achievement rather than the rewards of success. It is generally seen that achievement motivated people evidenced a significantly higher rate of advancement in their company compared to others. Programmes and courses designed, involves seven "training inputs." The first step refers to the process through which achievement motivation thinking is taught to the person. The second step helps participants understand their own individuality and goals. The third assist participants in practicing achievement-related actions in cases, role-plays, and real life. A fourth refers to practicing of achievement-related actions in business and other games.

A fifth input encourages participants to relate the achievement Behaviour model to their own Behaviour, self-image, and goals. The sixth Programme facilitates participants to develop a personal plan of action. Finally, the course provides participants with feedback on their progress towards achieving objectives and targets. Achievement motivation as a branch of study has greatly established its prominence. A number of companies are now training their employees in the same.

ENTREPRENEURIAL COMPETENCIES

Every career draws on the competencies of an individual. Some of these competencies may be general and some peculiar to the chosen career. You may understand competencies to mean abilities and skills. However, we would desist from calling these as personality traits as such a conceptualisation only reinforces the mistaken belief that entrepreneurs are born rather than made. We believe that recognition of these competencies as abilities and skills makes entrepreneurship as a teachable and learnable behaviour. We orient you towards a set of entrepreneurial competencies developed by the Entrepreneurship Development Institute of India Ahemdabad. These competencies were identified by a thorough research procedure based on critical analysis of the case studies of the successful entrepreneurs.

ENTREPRENEURIAL COMPETENCIES IDENTIFIED BY THE EDI

- Acting out of choice rather than compulsion, taking the lead rather than waiting for others to start.
- A mindset where one is trained to look for business opportunities from everyday experiences. Recall 'oranges' example.
- A 'never say die' attitude, not giving up easily, striving Information seeking continuously until success is achieved.
- Knowing who knows, consulting experts, reading of relevant material and an overall openness to ideas and information.
- Attention to details and observance of established standards and norms.
- Taking personal pains to complete a task as scheduled.
- Concern for conservation of time, money and effort.
- Breaking up the complex whole into parts, close examination of the parts and inferring about the whole *e.g.*, simultaneously attending to production, marketing and financial aspects (parts) of the overall business strategy (the whole).
- Observing the symptoms, diagnosing and curing.

- Not being afraid of the risks associated with business and relying on one's capabilities to successfully manage these.
- Conveying emphatically one's vision and convincing others of its value.
- Eliciting support of others in the venture.
- Providing leadership.
- Ensuring the progress of the venture as planned.
- Believing in employee well being as the key to competitiveness and success and initiating programmes of employee welfare.

The self-administered questionnaire in the annexure to this chapter would help you measure where you stand on these competencies. Given that these competencies matter in entrepreneurial success. EDI estimates that development of these competencies can substantially bring down incidence of business failures/industrial sickness.

DEVELOPING COMPETENCIES

'Awareness,' they say, is the first step towards 'improvement' and 'success.' Now that you are aware of the critical competencies for entrepreneurial success and also have a measure of your scores on these, it is appropriate that you also think in terms of how to improve your scores. Suppose, you find yourself lacking in the competency - 'opportunity spotting,' you may start practicing to think like an entrepreneur. With just a little change in perspective, the world changes for you. Similarly you may work on the other competencies as well.

MOTIVATION AND PRODUCTIVITY IN THE LIBRARY

Employee motivation is important in libraries, as in any other organisation. This chapter attempts to identify the place of motivation in developing human resources in the library. This attempt begins with the need to define human resources, human resources development, and motivation, and to discuss theories of motivation and the literature of motivation as they pertain to libraries.

THE CONCEPT OF HUMAN RESOURCES

UNECA conceptualises human resources as the body of knowledge, skills, attitudes, physical, and managerial efforts required to manipulate land, capital, and technology, to produce goods and services for human consumption and welfare. Human resources includes:

- Technical skill and abilities acquired from education, training, and experience. It indicates the ability to use knowledge, methods, and techniques in the performance of library tasks.
- Human skills, which is the ability to work with and through people. It includes the understanding of motivation and the application of effective leadership.

- Conceptual skill, which incorporates the ability to understand the complexity of the overall organisation.

Human resources includes two major activities. The first is recruitment, selection, compensation, discipline, appraisal, and welfare of employees. The second is working with employees to improve their efficiency and productivity. The activities that enable individuals and groups to acquire new knowledge and skills and assume new roles and responsibilities are usually referred to as human resources development.

HUMAN MOTIVATION AND ENTREPRENEURSHIP

Despite the importance of including individual-level factors in a comprehensive explanation for the entrepreneurial process, previous studies of entrepreneurial motivation have often led to disappointing results. However, we believe that researchers should not conclude from this failure that human motivation is irrelevant to the entrepreneurial process. Rather, we suggest that there are specific reasons for the limited results obtained in previous research.

CONTROLS FOR OPPORTUNITIES

Previous research has suffered from a lack of control for the variation in the opportunities that different entrepreneurs pursue. To accurately measure the effects of motivation on entrepreneurial decisions, researchers need to control the effects of opportunities. As Venkataraman argued, a valuable opportunity for an individual is one that generates a level of profit that exceeds the entrepreneur's opportunity cost, a premium for the illiquidity of money, time, and effort expended, and a premium for bearing risk and uncertainty. Because some opportunities will exceed this threshold by a greater amount than will others, the nature of the opportunity will influence entrepreneurial decisions.

Researchers need to know the magnitude of the force exerted by the opportunities themselves to accurately estimate the effect of the individual motivations on entrepreneurial decisions. In the absence of such controls, one cannot know if the effects observed represent the effects of individual motivations or are artifacts of unobserved correlation between the opportunities and the people who pursue them. Prior research has generally failed to control the effect of opportunities by examining entrepreneurs pursuing different opportunities without explicitly modeling the value of the different opportunities pursued. In addition, prior studies have generally compared managers with firm founders.

However, human motivations can influence the tendency of people to engage in entrepreneurial activities only if those activities are possible. If people have not discovered entrepreneurial opportunities or have discovered opportunities but cannot act on those discoveries, it is impossible to determine if their individual motivations make them more or less likely than others to act on entrepreneurial opportunities. Therefore, one cannot tell from studies that compare managers to firm founders whether certain motivations influence people to make entrepreneurial decisions unless researchers have ensured that the managers have discovered opportunities and have measured the value of those opportunities. Otherwise, researchers might only capture the fact that some managers have all of the right motivations, but no opportunities in which to use them. We offer four suggestions to researchers interested in examining the effect of motivations on entrepreneurial decisions about how to deal with variation in opportunities. First, researchers could explore settings in which potential entrepreneurs pursue reasonably identical opportunities. For example, every year, many potential entrepreneurs evaluate and pursue opportunities to purchase McDonald's franchises.

When a person applies to be a McDonald's franchisee or company-owned outlet manager, one applies only to be part of the system rather than to select a particular outlet. Therefore, the opportunities to which people respond in this setting are identical. By comparing the motivations of a sample of people seek to be McDonald's franchisees with people who seek to be McDonald's company-owned outlet managers, researchers can determine the contributions of particular motivations on the decision to entrepreneur. Second, as a variety of researchers are beginning to do, scholars could employ experimental designs in which potential entrepreneurs are asked to make a series of entrepreneurial decisions in a controlled simulation. By measuring the motivations of potential entrepreneurs and examining the correlation between the motivations and the decisions made in these simulations, researchers could determine how motivations influence entrepreneurial decisions.

Third, the most obvious means of controlling opportunity are to use a sample of entrepreneurs within the same industry and country and to measure aspects of the environment that might vary within industry and region. We recommend these approaches to limiting other sources of variance than motivations from studies of motivation and entrepreneurship. Fourth, as some researchers are beginning to do, scholars could employ third parties to code the value of potential opportunities. For example, researchers could explore the propensity of inventors to found companies based on their inventions. Because all inventors are at risk of exploiting their inventions through firm formation, this setting provides a useful context in which to explore the decision to entrepreneur. By partialing out the externally evaluated value of the opportunities, researchers could determine whether motivations influence the decision to entrepreneur, net of the effects of the value of the opportunity.

Entrepreneurship as a Process

Much of the prior research has looked at entrepreneurship as a profession that certain types of people adopt, rather than as a process that occurs over time.

This approach is problematic because the appropriate conceptual lens through which to look at entrepreneurship is as a dynamic process. Because entrepreneurship is episodic and much entrepreneurial action is not long lasting, it is unrealistic to model motivation as dividing entrepreneurs and other members of society into two groups. In fact, relatively little of the motivation research on entrepreneurship has considered the effects of motivation on specific steps in the entrepreneurial process. Most studies on motivation and entrepreneurship adopt static designs that seek to determine if firm founders are different from each other, managers, or the general population at the moment the two groups are measured.

This approach makes two problematic assumptions. First, it assumes that a given motivation influences all steps in the entrepreneurial process equally, and that the effects of a given motivation do not select out some people at earlier stages in the process. Second, it assumes that, at the moment in which the founders are compared to the others, the founders who are still in charge of the organisations that they founded represent the population of people who engage in entrepreneurial activity. Because entrepreneurship is a process, with tremendous selection at each step, we believe that these assumptions are quite faulty.

The motivations that allow progression from opportunity recognition to resource assembly might not lead from financial assembly to first sales. For example, to assemble resources, a person might need to be highly confident. Those people lacking sufficient overconfidence to assemble resources are selected out of the entrepreneurial process. If there is very little variation in over-confidence among the people who have resources and seek to reach first sales, overconfidence will have no effect on achieving first sales. For these reasons, we believe that it may not be possible to examine the direct effects of a lead entrepreneur's motivations on the financial performance of a new company that the individual founds.

The effects of motivation might be captured by the intervening variables in any causal model of the effects of motivation on firm performance. For example, those higher in nAch might be more likely to obtain venture capital financing. However, once venture capital financing is measured, there is no effect of nAch on firm performance. We offer several specific suggestions for how researchers could better think about how motivations influence the entrepreneurial process. First, researchers could incorporate motivations into a dynamic evolutionary perspective on entrepreneurship by using motivations to distinguish those individuals who select out at different steps in the entrepreneurial process. For example, motivations could separate those individuals who positively evaluate opportunities from those who do not, those who obtain outside funding from those who do not, those who continue to pursue opportunities from those who abandon the effort, or those who pursue rapid rather than slow growth.

The pursuit of opportunity provides a good example. As Aldrich and Zimmer explain, "opportunities are irrelevant unless taken advantage of, and people vary widely in their ability to seise opportunities". We agree, but would argue that people also differ widely in their motivation to seise opportunities. It would be interesting to know if certain motivations predispose people to take action in response to the discovery of opportunities. One might argue, for example, that people higher in self-efficacy will be more likely to seek financing to exploit opportunities than will people lower in self-efficacy.

Because the process of financing exposes a person's entrepreneurial ideas to the scrutiny of skeptical others, those people willing to expose their ideas to scrutiny might have to be more confident than those who will not. Second, researchers could theorise more deeply about how motivation might impact entrepreneurial decisions. Rather than falling back on the stock idea that firm founders must be fundamentally different types of people from other members of society, we suggest researchers consider how motivations might influence some people to make different decisions from others in the entrepreneurial process.

For example, inventors higher in selfefficacy might found firms to exploit their inventions while inventors lower in self-efficacy might license their technology to others. Similarly, entrepreneurs with a greater need for independence might self-finance new firms, whereas those with a lesser need for independence might seek venture capital. We also suggest that it is not necessarily important for entrepreneurship researchers to show that specific motivations influence the financial performance of new firms. If financial performance of a new firm is conditional on the ability of an entrepreneur to create the firm, and that act of creation depends heavily on human motivation, then human motivation matters to entrepreneurship even if motivation has no direct effect on the performance of the newly founded firm.

In fact, we would expect that the more significant a firm that an entrepreneur founds, the less their motivations influence the firm formation process. For example, the more significant the new firm that an entrepreneur builds, the less influence they will have personally on day-to-day operations, and the less that we would expect the financial performance of the firm to be affected by their personal motivations.

Meta-Analysis

The third criticism of previous research is the failure to use meta-analysis. The ability to combine the results of scores or hundreds of individual studies into a single statistic was not always available to researchers. This sometimes led people who conducted narrative reviews to underestimate the effect of the variable being considered; for example, non-significant results in single studies may be due to sampling error rather than invalidity. Although metaanalytic results are not available for all the motivations we discuss, such data, where available, throw new light on some motivations.

Wrong Motives

A fourth criticism of extant research is its tendency to study the wrong motives. Some motives are more relevant to entrepreneurial activity than others. For example, risk-taking propensity as measured by self-perception and tolerance for ambiguity has long been assumed to be an entrepreneurial motive, but the evidence so far is only equivocal. Regarding risk, perhaps the problem has been that people cannot perceive the riskiness of their own actions, or that what is risky to one person is not risky to another. For example, several recent studies using interviews and expert evaluations showed that entrepreneurs objectively have a higher propensity for risk than either entrepreneurs or the general population but that entrepreneurs do not perceive their actions as risky. Thus, the effects of risk-taking propensity may be confounded with the high self-efficacy of entrepreneurs.

We suggest that researchers better define the motives that they think are important and focus on more precise measures of them. One way to do that would be for researchers to go back to the underlying psychological literature and examine how researchers have dealt with the nuances of theorising about and measuring the same motives in other settings. If psychologists have figured a way around the problems of using self-perceptions in the measurement of risky Behaviour, like drug usage, those same techniques can be brought to bear on the measurement of risky behaviour in entrepreneurial settings. We believe that another important step for research on motivation and entrepreneurship would be for researchers to develop more complete models of the entrepreneurial process before examining the effects of particular motives on particular activities. A fuller understanding of the role of motivations in the overall process would require consideration of factors other than motives. We suggest that researchers develop explanations that include the variety of such influences.

Indirect Effects

A fifth criticism has been the failure to look for indirect effects of motivational traits. Most, though not all, researchers have assumed that traits and motives have direct effects on outcomes and this may be true to some extent. However, an increasing body of literature is revealing that traits affect action indirectly through other mechanisms. For example, in the general realm of work, conscientiousness is a reliable predictor of performance, but there is considerable evidence that the effects of conscientiousness on work performance are mediated by situation-specific factors such as goal setting and goal commitment. Similarly, Bandura has argued that locus of control is not a strong, direct predictor of performance in a task; and studies have shown that the effects of self-efficacy mediate the effects of locus of control when self-efficacy is added to the equation. Therefore, locus of control effects reported in the entrepreneurship literature might be proxying unobserved self-efficacy.

One recent study to have taken the approach of considering indirect effects of motivation in the setting of entrepreneurial action is that of Baum, who studied the growth of small companies in the architectural woodworking industry. They included variables from five separate domains: traits and motives, skills and abilities, situation-specific motivation, business strategies, and environmental factors. They combined the measures within each domain into single indexes and related these indexes to each other and to venture growth. All the domains played a role in venture growth but the effects of motives were all indirect. Motives worked through skills, situation-specific motivation, and strategies to affect growth. Given the indirect effects observed in this study, we suggest that researchers consider such indirect patterns in their explanations for the effect of motivation on entrepreneurial action.

Definitions

A sixth criticism has stemmed from a lack of consistent definitions of entrepreneurship. In general, the definition of what constitutes entrepreneurial activity varies significantly across studies. For example, McClelland viewed managerial positions of certain types such as sales as one that demanded entrepreneurial skills, whereas much of the recent work in the applied field of management has sought to compare entrepreneurs to managers. Therefore, it is unclear if the samples from these different studies are comparable, or even represent entrepreneurship in a meaningful way. This point, of course, brings us back to the importance of a common definition of entrepreneurship. As we indicated earlier, we advocate the definition proposed by Shane and Venkataraman. Whether researchers adopt this particular definition, however, is less important than the existence of a common definition. Without a common definition, it will not be possible to accumulate findings that are comparable from study to study.

LIBRARY MOTIVATIONS INFLUENCE ENTREPRENEURSHIP

We suggest how human motivations might influence the entrepreneurial process. We offer this example to help future researchers design empirical tests of the role of motivation in entrepreneurship.

We begin with the set of human motivations that psychologists have shown to influence many aspects of human Behaviour. These include the motivations that we described earlier in the study, in particular, nAch, locus of control, desire for independence, passion, and drive. We propose that entrepreneurship is a process that begins with the recognition of an entrepreneurial opportunity and is followed by the development of an idea for how to pursue that opportunity, the evaluation of the feasibility of the opportunity, the development of the product or service that will be provided to customers, assembly of human and financial resources, organisational design, and the pursuit of customers. We suggest that some or all of the motivations influence the transition of individuals from one stage of the entrepreneurial process to another. In some cases, all of the motivations might matter.

In other cases, only some of the motivations might matter. The relative magnitudes of how much each motivation matters will likely vary, depending on the part of the process under investigation. In fact, it is quite plausible that motivations that influence one part of the process have all of their effects at that stage in the process and have no effects on later stages in the process. In this example, motivations are not the only things that influence these transitions. Cognitive factors, including knowledge, skills, and abilities, certainly matter. All action is the result of the combination or integration of motivation and cognition. First, the entrepreneurs need to have some knowledge, especially of the industry and of any relevant technology that is critical to success.

They can hire people with certain specialised skills that they lack, but they must possess enough expertise to know that they are doing the right thing. Second, the entrepreneur must have skills. The necessary skills will depend on the circumstances, but they may include such factors as selling and bargaining, leadership, planning, decision-making, problem solving, team building, communication, and conflict management. Third, the entrepreneur needs to have the requisite abilities, including intelligence. Possessing the necessary KSAs enables the entrepreneurs to develop a viable vision, including a strategy for the organisation and to carry it out successfully.

Motivation helps the entrepreneur to acquire such KSAs in the first place and provide the impetus and energy to implement the needed actions. The human capital literature in entrepreneurship has begun to show the effect of certain types of knowledge and skills on the start-up and resource assembly parts of this process. The opportunities themselves certainly matter. Prior research has shown that such things as the possession of a patented technology make individuals more likely to engage in the entrepreneurial process. One would expect that identification of a large market or a high margin product would do the same.

First, opportunities may interact in interesting ways with the attributes of people. Second, as much of the macro-level research has shown, the willingness to engage in entrepreneurial activities depends on such things as the legal system of the country in which the entrepreneur operates, the age of the industry, the availability of capital in the economy, the condition of capital markets, and the state of the overall economy. We believe that these factors are important, but that it might also be interesting to know whether motivations of particular people lead to different types of entrepreneurial action under different environmental conditions.

Motivations might be more or less stronger than these other factors in the degree that they influence particular transition points. In addition, there might be important and interesting interaction effects between motivations and opportunities, KSAs, and environmental factors. The relative importance of different categories of factors, their independent and combined effects, and their relative importance at different stages of the entrepreneurial process are clearly important theoretical and empirical questions that remain largely unexplored. We hope that researchers will begin to explore them because they appear to us to be central issues in the field of entrepreneurship.

MOTIVATION FACTORS

- When we look at the psychology of human Behaviour we can begin to understand certain baseline motivations which draw adults to on line social networks. Abraham Maslow published his theory of human motivation in 1943. Its popularity continues unabated. Like his colleague Carl Rogers, Maslow believed that actualisation was the driving force of human personality, Motivation and Personality. Maslow's great insight was to place actualisation into a hierarchy of motivation. Self-actualisation, as he called it, is the highest drive, but before a person can turn to it, he or she must satisfy other, lower motivations like hunger, safety and belonging. The hierarchy has five levels.
- Physiological (hunger, thirst, shelter, sex, etc.).
- Safety (security, protection from physical and emotional harm).
- Social (affection, belonging, acceptance, friendship)
- Esteem (also called ego). The internal ones are self respect, autonomy, achievement and the external ones are status, recognition, and attention.
- Self-actualisation (doing things).

Maslow points out that the hierarchy is dynamic; the dominant need is always shifting. The hierarchy does not exist by itself, but is affected by the situation and the general culture. Satisfaction is relative. Douglas McGregor makes it the building block for his Theory X and Theory Y.

A 1990s example of self actualisation may be surfing the Internet. Empirical research has confirmed the first three levels, but has not done so for the fourth and fifth levels of esteem and self-actualisation. Some have noted that Maslow's hierarchy follows the life cycle. A newborn baby's needs are almost entirely physiological. As the baby grows, it needs safety, then love.

Toddlers are eager for social interaction. Teenagers are anxious about social needs; young adults are concerned with esteem and only more mature people transcend the first four levels to spend much time self actualising. Based on the observations across numerous networking platforms and reflect on the past definitions of human motivation we can see that social networks on line provide a primary motivation for adults in the category of self actualisation, or doing things. Maslow defines self actualisation as growth-motivated rather than deficiency-motivated:

- Based on observations and interview as suggested, provide a general categorisation of the factors that enhance individual growth for adults participating in on line social networks. Each of these factors will be defined in greater detail in future articles post.
- With all the hype, craze and media coverage of social networking platforms,,*i.e.*, Facebook and Linkedin, many adults are drawn to the medium to learn what the hype is all about.
- Once adults enter networks and learn the "tools of the trade" many are amazed to find the presence of other adults they know and many they don't already engaged with the medium.
- Adults begin to find association with groups, causes, forums, media and other affinities which relate to their interest both personally and professionally.
- The predominant business segment using social networks today is employment recruiters. However, as the medium and adult participation has grown there is an exponential growth of business opportunities that adults are learning to facilitate using social networks as the medium.
- Adults, and their businesses, are applying creative ways to use the technology behind social computing to extend its value to both personal and professional needs.
- When you consider the creative possibilities of social networks adults expect to the formation of some economic and social value to be derived from their participation whether currently or in the future.

The expectation of individual growth and satisfaction is high.These factors combined with the media hype over social networking are the motivating issues which are driving millions of adults to the medium at annual growth rates of 70 per cent and more. The opportunity to capitalise economically is emerging quickly. Word of mouth will fuel growth rates faster than any other technological medium in our past.

THEORIES OF MOTIVATION

Contribution of Robert Owen

Though Owen is considered to be paternalistic in his view, his contribution is of a considerable significance in the theories of motivation. During the early years of the nineteenth century, Owen's textile mill at New Lanark in Scotland was the scene of some novel ways of treating people. His view was that people were similar to machines. A machine that is looked after properly, cared for and maintained well, performs efficiently, reliably and lastingly, similarly people are likely to be more efficient if they are taken care of. Robert Owen practiced what he preached and introduced such things as employee housing and company shop. His ideas on this and other matters were considered to be too revolutionary for that time.

Jeremy Bentham's "The Carrot and the Stick Approach"

Possibly the essence of the traditional view of people at work can be best appreciated by a brief look at the work of this English philosopher, whose ideas were also developed in the early years of the Industrial Revolution, around 1800. Bentham's view was that all people are self-interested and are motivated by the desire to avoid pain and find pleasure. Any worker will work only if the reward is big enough, or the punishment sufficiently unpleasant. This view - the 'carrot and stick' approach - was built into the philosophies of the age and is still to be found, especially in the older, more traditional sectors of industry.

The various leading theories of motivation and motivators seldom make reference to the carrot and the stick. This metaphor relates, of course, to the use of rewards and penalties in order to induce desired Behaviour. It comes from the old story that to make a donkey move, one must put a carrot in front of him or dab him with a stick from behind.

Despite all the research on the theories of motivation, reward and punishment are still considered strong motivators. For centuries, however, they were too often thought of as the only forces that could motivate people. At the same time, in all theories of motivation, the inducements of some kind of 'carrot' are recognised. Often this is money in the form of pay or bonuses. Even though money is not the only motivating force, it has been and will continue to be an important one.

The trouble with the money 'carrot' approach is that too often everyone gets a carrot, regardless of performance through such practices as salary increase and promotion by seniority, automatic 'merit' increases, and executive bonuses not based on individual manager performance. It is as simple as this: If a person put a donkey in a pen full of carrots and then stood outside with a carrot, would the donkey be encouraged to come out of the pen ? The 'stick', in the form of fear-fear of loss of job, loss of income, reduction of bonus, demotion, or some other penalty–has been and continues to be a strong motivator.

Yet it is admittedly not the best kind. It often gives rise to defensive or retaliatory Behaviour, such as union organisation, poor-quality work, executive indifference, failure of a manager to take any risks in decision making or even dishonesty. But fear of penalty cannot be overlooked. Whether managers are first-level supervisors or chief executives, the power of their position to give or with hold rewards or impose penalties of various kinds gives them an ability to control, to a very great extent, the economic and social well-being of their subordinates.

Abraham Maslow's "Need Hierarchy Theory"

One of the most widely theories of motivation is the hierarchy of needs theory put forth by psychologist Abraham Maslow. Maslow saw human needs in the form of a hierarchy, ascending from the lowest to the highest, and he concluded that when one set of needs is satisfied, this kind of need ceases to be a motivator.

As per his theory this needs are: These are important needs for sustaining the human life. Food, water, warmth, shelter, sleep, medicine and education are the basic physiological needs which fall in the primary list of need satisfaction. Maslow was of an opinion that until these needs were satisfied to a degree to maintain life, no other motivating factors can work.

These are the needs to be free of physical danger and of the fear of losing a job, property, food or shelter. It also includes protection against any emotional harm. Since, people are social beings, they need to belong and be accepted by others. People try to satisfy their need for affection, acceptance and friendship. Once people begin to satisfy their need to belong, they tend to want to be held in esteem both by themselves and by others.

This kind of need produces such satisfaction as power, prestige status and self-confidence. It includes both internal esteem factors like self-respect, autonomy and achievements and external esteem factors such as states, recognition and attention. Maslow regards this as the highest need in his hierarchy. It is the drive to become what one is capable of becoming, it includes growth, achieving one's potential and self-fulfilment. It is to maximise one's potential and to accomplish something.

From the standpoint of motivation, the theory would say that although no need is ever fully gratified, a substantially satisfied need no longer motivates. So if you want to motivate someone, you need to understand what level of the hierarchy that person is on and focus on satisfying those needs or needs above that level. Maslow's need theory has received wide recognition, particularly among practicing managers. This can be attributed to the theory's intuitive logic and ease of understanding. However, research does not validate these theory. Maslow provided no empirical evidence and other several studies that sought to validate the theory found no support for it.

"Theory X and Theory Y" of Douglas McGregor

McGregor, in his book "The Human side of Enterprise" states that people inside the organisation can be managed in two ways. The first is basically negative, which falls under the category X and the other is basically positive, which falls under the category Y. After viewing the way in which the manager dealt with employees, McGregor concluded that a manager's view of the nature of human beings is based on a certain grouping of assumptions and that he or she tends to mold his or her Behaviour towards subordinates according to these assumptions. Under the assumptions of theory X:

- Employees inherently do not like work and whenever possible, will attempt to avoid it.
- Because employees dislike work, they have to be forced, coerced or threatened with punishment to achieve goals.
- Employees avoid responsibilities and do not work fill formal directions are issued.
- Most workers place a greater importance on security over all other factors and display little ambition.

In contrast under the assumptions of theory Y:

- Physical and mental effort at work is as natural as rest or play.
- People do exercise self-control and self-direction and if they are committed to those goals.
- Average human beings are willing to take responsibility and exercise imagination, ingenuity and creativity in solving the problems of the organisation.
- That the way the things are organised, the average human being's brainpower is only partly used.

On analysis of the assumptions it can be detected that theory X assumes that lower-order needs dominate individuals and theory Y assumes that higher-order needs dominate individuals. An organisation that is run on Theory X lines tends to be authoritarian in nature, the word "authoritarian" suggests such ideas as the "power to enforce obedience" and the "right to command". In contrast Theory Y organisations can be described as "participative", where the aims of the organisation and of the individuals in it are integrated; individuals can achieve their own goals best by directing their efforts towards the success of the organisation. However, this theory has been criticised widely for generalisation of work and human Behaviour.

Contribution of Rensis Likert

Likert developed a refined classification, breaking down organisations into four management systems:

- 1st System – Primitive authoritarian.
- 2nd System – Benevolent authoritarian.
- 3rd System – Consultative.
- 4th System – Participative.

As per the opinion of Likert, the 4th system is the best, not only for profit organisations, but also for non-profit firms.

Frederick Herzberg's Motivation-Hygiene Theory

Frederick has tried to modify Maslow's need Hierarchy theory. His theory is also known as two-factor theory or Hygiene theory. He stated that there are certain satisfiers and dissatisfiers for employees at work. Intrinsic factors are related to job satisfaction, while extrinsic factors are associated with dissatisfaction. He devised his theory on the question: "What do people want from their jobs ?" He asked people to describe in detail, such situations when they felt exceptionally good or exceptionally bad. From the responses that he received, he concluded that opposite of satisfaction is not dissatisfaction. Removing dissatisfying characteristics from a job does not necessarily make the job satisfying. He states that presence of certain factors in the organisation is natural and the presence of the same does not lead to motivation. However, their non-presence leads to demotivation. In similar manner there are certain factors, the absence of which causes no dissatisfaction, but their presence has motivational impact.

Examples of Hygiene factors are:

- Security, status, relationship with subordinates, personal life, salary, work conditions, relationship with supervisor and company policy and administration.

Examples of Motivational factors are:

- Growth prospectus job advancement, responsibility, challenges, recognition and achievements.

Contributions of Elton Mayo

The work of Elton Mayo is famously known as "Hawthorne Experiments". He conducted Behavioural experiments at the Hawthorne Works of the American Western Electric Company in Chicago. He made some illumination experiments, introduced breaks in between the work performance and also introduced refreshments during the pause's.

On the basis of this he drew the conclusions that motivation was a very complex subject. It was not only about pay, work condition and morale but also included psychological and social factors. Although this research has been criticised from many angles, the central conclusions drawn were:

- People are motivated by more than pay and conditions.
- The need for recognition and a sense of belonging are very important.
- Attitudes towards work are strongly influenced by the group.

Vroom's Valence x Expectancy Theory

The most widely accepted explanations of motivation has been propounded by Victor Vroom. His theory is commonly known as expectancy theory. The theory argues that the strength of a tendency to act in a specific way depends on the strength of an expectation that the act will be followed by a given outcome and on the attractiveness of that outcome to the individual to make this simple, expectancy theory says that an employee can be motivated to perform better when their is a belief that the better performance will lead to good performance appraisal and that this shall result into realisation of personal goal in form of some reward. Therefore an employee is:

- Motivation = Valence x Expectancy.

The theory focuses on three things:

- Efforts and performance relationship.
- Performance and reward relationship.
- Rewards and personal goal relationship.

This leads us to a conclusion that:

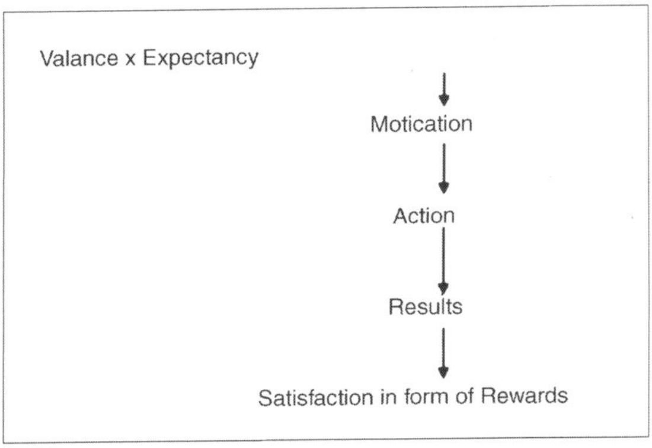

The Porter and Lawler Model

Lyman W. Porter and Edward E. Lawler developed a more complete version of motivation depending upon expectancy theory.

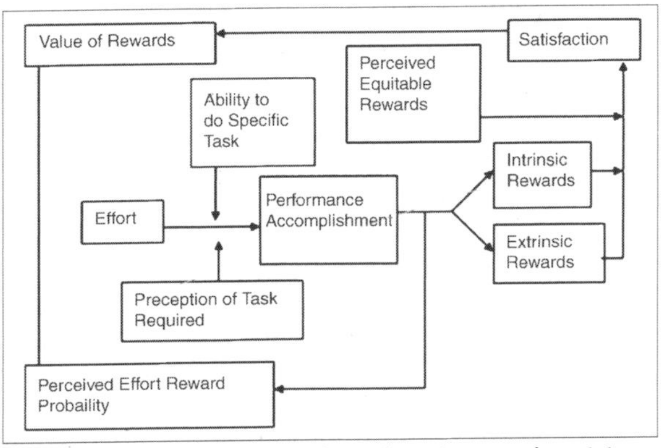

Actual performance in a job is primarily determined by the effort spent. But it is also affected by the person's ability to do the job and also by individual's perception of what the required task is. So performance is the responsible factor that leads to intrinsic as well as extrinsic rewards. These rewards, along with the equity of individual leads to satisfaction. Hence, satisfaction of the individual depends upon the fairness of the reward.

Clayton Alderfer's ERG Theory

Alderfer has tried to rebuild the hierarchy of needs of Maslow into another model named ERG, *i.e.*, Existence–Relatedness–Growth. The existence group is concerned mainly with providing basic material existence.

The second group is the individuals need to maintain interpersonal relationship with other members in the group. The final group is the intrinsic desire to grow and develop personally. The major conclusions of this theory are:

- In an individual, more than one need may be operative at the same time.
- If a higher need goes unsatisfied than the desire to satisfy a lower need intensifies.
- It also contains the frustration-regression dimension.

McClelland's Theory of Needs

David McClelland has developed a theory on three types of motivating needs:

- Need for Power.
- Need for Affiliation.
- Need for Achievement.

Basically people for high need for power are inclined towards influence and control. They like to be at the center and are good orators. They are demanding in nature, forceful in manners and ambitious in life. They can be motivated to perform if they are given key positions or power positions. In the second category are the people who are social in nature. They try to affiliate themselves with individuals and groups. They are driven by love and faith.

They like to build a friendly environment around themselves. Social recognition and affiliation with others provides them motivation. People in the third area are driven by the challenge of success and the fear of failure. Their need for achievement is moderate and they set for themselves moderately difficult tasks.

They are analytical in nature and take calculated risks. Such people are motivated to perform when they see atleast some chances of success. McClelland observed that with the advancement in hierarchy the need for power and achievement increased rather than Affiliation. He also observed that people who were at the top, later ceased to be motivated by this drives.

Equity Theory

As per the equity theory of J. Stacey Adams, people are motivated by their beliefs about the reward structure as being fair or unfair, relative to the inputs. People have a tendency to use subjective Judgement to balance the outcomes and inputs in the relationship for comparisons between different individuals. Accordingly:

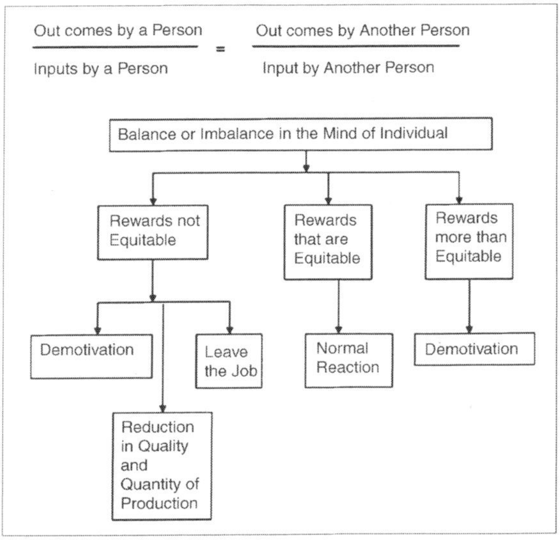

If people feel that they are not equally rewarded they either reduce the quantity or quality of work or migrate to some other organisation. However, if people perceive that they are rewarded higher, they may be motivated to work harder.

Reinforcement Theory

B.F. Skinner, who propounded the reinforcement theory, holds that by designing the environment properly, individuals can be motivated. Instead of considering internal factors like impressions, feelings, attitudes and other cognitive Behaviour, individuals are directed by what happens in the environment external to them.

Skinner states that work environment should be made suitable to the individuals and that punishments actually leads to frustration and de-motivation. Hence, the only way to motivate is to keep on making positive changes in the external environment of the organisation.

Goal Setting Theory of Edwin Locke

Instead of giving vague tasks to people, specific and pronounced objectives, help in achieving them faster. As the clarity is high, a goal orientation also avoids any misunder-standings in the work of the employees. The goal setting theory states that when the goals to be achieved are set at a higher standard than in that case employees are motivated to perform better and put in maximum effort. It revolves around the concept of "Self-efficacy", *i.e.*, individual's belief that he or she is capable of performing a hard task.

Cognitive Evaluation Theory

As per this theory a shift from external rewards to internal rewards results into motivation. It believes that even after the stoppage of external stimulus, internal stimulus survives. It relates to the pay structure in the organisation. Instead of treating external factors like pay, incentives, promotion etc and internal factors like interests, drives, responsibility etc, separately, they should be treated as contemporary to each other.

The cognition is to be such that even when external motivators are not there the internal motivation continues. However, practically extrinsic rewards are given much more weightage.

MOTIVATION IN THE DEVELOPMENT OF HUMAN RESOURCES IN THE LIBRARY

A library is an organisation whose mission is to provide information to its users. The library staff are the human resources, who provide information services using library resources. How well the services are provided depends on how well the human resources are motivated and developed. Motivation is crucial to the development of human resources in the library in the following ways:

- Maslow's hierarchy of needs is apparent in library employment. Acquiring a job and looking for job security help satisfy physiological and safety needs. When those needs are satisfied, employees look to their need for belonging and self-esteem. The need for self-esteem and self-actualisation are represented in library human resources development efforts that focus on training, creativity, problem-solving, and so on.
- The maintenance and motivational factors of Herzberg's two-factor theory play important roles in the development of human resources in the library. Herzberg's believed that motivators must be build into the job. These include responsibility, autonomy, respect and recognition from superiors, a sense of wellbeing, and the opportunity to have one's ideas adopted.
- Equity theory indicates likewise has a place in the library. Workers compare their pay, work schedules, benefits, or any reward with what is being received by other employees. Unless the reward system is carefully administered, it could result in problems of perceived or actual inequity.
- Expectancy theory can be used in the development of human resources in libraries. The logic of expectancy theory is that individuals exert effort for a performance that results in preferred rewards. Expectancy can be influenced by selecting individuals with particular skills and abilities, providing training, and providing support to achieve a particular level of performance.

HUMAN RESOURCES DEVELOPMENT

Nadler defines human resources development as a "series of organised activities conducted within a specified time and designed to produce Behaviour change" in individuals and organisations. The key point is learning. Ojo remarks that, the "organised activities contained in the definition provided above embraced a carefully developed learning activity with identifiable components of objectives, actions, and evaluation. These conditions must exist in all forms of human resources development." Ideally, human resources development should provide solutions to problems such as a shortage of employees, employees who are inadequately skilled and efficient, high turnover, organisational expansion, career planning, and training needs.

STRATEGIES FOR INCREASING MOTIVATION

Job Enrichment

The idea of quality work life has received attention for several decades. Workers become increasingly dissatisfied and frustrated by routine tasks. The result may be lower output, poor attitude, lower quality, absenteeism, high turnover, and pressure for better conditions and greater participation in decision-making. Herzberg contributed the theory of job enrichment as a motivational technique. Job enrichment provides employees with an opportunity to grow psychologically and mature in a job. Job enrichment attempts to make the job itself motivational. Research indicates that jobs higher in enrichment factors result in higher satisfaction; however, research also indicates that enriched jobs require more training time and result in slightly higher anxiety and stress. Job enrichment increases a job's range and depth, which refers to the number of activities and the autonomy, responsibility, discretion, and control.

Merit Pay

The money that employees receive is actually a package made up of salary, and other fringe benefits such as transport, housing, furniture, medical allowance. Others include meal subsidy and utility allowances. The motivation theories discussed, suggest that and fringe benefits can have some influence on effort and persistence. The money that employees receive is actually a package of salary and benefits. Theories of motivation suggest that salary and benefits have influence on effort and persistence.

Pay has the potential to satisfy each of the five needs in Maslow's hierarchy. In Herzberg's two-factor model pay is a maintenance factor that should not contribute significantly to motivation. In expectancy theory, pay can satisfy a variety of needs and influence choice and Behaviour, while in equity theory, pay is a major outcome that one compares with other employees. A number of studies reveal that, in order to motivate, a salary plan must demonstrate that good performance leads to higher levels of pay, minimise any negative consequences of good performance, and relate other rewards to good performance.

Flexible Working Hours

Libraries are faced with an increasingly diverse workforce that includes nursing mothers, single parents with young children, employees with very different responsibilities, and those taking classes or pursuing degrees to improve skills and abilities or for self-improvement. The concept of flexible working hours has motivational appeal to many library staff. Flexible time is intended to ensure that the work of the organisation is accomplished and, at the same time, to permit library staff and their supervisors to establish work schedules that recognise individual and family needs. Research indicates that flexible scheduling can be motivational in that job satisfaction is improved and absenteeism reduced. The ability to accommodate employee needs is a healthy and positive approach to motivation.

6

Approach to Training and Development in Library

INTRODUCTION

Unfortunately, the procedures of employee training and development within our organisations are undeveloped. They are mainly performed occasionally, and not connected with organisational strategy, nor do they have some strategic significance. They are mostly enforced when such business problems occur or are perceived that are considered relievable or solvable by organising a training, course or seminar for some of the employees. Employees view the training as an imposed obligation, rather than a way to maximise their potential and they do not realise that by improving their performances and innovation of their knowledge they may contribute to better business results of the organisation they belong to. Unfortunately, top managers do not realise this as well. From their relationship with the employees it is plain to see that the employees are still treated as an expense, rather than an investment worthy of investing. In our organisations there is no culture of obtaining and sharing of knowledge. Many of our managers are under the influence of prejudices such as: training is expensive, training is an expense burdening the current business, it is not rewarding, training is for the young, etc., Knowledge is expensive, but ignorance is even more expensive.

Human possibilites to learn are unlimited, unless idviduals do not limit their abilities within their minds. Many studies have shown that investing in employee training and development has larger business effects than investing in equipment and other material resources. Our organisations must harmonise their approach to employee development with the changes. Employee training and development has to be connected with the organisational goals and strategy, they need to fulfil the new reqiurements of the environment.

Employee training and development needs to become a managerial function. It is a managerial challenge to consider the employees of the organisation from a strategic perspective (future orientedness) and constantly monitor and encourage the development of new skills and knowledge as the foundation of organisational development. This is not about assigning the employees to appropriate jobs, but rather about the constant dynamic of encouraging and discovering new possibilities. This is a new type of leadership, significantly different from the classical model of organisational management.

The leaders are no longer expected to be all-knowing bosses and supervisors, but rather moderators and inspirators. Since, people do not share the information which is the source of their power instictively, the leaders need to recognise, attract and release knowledge in the organisation. One of the main challegnes of modern organisations therefore is how to manage the process of knowledge transfer. "The answer is that wisdom, just because it is the most important, doesn't need to be located inside a tall building where the chief executive and his main assistants hang their hats (and soon their heads as well – unless they join the revolution of the mind). This pictoresque answer of Tom Peters refers to decentralisation and substantivity of employees (turning every workplace into business), which implies a high degree of employee competence and orientation Towards the participative style of management.

The process of democratisations, transitions, opening towards the EU, privatisations and arrival of foreign companies and praxis contributed considerably to transformation of approach to employee training and development within our organisations, from the *ad hoc* processes that originate from the goals and strategies, to a modern approach where human resources and their knowledge are gaining more and more significance.

IMPORTANCE OF TRAINING OBJECTIVES

Training objectives are one of the most important parts of training Programme. While some people think of training objective as a waste of valuable time. The counterargument here is that resources are always limited and the training objectives actually lead the design of training. It provides the clear guidelines and develops the training Programme in less time because objectives focus specifically on needs. It helps in adhering to a plan. Training objective tell the trainee that what is expected out of him at the end of the training Programme.

Training objectives are of great significance from a number of stakeholder perspectives:

- Trainer.
- Trainee.
- Designer.
- Evaluator.

Trainer

The training objective is also beneficial to trainer because it helps the trainer to measure the progress of trainees and make the required adjustments.

Also, trainer comes in a position to establish a relationship between objectives and particular segments of training.

Trainee

The training objective is beneficial to the trainee because it helps in reducing the anxiety of the trainee up to some extent. Not knowing anything or going to a place which is unknown creates anxiety that can negatively affect learning.

Therefore, it is important to keep the participants aware of the happenings, rather than keeping it surprise. Secondly, it helps in increase in concentration, which is the crucial factor to make the training successful. The objectives create an image of the training Programme in trainee's mind that actually helps in gaining attention. Thirdly, if the goal is set to be challenging and motivating, then the likelihood of achieving those goals is much higher than the situation in which no goal is set. Therefore, training objectives helps in increasing the probability that the participants will be successful in training.

Designer

The training objective is beneficial to the training designer because if the designer is aware what is to be achieved in the end then he'll buy the training package according to that only.

The training designer would then look for the training methods, training equipments, and training content accordingly to achieve those objectives. Furthermore, planning always helps in dealing effectively in an unexpected situation.

Consider an example; the objective of one training Programme is to deal effectively with customers to increase the sales. Since, the objective is known, the designer will design a training Programme that will include ways to improve the interpersonal skills, such as verbal and non- verbal language, dealing in unexpected situation, *i.e.*, when there is a defect in a product or when a customer is angry. Therefore, without any guidance, the training may not be designed appropriately.

Evaluator

It becomes easy for the training evaluator to measure the progress of the trainees because the objectives define the expected performance of trainees. Training objective is an important to tool to judge the performance of participants.

TRAINING AND DEVELOPMENT: CONCEPT, IMPORTANCE AND METHODS OF TRAINING

Changes in technology, especially information technology, generate knowledge spreading up at tremendous speed, as well as its quick obsolence.

In the period between 1900 and 1950, the amount of human knowledge doubled, and Since, then it has doubled every 5 to 8 years. Knowledge is becoming obsolete so quickly that all of us need do double our knowledge every 2 to 3 years in order to keep up with the changes. On the other hand, the increasing complexity, turbulency and uncertainty of the environment requires different and greater knowledge. Modern business requires more and more knowledge and skills that are still inadequatly present in the formal school education, *i.e.*, the gap between business reqiurements and the knowledge acquired at school is growing.

The period of mass producing is over and the customers are very selective. Increased consumer demands require new solutions and knowledge. Due to increasing competition, the organisation is required to constantly revise its product and service mix, managerial methods, and to increase productivity. Modern conditions of dynamic competition, sophisticated information technology, knowledge economy, market globalisation, has changed the relation to importance of human resources in organisation. These conditions actualise the human capital as the strategic resource of every organisation. Differences between the organisations exist exactly due to the differences between human capital, *i.e.*, the organisations human resources, ways of their management and development.

In a more and more global, complex and turbulent environment, knowledge is the only reliable source of competitive advantage. Traditional factors of manufacturing as the soil, Labour and capital did not disappear, but their significance is not primary anymore. Knowledge is viewed as the key of realisation of a competitive advantage. And therefore the question of where the corporative knowledge is located, how to release it and develop to achieve organisational goals has become very important.

Since, the organisational knowledge is largely located inside the human mind, *i.e.*, the head of employees, as carriers of knowledge and activities, human resources are becoming the key factor of business success. Organisational development is always conditioned by human knowledge and skills. That is why, contemporary organisations pay more and more attention to the development of their emplozees. Thus, employee education and training are becoming an optimal answer to complex business challenges, and the management of human resources is taking central role in modern management.

Through the process of employee training and development, the management of human resources provides constant knowledge innovation, creates conditions for mutual knowledge and experience exchange and proactive behaviour, in this way contributing to competitive advantage and satisfaction of all participants in business procedures. As a consequence of these procedures a learning organisation has formed. The aim of this chapter is to point to the fact that education and development of human potential are the basic factor for creation of basis for transformation from traditional to a learning company.

Learning organisation is organisation that promotes learning of all of its members and it transforms permanently. Individuals and societies that do not have enough knowledge are in inferior position, compared to societies and organisations that have it and even permanently acquire new knowledge. That is the reason why we say that success is not among the educated but among those that are learning permanently, and everything changes except knowledge acquirement, which is constant.

EMPLOYEE TRAINING AND DEVELOPMENT

Understanding the phenomenon of employee training and development requires understanding of all the changes that take place as a result of learning. As the generator of new knowledge, employee training and development is placed within a broader strategic context of human resources management, *i.e.*, global organisational management, as a planned staff education and development, both individual and group, with the goal to benefit both the organisation and employees. To preserve its obtained positions and increase competitive advantage, the organisation needs to be able to create new knowledge, and not only to rely solely on utilisation of the existing. Thus, the continous employee training and delopment has a singnificant role in the development of individual and organisational performance.

The strategic procedure of employee training and development needs to encourage creativity, ensure inventiveness and shape the entire organisational knowledge that provides the organisation with uniqueness and differentiates it from the others. Education is no longer the duty and privilege of those in higher positions and skilled labour, but it is becoming the duty and need of everyone. The larger the organisations, the more funds they spend on education and provide their employees with greater and diverse possibilities of education and development.

Understanding the tremendous significance of education for the modern organisation and confident that it represents a good and remunirative investment, present day organisations set aside more and more resources for this activity. Most of the organisations invest 3 to 5 per cent of their revenue into adult education. It is estimated that the organisations that desire to keep the pace with changes need to provide their employees with 2 per cent of total annual fund of working hours for training and education. Thus, it is necessary to accept the model of permanent, continuous learning. That truth has been known for more than two centuries. Denis Diderot, a French philosopher and literate of the Age of Enlightment, wrote the following: "Education shouldn't be finished when an individual leaves school, it should encompass all the ages of life... to provide people in every moment of their life with a possibility to maintain their knowledge or to obtain new knowledge". The only way for present day organisations to survive is the imperative to innovate or perish.

Since, this depends on the knowledge the organisation possesses, this imperative could be read as: learn faster than competition. The logical sequence is: knowledge creation – innovation – competitive advantage. If knowledge is good, is it not true that the more knowlegde we have, the better we are? Many organisations which consider knowledge as a good thing are trapped into the pitfall of gathering as much knowledge as possible. Knowledge that is not necessary is exatly what it is: unnecessary. And the efforts to obtain it are wasted efforts.

The only important knowldege is the knowledge with strategic importance to the company, knowledge that helps to increase the value of the company, knowledge with significance to the strategy of the company. It is not about knowledge for the sake of knowledge, but rather knowledge according to the needs, applicable knowledge, knowledge to create innovation and competitive advantage. Obtaining knowledge, learning, education, all could have a real effect on the quality of labour only if they are harmonised with the needs of a particular organisation, its goals and the goals of its employees.

The further choice of educational contents and educational methods, and the efficiency of educational effectiveness control depend on clearly defined educational goals and needs, answers to the questions of which knowldege is necessary to realise the strategy and the survival of the organisation in general, which employees need to possess this knowledge and will this knowledge solve certain problems. Employee training and development does not imply only obtaining new knowledge, abilities and skills, but also the possibility to promote entrepreneurship, introduce employees to changes, encourage the changes of their attitude, introduce the employees to important business decisions and involve them actively in the process of decision making.

To precisely define expectations and attract skilled workforce, more and more employment advertisings offer a certain number of annual hours or days for education. The most wanted resources are the people with particular knowledge, skills and abilities. Managers must learn to manage them, and the organisations to employ and retain them. Knowledge based organisations must preserve their competitive advantage by retaining skilled workforce, workers of knowledge, strengthening their motivation and improving the reward and compensation systems according to the workers' performances.

Within the context of learning organisation, it is not sufficient for the worker only to add value to the organisation based on his knowledge, but he also has to receive knowledge. He gives as much knowledge as he receives. For the present day employees the wage by itself is not a sufficient incentive, but they also need investment into themselves in a sense of investing in their knowledge. Empolyees no longer work for money alone, nor can they be influenced by traditional attractive financial packages.

CONCEPT OF A LEARNING ORGANISATION

Every individual should appreciate lifelong learning, and every successful organisation has to become a permanently learning organisation. Many successful organisations describe themselves as learning organisation or one of their strategic goals is to become such an organisation. Companies such as Coca-Cola, Motorola, General Electrics and Cisco have assigned vice presidents for knowledge, learning or intellectual capital whose task is to create knowledge management systems that enable them to quickly adopt development tendencies, influencing in that way the customers, competitors, distributors and suppliers.

The organisation is not only the user of knowledge, but also its creator. Peter Senge described in the book named "The Fifth Discipline", the learning organisation implies free flow of knowledge, *i.e.*, lifting of all barriers on developing knowledge and new ideas at the very beginning. In the future it will not be possible to "unthread things from above" and for all the others to follow the "big brother's" instructions anymore. The top organisations of the future will be distinguished by their knowledge about how to encourage engagement and develop the learning potential on each organisational level. Peter Senge's model of a learning organisation is very interesting Since, it recognises the organisation as a whole, *i.e.*, in his organisation, through their functions and sectors within the organisation, all the employees influence the course of business procedures, and the knowledge creation, consequently the creation of new values both for the organisation and its customers. With this definition, Senge has made significant qualitative progress compared to the classical organisation, Since, he emphasised the necessity of ability development through the process of learning.

Besides Senge, Chris Argyris was a great populariser of a learning organisation as well. In his book "Teaching smart people how to learn", he says: "Any company that aspires to succeed in the tougher business environment must first resolve a basic dilemma: success in the marketplace increasingly depends on learning, yet most people don't know how to learn.

What's more, those members of the organisation that many assume to be the best at learning are, in fact, not very good at it. I am talking about the well-educated, highpowered, highly committed professionals who take up key leadership positions in the modern corporation." Organisations learn only through the learning individuals. Individual learning does not guarantee organisational learning. But without it there is no organisational learning as well. The ablity to learn faster than the competitors may be the only sustainable competitive advantage.

Thus, the learning organisation is the organisation that learns and encourages people to learn in the organisation. It motivates information exchange between employees and creates staff with different knowledge. Chris

Argiris explains this: "On the other hand, there is a problem of existence of individuals within the organisation who know how to learn, but that doesn't create automatically conditions for the organisation to learn as well. This is due to the indisputable view that knowledge is still the only private property the man owns. This means that individual learning, and even learning of all the employees, doesn't imply the existence of a learning organisation. To have a learning organisation, it is necessary to know how to transfer individual into organisational knowledge, *i.e.*, into organisational learning." The starting point of knowledge management concept is in the fact that power does not come from knowledge, but from the exchange of knowledge.

It starts from the synergic effect. By exchanging knowledge, combining individual knowledge, we get much more qualitative knowledge than the individual knowledge. Obtaining and sharing knowledge is the core of the learning organisation. The reasons to become a learning organisation are the following: people are developing (greater motivation, flexibility of employees, people are more creative, improved social interaction), better working teams and groups (knowledge sharing, mutual dependence), benefiting organisations (greater work productivity, more qualitative products/services/ procedures, competitive advantage, profit).

METHODS OF TRAINING

There are various methods of training, which can be divided in to cognitive and Behavioural methods. Trainers need to understand the pros and cons of each method, also its impact on trainees keeping their background and skills in mind before giving training. Cognitive methods are more of giving theoretical training to the trainees.

The various methods under Cognitive approach provide the rules for how to do something, written or verbal information, demonstrate relationships among concepts, etc., These methods are associated with changes in knowledge and attitude by stimulating learning.

The various methods that come under Cognitive approach are:

- Lectures.
- Demonstrations.
- Discussions.
- Computer based training (cbt).
  - Intellegent tutorial system(its).
  - Programmed instruction (pi).
  - Virtual reality.

Behavioural methods are more of giving practical training to the trainees. The various methods under Behavioural approach allow the trainee to Behaviour in a real fashion. These methods are best used for skill development. The various methods that come under Behavioural approach are:

- Games and simulations.
  - Behaviour-modeling.
  - Business games.
  - Case studies.
  - Equipment stimulators.
  - In-basket technique.
  - Role plays.

Both the methods can be used effectively to change attitudes, but through different means.

INSTRUCTIONAL SYSTEM DEVELOPMENT MODEL (ISD) MODEL

Instructional System Development model or ISD training model was made to answer the training problems. This model is widely used now-a-days in the organisation because it is concerned with the training need on the job performance. Training objectives are defined on the basis of job responsibilities and job description and on the basis of the defined objectives individual progress is measured. This model also helps in determining and developing the favourable strategies, sequencing the content, and delivering media for the types of training objectives to be achieved. The Instructional System Development model comprises of five stages:

- This phase consist of training need assessment, job analysis, and target audience analysis.
- This phase consist of setting goal of the learning outcome, instructional objectives that measures Behaviour of a participant after the training, types of training material, media selection, methods of evaluating the trainee, trainer and the training Programme, strategies to impart knowledge, *i.e.*, selection of content, sequencing of content, etc.
- This phase translates design decisions into training material. It consists of developing course material for the trainer including handouts, workbooks, visual aids, demonstration props, etc, course material for the trainee including handouts of summary.
- This phase focuses on logistical arrangements, such as arranging speakers, equipments, benches, podium, food facilities, cooling, lighting, parking, and other training accessories.
- The purpose of this phase is to make sure that the training Programme has achieved its aim in terms of subsequent work performance. This phase consists of identifying strengths and weaknesses and making necessary amendments to any of the previous stage in order to remedy or improve failure practices.

The ISD model is a continuous process that lasts throughout the training Programme. It also highlights that feedback is an important phase throughout the entire training Programme. In this model, the output of one phase is an input to the next phase.

Another Method is Management Development Method

- The more future oriented method and more concerned with education of the employees. To become a better performer by education implies that management development activities attempt to instill sound reasoning processes. Management development method is further divided into two parts:
- The development of a manager's abilities can take place on the job.

The four techniques for on the job development are:

- Coaching.
- Mentoring.
- Job rotation.
- Job instruction technique (jit).

Off the Job Training

There are many management development techniques that an employee can take in off the job. The few popular methods are:

- Sensitivity training.
- Transactional analysis.
- Straight lectures/ lectures.
- Simulation exercises.

TRAINING AND SUPPORT TO USERS

The importance of the library as a resource centre and the endeavor of the management to exploit the resources gathered over the years with a lot of investment, need not be over emphasized. However, it has been the experience of many a library, especially those attached to organisations, the use of their resources appear to be little compared to the efforts put in building up the resources. As such there appears to be a constant need to initiate outreach programmes in order to enhance the usage of the library to the maximum extent. Library is looked upon as a centre for learning. The Library has to strive to repackage the material that is received in the library in the form of Alerts, reviews, digests, abstracts and databases to enhance library utilization and improve readership. Also, in view of the rapid developments in Information and Communication Technologies, the role of a librarian is not like what it used to be a few decades ago. Added to IT, satellite communication systems, networking, Internet and intellectual property rights, have all made the library environment more complex. Further, the budgetary constraints, inadequate infrastructure, falling standards in human resources are all compelling the librarian to change his attitude from a mere custodian of information to that of a facilitator. As the library is a service institution there should be close interaction between the information providers, processors and users to enhance the effectivity of any resource centre Keeping in view the above factors, National Institute of Rural Development (NIRD) conducted a learning programme on. This programme provided a forum for the users of information and the library personnel to come together, to understand each others way of dealing with information and how the information barriers can be overcome and what best practices are to be adopted to increase the utilization of the resources of the Library through various training programmes.

LIBRARY UTILIZATION AND READERSHIP ENHANCEMENT (LURE)

When CORD conducted the one-day programme LURE I in 1991, had a modest goal to find out the ways and means to increase the library utilization by adopting innovative methods tolure the readers. This was based on a feeling that we have been investing in the library huge amounts of money year after year, trying to equip the library with more relevant reading material and also recruit trained personnel to make the resources more useful. While we are trying to build up a tempo, we had a feeling somewhere along the line that the readers or users are still not coming along with us. This feeling lead us to an introspection which gave rise to the impetus for conducting a programme for the first time on LURE in 1991. As stated earlier, the learning programme provided an opportunity for interaction between the library professionals and our own users in understanding the lacunae in promoting exploitation of library resources. In the first workshop on LURE in 1991 several issues were thrown up such as the following:

Issues for Consideration

As the reader is reluctant to come to library, it may be necessary that the library has to go to the reader. Naturally, that situation will determine the kind of services that are planned or envisaged to enhance the usage of the library. The issues that influence the usage hinge upon how the information needs are gauged and the methods that are adopted to identify those needs. Some of the other major issues identified are:

- Focus of the parent organisation
- Information collection
- Information processing
- Information search in the Internet era
- Information dissemination
- Information barriers

The workshop offered a set of simple but effective steps to increase the library use with suggestions like involvement of users in procurement of literature, client based services etc., The other major recommendations include:

- The book selection and acquisition are both important and modalities like participatory practices have to be followed;
- User education and user services have to be frequently conducted by the library to improve the interaction between users and the library personnel;
- A brochure on the library highlighting the library collection, cataloging and classification system followed and the services offered would be more useful;
- Immediate computerization of all activities of library;
- Creation of new services like abstracting, alerting service, reference and making digests on specific topics etc.,
- Augmentation of facilities for document supply and other physical facilities like proper sign boards, stools to reach higher shelves, etc., and
- Strengthening of the resource sharing at the local level.

These recommendations were taken seriously as they were particularly important in the over all development of the library utilization. Fortunately, most of the suggestions would be implemented with a telling effect on the positive response of the readers.

LURE – II

After a gap of nearly two years, CORD thought of again reviewing the library utilization with the completion of library automation. Accordingly, in 1993 a second programme on LURE was conducted. This time with a difference. The impetus came from the management of parent organization. There was a constant refrain from the management that with automation is there any improvement in the utilization of library resources? How many faculty are visiting the library? What is the ratio between faculty and participants of various training programmes that visit the library? What special arrangements were made to familiarize the participants with the new automation etc.,

These were a few of the questions that were bothering the management. Also, with computerization of library procedures, a new barrier is likely to be perceived by the users. Such 'Automation anxiety' may have to be taken into consideration in designing training programmes on library initiation.

Accordingly, the participants were chosen from not only the users of the library but also the participants of the then running courses, besides other librarians of neighbouring institutions. The programme was conducted in 3 sessions.

In these sessions several papers based on cases illustrating the circulation facility, visitors register, pattern of usage of library on different dates and use of various information products of CORD were presented. These studies provided a picture of the pattern of library usage after the automation which appeared to be promising and provided the guidance as to how to increase awareness and access to information. Several suggestions emerged based on the discussions and some of which are as follows:—

- Information Products:
  - The coverage of indexing and abstracting services done through CORD Index and CORD Abstracts is found to be satisfactory. However, emphasis may have to be given to the immediate interest of the faculty members depending on their research and training programmes.
  - The journals that are covered in CORD Alerts may have to be displayed at a designed place for their immediate location and identification of articles given in the service.
- Maintenance:
  - Upkeep and maintenance of various sections will provide the necessary incentive for the users to browse.
  - Library staff should be trained and motivated to assist the readers.
- User Studies:
  - Though the faculty members are patronising the library, there is a scope for improvement.
  - Visitors to the Library are not always recording their visits in the prescribed register and so it did not reflect the total visits made by the academic staff in comparison with non-academic staff. A strict vigil on the visitors register may have to be maintained to satisfy the management.

The other major recommendations include:

- Promotion of library with a professional image is essential;
- Library staff should be trained in inter-personnel communication skills;
- There is a need to display current journals in more attractive and useful manner like displaying latest issues at a prominent place, rearranging of primary journals in alphabetical sequence, etc.,
- NIRD publications should be displayed prominently for outside visitors.
- A marketing approach to its library and information products is essential. For this purpose Library counters and surrounding areas should be used for display of not only for acquired publications but also NIRD publications.
- There are about 3000 participants in a year coming to NIRD to participate in the training programmes, who should be given orientation tour to the library for better appreciation of the resources. Also, a session on information resources, and information management relevant to the theme of any course wherever possible should be arranged apart from display of the publications pertaining to the training programme.

- A faculty directory, user manual, training of staff on information technology etc., are other suggestions that emerged from the programme.

After LURE-II in 1993 there was marked improvement in the appreciation of library services, the physical facilities and the environment in the library. Non-book material like CD-ROMS, videos, electronic journal have slowly started to show their presence. In the mid 90s internet opened gates to the Information sources world wide, and made possible access to information from a remote location. As a result it has become more important to look into the problems of transforming a traditional library into an information clearing house.

LURE – III

Against this backdrop a 3rd LURE programme was conducted in the year 1998 after a gap of 5 years. This learning programme was made into a National Workshop inviting papers from all over India on various themes such as library utilisation; techniques of readership enhancement; evaluation of library services; internet and changing role of the librarian etc. Participants from several parts of the country made their presentations based on their own back-home experience in user education and identification of user needs. This workshop revealed various kinds of experiments that are on-going in several parts of the country by innovative librarians and demystifying the Internet for the librarian and the user. Information search in the Internet era has totally changed the way the readers look for information. Searching Internet should become a matter of routine in any special library, to make the expression "Internet is Librarianship" truly applicable. Some of the other major recommendations of the workshop were:

- Continuous study of user needs.
- Development of communication skills of the library personnel.
- Role of parent organization in recognising the contribution of their libraries and supporting their activity.
- Design and update of user manual in the fast changing information technology environment.
- Change of attitude of librarians to the market driven economy and interact with the users more closely and make users appreciate the library services.
- A thematic approach to all the library services have to be *i.e.*, the information products of the library like CORD INDEX, CORD ABSTRACTS should follow the themes identified for the research and training of the institute.
- The Selective Dissemination of Information (SDI) service can perhaps be concentrated on a faculty or a discipline at a time. Once a faculty is studied for a period of 6 months or so as a focussed group the impact on the group and its activities perhaps be quantitatively measured.

CORD is giving continuous training to the Library staff in the above areas in order to serve the clientele for effective use of Library Resources. They are also deputing the staff to other training programmes to get trained in these as well as new emerging areas. Simultaneously providing training and support to the users for better utiliztion of the resources without any barriers. Thus a new era emergd where information driven activities gained importance which will hopefully energize the users as well as information specialists to come together and work for the better uilization of information following the best practices in information dissemination through regular training programmes.

DIFFERENT TYPES OF TRAINING AND ACTIVITIES

INFORMAL VERSUS FORMAL TRAINING, SELF-DIRECTED VERSUS OTHER-DIRECTED TRAINING

There are different major forms of learning and development. We're most familiar with formal and other-directed forms of learning and development, that include the strong attention to the systematic structure and evaluation of the learning and development, especially as used in schooling. That is somewhat ironic, because the most common forms of learning and development are informal and self-directed — they occur without strong attention to a systematic design and evaluation and without many experts guiding us through those experiences.

TYPES OF ACTIVITIES FOR LEARNING AND EVELOPMENT

There are many approaches to learning and development and many types of activities that can be undertaken to learn. We're most used to thinking of the formal, other-directed activities, such as attending courses or lectures. However, most of the types of learning are informal and unstructured. An awareness of these other types will broaden your possibilities for intentional learning and for designing training for yourself and others.

MOVEMENTS IN ORGANIZATIONAL TRAINING AND DEVELOPMENT

The field (or many would argue, the profession) of training and development has undergone dramatic improvements, especially with the inclusion of computer- and Web-based technologies. We're also expanding the concept of learning beyond the learning of individuals — we're thinking that groups and organizations can learn, too. (Although the topics of the learning organization and knowledge management are fairly recent and still popular, many people would disagree that they're actually learning and development programmes — those people might assert that they're actually forms of organizational performance management. However, the two topics still seem to be so broad and changing, that they're referred to here as movements.)

EXAMPLES OF PROGRAMMES IN THE WORKPLACE

Before this Library topic goes on to explaining how to design and develop training programmes, it's useful to get a quick impression of various types of training programmes. A training programme is an intentionally designed, (hopefully) highly integrated set of activities that are aligned to accomplish a certain set of results among learners. Many of us might not be used to thinking of the following as programmes in the workplace.

HOW TO ENSURE TRANSFER OF TRAINING — TRAINING THAT STICKS

One of the biggest concerns of trainers — and those paying for training — is whether the learners will indeed understand and apply the new information and materials from the learning and development activities, that is, whether the new information and materials will transfer to the learners.

INSTRUCTIONAL SYSTEM DESIGN (ISD) AND THE ADDIE MODEL

Formal approaches to learning and development often have the highest likelihood of transfer of training. A formal approach to learning and development usually follows a systematic and consistent framework. Systematic means that the framework is designed to guide learners to achieve an overall set of goals — goals to address a need or situation, then associates objectives and activities to achieve those overall goals, and evaluates the activities and results to be sure the goals were achieved. Instructional system design (ISD) is the activities to ensure that the design of training is very successful in achieving the goals of the training. One of the most common ISD models is ADDIE, which is an acronym for assessment, design, development, implementation and evaluation — you can discern from the acronym that ADDIES is a systematic design of training.

- *ADDIE Phase 1 — Assessing Your Training Needs:* Needs Assessment to Training Goals: What overall results or outcomes should be accomplished by learners? Those outcomes usually are identified from the results of assessments, or measurements, of what a person or workplace needs to accomplish in order to achieve some desired level of performance. An outcome might be the ability to perform a complex job.
- *ADDIE Phase 2 — Designing Training Plans and Learning Objectives:* What learning objectives must be accomplished by learners in order to achieve the overall outcomes, and what activities must be undertaken by trainers and learners to accomplish those objectives?

The integration of the overall outcomes, objectives and activities and also how they will be evaluated comprise the design of the learning and development programme. Learning objectives often are described in terms of new learning — new knowledge, skills and competencies.

- *ADDIE Phase 3 — Developing Training Activities and Materials:* Now it's important to get even more clear on what resources must be obtained and developed in order to undertake the activities to achieve the objectives. Resource might include certain expertise, facilities and technologies. Development might include several trainers and learners reviewing the design of the training to ensure it meets their nature and needs.
- *ADDIE Phase 4 — Implementing Your Training Programme:* Now you're ready to have trainers and learners participate in the programme, to undertake the activities and evaluations of learning. Implementation often results in refining the original design of the training programme.
- *ADDIE Phase 5 — Evaluating Your Training Programme:* As trainers and learners participate in the programme, evaluation should occur of the quality of the activities and the extent of achievement of the objectives. After the programme, evaluation should occur to assess the extent of achievement of the overall goals of the programme. Evaluation might focus on short-term, intermediate and long-term outcomes.

TRAINING AND HUMAN RESOURCE MANAGEMENT

The HR functioning is changing with time and with this change, the relationship between the training function and other management activity is also changing. The training and development activities are now equally important with that of other HR functions.

Gone are the days, when training was considered to be futile, waste of time, resources, and money. Now a days, training is an investment because the departments such as, marketing and sales, HR, production, finance, etc. depends on training for its survival. If training is not considered as a priority or not seen as a vital part in the organisation, then it is difficult to accept that such a company has effectively carried out HRM. Training actually provides the opportunity to raise the profile development activities in the organisation.

To increase the commitment level of employees and growth in quality movement (concepts of HRM), senior management team is now increasing the role of training. Such concepts of HRM require careful planning as well as greater emphasis on employee development and long term education.

Training is now the important tool of Human Resource Management to control the attrition rate because it helps in motivating employees, achieving their professional and personal goals, increasing the level of job satisfaction, etc., As a result training is given on a variety of skill development and covers a multitude of courses.

ROLE OF HRD PROFESSIONALS IN TRAINING

This is the era of cut-throat competition and with this changing scenario of business; the role of HR professionals in training has been widened.

HR role now is:

- Active involvement in employee education
- Rewards for improvement in performance
- Rewards to be associated with self esteem and self worth.
- Providing pre-employment market oriented skill development education and post employment support for advanced education and training.
- Flexible access, *i.e.*, anytime, anywhere training.

The Training System

A System is a combination of things or parts that must work together to perform a particular function. An organisation is a system and training is a sub system of the organisation.

The System Approach views training as a sub system of an organisation. System Approach can be used to examine broad issues like objectives, functions, and aim. It establishes a logical relationship between the sequential stages in the process of training need analysis (TNA), formulating, delivering, and evaluating. There are four necessary inputs, *i.e.*, technology, man, material, time required in every system to produce products or services. And every system must have some output from these inputs in order to survive. The output can be tangible or intangible depending upon the organisation's requirement. A system approach to training is planned creation of training Programme.

This approach uses step-by-step procedures to solve the problems. Under systematic approach, training is undertaken on planned basis.

Out of this planned effort, one such basic model of five steps is system model that is explained below. Organisation are working in open environment, *i.e.*, there are some internal and external forces, that poses threats and opportunities, therefore, trainers need to be aware of these forces which may impact on the content, form, and conduct of the training efforts. The internal forces are the various demands of the organisation for a better learning environment; need to be up to date with the latest technologies. The three model of training are:

- System Model.
- Instructional System Development Model.
- Transitional model.

MODELS OF TRAINING

Training is a sub-system of the organisation because the departments such as, marketing and sales, HR, production, finance, etc depends on training for its survival. Training is a transforming process that requires some input and in turn it produces output in the form of knowledge, skills, and attitudes (KSAs).

SYSTEMATIC MODEL TRAINING

The system model consists of five phases and should be repeated on a regular basis to make further improvements. The training should achieve the purpose of helping employee to perform their work to required standards:

- *Analyse and identify the training needs, i.e.*, to analyse the department, job, employees requirement, who needs training, what do they need to learn, estimating training cost, etc The next step is to develop a performance measure on the basis of which actual performance would be evaluated.
- *Design and provide training to meet identified needs*. This step requires developing objectives of training, identifying the learning steps, sequencing and structuring the contents.
- *Develop* - This phase requires listing the activities in the training Programme that will assist the participants to learn, selecting delivery method, examining the training material, validating information to be imparted to make sure it accomplishes all the goals and objectives
- *Implementing* is the hardest part of the system because one wrong step can lead to the failure of whole training Programme.
- *Evaluating* each phase so as to make sure it has achieved its aim in terms of subsequent work performance. Making necessary amendments to any of the previous stage in order to remedy or improve failure practices.

TRANSITIONAL MODEL

Transitional model focuses on the organisation as a whole. The outer loop describes the vision, mission and values of the organisation on the basis of which training model, *i.e.*, inner loop is executed.

- *Vision*—focuses on the milestones that the organisation would like to achieve after the defined point of time. A vision statement tells that where the organisation sees itself few years down the line. A vision may include setting a role mode, or bringing some internal transformation, or may be promising to meet some other deadlines.
- *Mission*—explain the reason of organisational existence. It identifies the position in the community. The reason of developing a mission statement is to motivate, inspire, and inform the employees regarding the organisation. The mission statement tells about the identity that

how the organisation would like to be viewed by the customers, employees, and all other stakeholders.

- *Values*—is the translation of vision and mission into communicable ideals. It reflects the deeply held values of the organisation and is independent of current industry environment. For example, values may include social responsibility, excellent customer service, etc.

BENCHMARKING BEST PRACTICE IN LIBRARY STAFF DEVELOPMENT

Most university libraries throughout the world are engaged in some level of staff development. Benchmarking of staff development activities however is not widespread and little useful data exists to enable meaningful comparisons between university libraries within national borders, let alone provide meaningful international perspectives. Three studies in the first half of this decade examined staff development policy and practice in the university library sector in Australia and the United Kingdom. Significantly, the studies enabled limited international comparisons where none had been previously possible. In January 2008, two university library organisations – CAVAL in Australia and EMALINK in the United Kingdom - commenced a joint project to further develop this process of comparison by benchmarking staff development practices within their member libraries. Although located in different hemispheres and literally half a world away from each other, CAVAL and EMALINK were assessed as good candidates for a benchmarking study.

Both organisations are roughly similar in terms of their size, composition and orientation. Prior to 2008, they had also already shared expertise relating to staff development and key personnel had worked together as members of IFLA's Continuing Professional Development and Workplace Learning Section.

A collaborative project thus appeared to offer CAVAL and EMALINK a unique opportunity to provide value to their member libraries in two key ways:

- By identifying, comparing and generally sharing knowledge about current staff development practices and processes; and,
- By establishing common measurement points, indicators and best practice benchmarks to assist with planning improvements in future staff development practices and processes.

On the ground, the project aimed to obtain data and test various assumptions that would enable the development of a practical tool to facilitate ongoing benchmarking between CAVAL and EMALINK member libraries. Longer term, the project hoped to inform the development of a marketable "dashboard" of indicators for benchmarking staff development activities in other libraries at national and international levels. CAVAL also planned to establish a database of indicators in order to build up a longitudinal data set to facilitate trend analysis.

In tandem with these aims, the project also sought to demonstrate how recent developments in information and communications technology (ICT), particularly social networking technology, have helped to facilitate international collaborative library research projects. Originally projected for completion in late 2008, the project encountered logistical challenges on the Australian side within several months of commencement. Rather than delay or compromise the entire project, CAVAL withdrew temporarily, thereby allowing EMALINK to push ahead with a pilot survey of its members in the United Kingdom. In this way, EMALINK was able to complete base level data collection already undertaken by CAVAL in 2006.

This chapter constitutes a progress report and case study of the CAVAL – EMALINK library staff development benchmarking project to July 2008. The chapter outlines the drivers for benchmarking in library staff development and discusses why applied research of this kind is of potentially such great value to university and other libraries in the context of current issues impacting staff development: for example, recruitment and retention of staff. Details are provided of the research methodology agreed by CAVAL and EMALINK, and the benchmarking dimensions investigated by the project. With preliminary data from EMALINK available in early July 2008, the paper reports on initial findings and considers important practical lessons in international collaboration learned to date.

STAFF DEVELOPMENT RESEARCH IN AUSTRALIA AND THE UNITED KINGDOM

Attempts to examine and benchmark staff development practice in Australian university libraries can be traced back more than twenty years; with more recent work in Australia and the United Kingdom attempting to update and expand that work. Both early Australian surveys by Trask and Gray revealed a paucity of human resource development in the university library sector, albeit balanced by an emerging recognition at that time of the importance of developing people.

In 2001 and then again in 2005, Smith explored the extent of commitment to staff development, linkages to strategic organisational priorities, and the focus of staff development activity. The overall picture presented by these 2001 and 2005 surveys was of a strong commitment to investment in human resource development – a picture very different to that found in the earlier 1983 and 1986 analyses.

Smith concluded that the major influences on the focus of staff development programmes in Australian university libraries included:

- Increasing scope and volume of electronic publishing, with consequent changes in required staff skills and knowledge;
- Increasing involvement of university library staff in teaching information literacy (with needs for skill development on the part of those staff doing such teaching);

- Changing organisational demographics (in particular ageing workforces), and actual or impending retirements of staff (particularly senior staff) – this resulting in the need for succession planning and development of new leadership and management capability; and,
- The imperative for regionally isolated libraries to grow and develop skills and capability within their existing workforce.

For the first time, the 2005 survey explored budget allocations for staff development. This was interesting as a measure in its own right of the level of commitment to staff development activity. It also enabled benchmarking against a comparable survey undertaken in the United Kingdom, and several other available benchmarks including those of the *American Society for Training and Development* and *UNESCO*. In 2004, motivated partly by the 2001 Australian study, Yeoh investigated staff development in a cross section of university libraries in England, Scotland and Ireland. That survey found, *inter alia:*

- A strong commitment to staff development as part of institutional strategic organisational management;
- Formal written statements of commitment to staff development in just over half of the organisations surveyed;
- A planned and structured approach to staff development in most organisations; and,
- A structured appraisal and review of these activities in two thirds of organisations.

It was also keen to develop common staff development indicators and a database to enable longitudinal studies. In retrospect, the survey instrument developed by the project team was arguably too broad, encompassing 97 questions over 46 pages, and too complex; partly a outcome of trying to align the survey with international studies.

As a result of the CAVAL survey's complexity, details of staff development practice within member libraries were largely obscured by other issues relating to recruitment and retention and succession planning. Although providing a highly detailed and ultimately fascinating snapshot of human resources in CAVAL member libraries in late 2006, the project stalled after presentation of the preliminary findings in March 2007. "The research project generated an immense amount of data that is of varying degrees of completeness and indeed of value."

The research instrument itself was complex, which potentially added further complications to the ability to undertake an effective comparative analysis and interpretation of the responses." Interestingly, researcher comments echo those of Ford, writing on benchmarking HRD: "choosing the wrong set of metrics is one of the surest ways to doom a benchmarking study." For CAVAL, the over-riding challenge of the 2006 *Benchmarking of Staff Development Practice in CAVAL Member Libraries* project was how to go about "extracting the desired key measurement points needed if benchmark levels of practice and processes are to be established within the membership of the consortium."

With resources allocated to the CAVAL project exhausted by early 2007 and other projects moving to the fore, further progress on benchmarking staff development seemed unlikely in the short term. As one door closes, however, sometimes another opens. Enter at this point EMALINK, the East Midlands Library Information Network, representing the 10 university and higher education libraries comprising the United Kingdom's East Midland University Association (EMUA).

WHY BENCHMARK BEST PRACTICE IN LIBRARY STAFF DEVELOPMENT?

Before reporting on the methodology and early findings of the 2008 CAVAL-EMALINK study, it is important to understand the significance of benchmarking best practice in staff development to libraries in general. Libraries, it was long argued, were simply the sum of their collections – print and later electronic.

A big library was ipso facto a good library. The majority of contemporary library measures still reflect this preoccupation with the physical item, even where electronic resources have taken precedence. The rise of the internet and increasing demands from customers have however progressively turned the focus of library managers to their people – arguably always their best information 'assets'.

People and the environments in which they live and work are not static though, and the parallel processes of personal and professional development must be ongoing.

Thus libraries, particularly university libraries, have come to realise the significance of better understanding staff development through benchmarking. Many are returning to the origins of benchmarking as an organisational improvement tool, and Spendolini's simple elevator definition of benchmarking as "learning from others". Researcher that "changes in the academic library workplace mirror those of other workplaces in the new millennium." Expanding on this theme, researcher observes:

- Following the nature of the work, the organisation of the institution is constantly shifting, requiring staff in all areas to perform a greater variety of tasks. The operations daily become more automated and more technical. The workforce becomes more diverse. The pace quickens. The budget tightens. And the tensions mount.

For libraries, particularly university libraries, there are also specific challenges to address. The last two decades have seen greatly increased emphases on access to information and knowledge management. Changes and developments in the ways and means of organising and accessing recorded knowledge have been both rapid and profound; with increasingly sophisticated information systems evolving as a result.

As IFLA acknowledges, libraries and those who work in them have an increasingly important role to play in such an environment:

- The quality of service provided to the public by library and information science institutions depends on the expertise of their staff. Constant flux in the needs of societies, changing technologies, and growth in professional knowledge demand that information workers must expand their understanding and update their skills on an ongoing basis.

As a consequence of this transformation, human resource professionals in libraries are observing a range of issues impacting on and influencing staff development. Focusing on university libraries, the issues are as follows:

- The need for library staff to keep current with continuous changes in information technology and with information itself;
- A related need to coordinate technical training for library staff, and find the expertise and resources to provide it;
- A strengthening of libraries' traditional customer service orientation in order to compete with Internet search engines and online booksellers;
- Further development of libraries' orientation towards teamwork, made necessary by shrinking budgets, decreases in staff numbers, and the rise of multifunctional teams;
- Additional support required for both new and experienced managers;
- Growth of the teaching and training role of university library staff, particularly but not exclusively those in professional positions; and finally,
- The need to provide meaningful staff development as a means of recruiting and retaining staff.

The imperative to maintain and upgrade the skills, knowledge, and abilities of library and information staff has been recognised, and is reflected, in the significant priority allocated to human resource development (HRD) activity in many libraries. As a strategic organisational priority it is important that HRD is assessed and, where necessary, improved and that this be a continuing cyclical activity. Benchmarking has clear potential to achieve that end. Indeed, benchmarking has particular applicability for HRD because the activity naturally lends itself to cooperative and collaborative working between institutions. Ford proposes a series of metrics which may be usefully applied to benchmarking staff development. Some are relatively straightforward to measure and calculate, while others are more challenging.

In broadly escalating degrees of difficulty in measurement these metrics include:

- Expenditure on staff development activities expressed as a percentage of payroll;

- Average hours spent on staff development per employee per annum;
- Average staff development cost per participant per hour;
- Percentage of employees undertaking staff development activity per annum;
- Average percentage of positive ratings of staff development activities by participants;
- Average percentage of gains in learning reported by participants in staff development activities;
- Average percentage of improvement in on-the-job performance as a result of participation in staff development activities;
- Cost savings and efficiency gains as a result of participation in staff development activities.

The eventual goal is to take raw data and convert it to ratios or percentages that can be monitored easily over time – in effect, a staff development 'dashboard'. Although nowhere near this level of sophistication, IFLA's *Continuing Professional Development and Workplace Learning Quality Guidelines Project* has published useful best practice indicators for staff development. IFLA requires that there be:

- Regular learning needs assessment.
- Broad range of learning opportunities, both formal and informal; formal offerings in a choice of formats, designed to meet identified needs, in modules structured to cover topics from introductory through advanced.
- Organizational commitment and leadership from staff development and continuing education administrators with expertise in adult continuing education.
- Widely disseminated information about continuing education and resources, accurately described.
- C[ontinuing] E[education] activities design that includes learning objectives aligned with identified needs; follows principles of instructional design and learning theory; selects course instructors on the basis of both subject knowledge and teaching ability; attends to transfer of training and feedback.
- Consistent documentation of individuals' participation in learning and recognition of continuing learning in hiring and promotion decisions.
- A minimum of 0.5 to 1.0 per cent of institutional budget earmarked for staff development, as stated in *The public library service: IFLA/ UNESCO guidelines for developmen.*
- About 10 per cent of work hours provided for attendance at workshops, conferences, in-service training, and other educational activities, and for informal learning projects.
- Evaluation of continuing education and staff development offerings and programmes.

- Research that assesses the state of CPD and examines the efficacy and outcomes of continuing education and staff development programmes.

CAVAL-EMALINK STUDY METHODOLOGY

In October 2007, Ian Smith and Graham Walton proposed that CAVAL in Australia and EMALINK in the United Kingdom undertake a joint study to identify best practice in staff development in member libraries.

They highlighted a number of benefits to individual member libraries, including:

- Acquisition of staff development data to inform and guide ongoing change processes;
- Opportunity to undertake national and international level comparisons; and,
- Opportunity for international partnering and skills exchange.

Within the context of developing and delivering the project, the proposal acknowledged that university libraries are busy organisations and that no funds had been budgeted for the project by CAVAL or EMALINK in 2008. It was considered crucial therefore that the work should not be time or resource intensive, particularly in relation to project management and data collection.

A relatively brief web based questionnaire was suggested to minimise the time and effort required for survey development, administration and analysis. Smith and Walton proposed that the project should be jointly overseen by a small team of nominated representatives from the CAVAL Human Resources Group and EMALINK.

This working group would take responsibility for jointly developing and administering the survey questionnaire, analysing the data obtained, and producing a summary report for dissemination to individual member libraries. The proposed study methodology called for data collection to take place through a web based questionnaire, with questions taking no more than 20 minutes in total to complete.

In scoping the 2006 staff development benchmarking study involving CAVAL member libraries, Smith originally proposed eight benchmarking dimensions:

- Budget allocation for staff development expressed as a percentage of total payroll costs. Further, what elements are covered by that budget and what budget model is applied for staff development (*e.g.*, centralised or distributed)?
- Approval criteria and processes – how are staff development applications assessed and approved?
- Links between staff development priorities and strategic planning;
- Organisational approaches to the development, documentation and evaluation of staff development plans;

- Common themes and priorities in staff development plans;
- Application of *Rodski* results in setting staff development objectives - have staff development investments in turn improved *Rodski* ratings?
- Coordination of staff development in CAVAL member libraries – how and by whom?
- Evaluation of staff development programmes by the organisation and measurement of the return on investment (ROI).

By mid-July 2008, EMALINK had received an encouraging seven responses from a total membership of ten university libraries. In 2006, CAVAL received responses from all eleven members.

UNDERSTANDING THE VALUE OF BENCHMARKING

In the context of libraries, benchmarking may be defined as an ongoing structured process by which we evaluate the functions, work processes and services of other organisations (not always libraries) recognised for their leadership and innovation.

This process of evaluation is undertaken for the purpose of organisational comparison and improvement. The concept of *competitive benchmarking*, later 'benchmarking', was first popularised by the Xerox Corporation in the late 1970s as an innovative response – at that time – to strong competition in a market segment that it had hitherto dominated.

Xerox refined the concept of benchmarking through the 1980s and eventually promulgated a ten-step benchmarking process. Despite there now being many competing process models for benchmarking, most can trace their origins back twenty years to the original Xerox process, and early variations. Other influences cited as significant in the development of the concept of benchmarking include the quality assurance movement and just-in-time manufacturing methods.

Indeed, Deming's classic four step quality improvement process still forms the basis of many benchmarking exercises. Benchmarking is essentially concerned with understanding how processes work – through observing and studying work methods and practices – and then identifying good or best practice.

Benchmarking seeks to learn from the observation of such good and best practice, and to make improvements necessary to reach identified standards of good and best practice. Assessment of improvement is based on review and comparison with other like organisations; hence the significance of a good match between CAVAL and EMALINK. Drawing on Deming's four step process, Ford and Longbottom each propose useful models for benchmarking; Ford specifically in the context of benchmarking human resource development (HRD). It is Longbottom's 'PAIR' approach however that resonates through the methodology applied in the CAVAL-EMALINK project:

- Planning - investigation, measurement and examination of the strengths and weaknesses of current processes;
- Analysis – identifying potential benchmarking partners and then exchanging information, and observing and comparing processes;
- Implementation – adaptation and modification of processes based on learning from the analysis stage;
- Review – ongoing review and refinement with the intention of achieving continuous improvements.

Within the higher education sector, libraries have frequently been early and enthusiastic adopters of benchmarking techniques. University libraries in Australia, New Zealand and the United Kingdom, for example, have all been at the forefront in adopting and applying benchmarking processes to various aspects of their operations. In the case of Australia, the work of scholars has been important in outlining suitable frameworks and encouraging the adoption of benchmarking methods in university libraries.

Noting the need to identify benchmarks which would assess efficient use of resources and the quality of the contributions which university libraries make to the realisation of university objectives, McKinnon *et al* proposed a range of criterion reference benchmarks with the intention firstly of identifying attributes of good practice and then using those attributes as benchmarks for further evaluation.

The *Council of Australian University Librarians* has encouraged benchmarking between its members and has facilitated a range of studies in various operational areas including client satisfaction with library services, performance and effectiveness of document delivery services, availability of sought materials, cataloguing, and the re-shelving of library materials. Several trans-national benchmarking projects have also been undertaken with Australian libraries as a key partner, for example between libraries in Australia and New Zealand and Australia and the United Kingdom.

IMPORTANCE OF TRAINING AND DEVELOPMENT

- Training and Development helps in optimising the utilisation of human resource that further helps the employee to achieve the organisational goals as well as their individual goals.
- Training and Development helps to provide an opportunity and broad structure for the development of human resources' technical and Behavioural skills in an organisation. It also helps the employees in attaining personal growth.
- Training and Development helps in increasing the job knowledge and skills of employees at each level. It helps to expand the horizons of human intellect and an overall personality of the employees.

- Training and Development helps in increasing the productivity of the employees that helps the organisation further to achieve its long-term goal.
- Training and Development helps in inculcating the sense of team work, team spirit, and inter-team collaborations. It helps in inculcating the zeal to learn within the employees.
- Training and Development helps to develop and improve the organisational health culture and effectiveness. It helps in creating the learning culture within the organisation.
- Training and Development helps building the positive perception and feeling about the organisation. The employees get these feelings from leaders, subordinates, and peers.
- Training and Development helps in improving upon the quality of work and work-life.
- Training and Development helps in creating the healthy working environment. It helps to build good employee, relationship so that individual goals aligns with organisational goal.
- Training and Development helps in improving the health and safety of the organisation thus preventing obsolescence.
- Training and Development helps in improving the morale of the Workforce.
- Training and Development helps in creating a better corporate image.
- Training and Development leads to improved profitability and more positive attitudes towards profit orientation.
- Training and Development aids in organisational development, *i.e.*, Organisation gets more effective decision making and problem solving. It helps in understanding and carrying out organisational policies
- Training and Development helps in developing leadership skills, motivation, loyalty, better attitudes, and other aspects that successful workers and managers usually display.

TRAINING AS CONSULTANCY

Training consultancy provides industry professional to work with an organisation in achieving its training and development objectives.

Training Courses that Consultancies Offer

- Business Training Courses:
  - Management Development:
    i. Conflict Management;
    ii. Managing Diversity;
    iii. Project Management;
    iv. Stress Management;

v. Time Management; and
vi. Senior Management Workshops.

- Sales:
  i. Negotiation Skills; and
  ii. Sales Technique.
- Customer Care:
  i. Customer Care Training; and
  ii. Managing Customers.
- Human Resource:
  i. HR Administration;
  ii. Induction Training;
  iii. Recruitment and Selection; and
  iv. Successful Appraising.
- Personal Development Courses.
- Workshops on:
  i. Assertive Skills;
  ii. Building Confidence;
  iii. Coping with Change;
  iv. Interview Techniques; and
  v. Maximise Potential.
- One to One Coaching:
  i. Focused entirely on personal objectives;
  ii. Move forward at individual pace;
  iii. Material used in tailor made to specific development Need; and
  iv. A strict code of confidentiality.

Importance of Training Consultancies:

- It helps in enhancing company's image.
- It helps in strengthening the team spirit.
- It helps in applying knowledge, developing core competencies, and reducing work load.
- It helps in improving the work relations.
- It helps in developing focused and inspired staff.
- It leads to greater chances of success.

Consultants can provide help on following areas:

- Management Development.
- Team Building Leadership.
- Health and Safety Training.
- Interpersonal Skills.
- Sales Training.

7

Strategies for Staff Learning

UNDERSTANDING LEARNING AND DEVELOPMENT

It's amazing how so many of us go through so many years of schooling, but have such little understanding of learning and development. Before reading about the many aspects of learning and development in this topic in the Library, including learning and development programmes and practitioners, it's best to start with a basic understanding of what learning and development is and how to best benefit from it. Also, it's useful to understand the common terms and the sometimes subtle differences between them.

If you will be doing training and development with yourself (and almost every adult will be at some time in their lives) or with others, you should know the differences between training children and teens versus training adults. Adults have very different nature and needs in training. Also, there are some common beliefs about training that just aren't true. Understand those misconceptions so you don't build your training around those illusions.

BENEFITS OF LEARNING AND DEVELOPMENT

We often think that the biggest benefit of learning is that we get a diploma or credential. As we get wiser, we realize there are so many more benefits than that. Knowing the benefits will help motivate you to design your own training plans and programmes, and to motivate others to participate as well. Perhaps one of the biggest benefits is the appreciation that you can be learning all the time, even if you are not in a formal training programme.

RELATIONSHIP OF LEARNING AND DEVELOPMENT TO PERFORMANCE

We tend to assume that training leads to learning, which leads to doing better in our lives and work — it leads to increased performance. However, you will very likely get more out of your trainings and be more successful in promoting trainings to others if you understand more about the relationship between training and performance. That understanding is especially useful when designing training to increase performance or to redesign training programmes that don't seem to be as successful as you wish.

GROW YOUR OWN WORKFORCE

There are many ways to provide support for employees seeking a bachelor's degree or MLS. Give employees who are working full-time while attending college or library school tuition assistance (any little bit helps) as well as some time off to study every week. Just an hour or two makes a huge difference to a working student. If you cannot afford tuition assistance or paid time to study—or even if you can—support students in developing practical projects for their course work, and use those projects to benefit customers.

A student who can point to her project being used by the library can see the value of her education *and* see how the library values her contribution. Support may also be more formal. For example, the Fresno County Public Library has a librarian trainee programme in which an MLS student may be selected to work under the direction of a librarian and receive mentoring along with pre-professional training and work experience.

ACTION OF STAFF LEARNING

Learning through action serves to help employees develop critical competencies by completing important library work. An action learning team tackles a strategic issue and makes recommendations to library leadership. Action learning has also been used to select, assess, and develop stars and high-potential employees to new levels of knowledge, skills, experience, and competencies. The characteristics of action learning are as follows:

- It is a team-based approach to learning.
- The team works on real-world problems or business challenges that are often for high stakes.
- There is often a training component such as team functioning or problem solving built in.
- The real-world challenge is a stretch assignment that extends beyond members' experience. Thus, teams are challenged and put into a stressful situation while knowing their work will be reviewed and supported by leadership.

Action learning is a prime source of development at the County of Los Angeles Public Library, reports county librarian Margaret Donnellan Todd. When Todd took on the director's role in 2001, she found a gap in candidates for potential leadership positions and few employees between the ages of 40 and 50. She was not too surprised; the library, like many in California, had faced several waves of financial problems, resulting in hiring freezes and talented employees moving on. She realized that she had to promote sooner than she might have wanted in order to fill vacancies, from employees who had the tools but not the experience; she likened it to skipping a grade in school. Action learning became her way to fill the gap.

The library began this strategy after one of its librarians attended an Urban Libraries Council Executive Leadership Institute (ELI) programme. The library's action learning teams do not include senior managers and are limited to librarians early in their career. A chair is appointed and a charter provided. Management helps shape the scope of work and then steps out of the picture. Action learning teams engage in real work, often advancing strategic initiatives of the library. Teams have engaged in practical as well as theoretical (policy) work, including providing services to seniors, studying the future of electronic services, and creating a model for warehousing lesser used books. Todd reports that the system has seen many librarians rise to the occasion, acquire new skills and confidence, and flourish as leaders.

IMPLEMENT A 360-DEGREE FEEDBACK PROGRAMME

In a 360-degree feedback programme, performance data are obtained from peers, subordinates, and the supervisor in order to provide an assessment of an employee's performance up, down, and sideways in the organization. It provides full circle, or 360-degree, feedback. This type of evaluation process offers employees a learning tool and feedback mechanism to promote growth and development. There are a variety of ways to conduct a 360-degree feedback programme, and not all are expensive. As with other approaches to employee performance evaluation, it is essential that everyone involved understand the purposes of the evaluation and receive thorough training in applying the process.

OFFER ON-THE-JOB TRAINING

Both formal and informal on-the-job training can be offered. The informal situation is like shadowing. It requires matching a high-potential employee with a star performer and permitting observation and dialogue about the work, situations encountered, how they were handled in the manner they were, and why. Formal on-the-job training is more akin to reference or the training offered on databases or a new integrated library system. In this approach a training plan is developed, usually following a tell/show/do/follow up format of instruction. Formal on-the-job training is a popular approach to staff development. All of the following programmes have a leadership or management curriculum as their cornerstone, but most use more than one strategy—not only classroom learning or on-the-job training—to help staff grow.

BALTIMORE COUNTY PUBLIC LIBRARY

- Did you know that twenty percent of our top management team (Branch Managers, AO Department Heads, and Executive Leadership) are eligible to retire today? We are in the midst of the "graying of

> the profession" and must position ourselves to be ready for inevitable staff retirements in the near future. That is where you enter the picture. This memo describes three different succession management initiatives for FY-2009 designed for staff members that a) wish to improve upon management and leadership skills to be more effective in their current role; or b) aspire to move into higher-level supervisory and management positions within BCPL. Please note that while these programmes serve to strengthen your skills in leadership, supervision, and management, participation does not guarantee promotion into future management vacancies.

This is how Jean Mantegna, HR manager of Baltimore County Public Library (BCPL), opens the invitation sent to all staff to participate in the library's succession management initiatives. She then goes on to describe the three succession management initiatives: Leadership Development Programme, Supervisory Skills for New Supervisors, and the Effective Managing Series. BCPL's philosophy is one of creating a pipeline—a pool of viable candidates ready to fill management vacancies when, as Mantegna puts it, "the baby boomers bust out to retirement." Individual staff members are not selected for grooming into targeted positions, and it is acknowledged that leadership competencies are desired at every level in the organization.

Leadership Development Programme

In its third year, the Leadership Development Programme is intended "to provide learning opportunities around qualities of leadership for staff members that aspire to future management roles." The programme is both theoretical and practical (mostly the later) and very experiential. Increasing competencies around self-awareness and learning by doing are critical components. Mantegna and Jim Fish, the library's director, partnered with the Community Colleges of Baltimore County to design the programme. Sessions take place in half- to full-day sessions on a college campus covering the following topics: communications, team building, project management, problem solving, conflict resolution, and managing change. Participants learn how to work as a member of a cross-functional team with other leaders at varying levels of the organization.

They are also developing their leadership competencies from the list of twenty selected by the system. Phase two of the programme begins six months into the programme, after participants learn how to function as a team. They begin to work on a team project—a project of key importance to the library, one that drives its work plan forward. The most recent project is to develop virtual new staff orientation. Prior projects include service to new populations; self-check evaluation and recommendations for improvement; service to teens; and improving the telephone system. Each project has a sponsor (a seasoned manager within the library system), and seasoned managers provide developmental coaching throughout the experience as an aid to the learning process. Continuing education units are provided for the full-day programmes with the college. Peer feedback is provided to and by all (a skill also practiced in the programme). At project completion, presentations are made to the administrative council. Feedback is unfailingly followed by a well-deserved celebration. BCPL, always a learning organization, has made some recent changes to the programme.

The current class is limited to seven participants, and the length of the programme has increased from nine to sixteen months. Feedback from the first year demonstrated that the class size of twenty-one was too large and the nine month time line too short. To date, thirty-four employees have completed the programme with excellent results. Seven participants have been promoted into managerial positions, and several learned that management is not for them. A few left BCPL, taking their newly acquired leadership skills to another library system. Regardless of whether anyone is actually promoted, there are many positive outcomes. According to Jean, programme graduates are more self-aware, have a better sense of what they want their career to look like, have acquired project management skills, have learned new skills and competencies, and, most important, are leaders in their position.

Supervisory Skills for New Managers

BCPL offers Supervisory Skills for New Managers in a blended learning environment (face-to-face, independent, and group) as a way to introduce supervisory skills to employees new to their role or aspiring to supervisory positions. The curriculum is broadly shaped around the topics of communications, leadership, management, personal development, and team building. The Division of Library Development and Services of the Maryland State Department of Education purchased the license to online business skills courses provided by Skill soft, a provider of on-demand e-learning training programmes of both business and technical topics. Participants complete three courses selected by BCPL.

The schedule alternates, with participants completing a self-paced course individually one month and meeting as a group to debrief it the following month. During the debriefing, in a highly interactive way, supervisors share their learning and discuss how it applies to supervising staff at BCPL. The first three topics of independent learning taken over a six-month period are "Becoming a Manager— Responsibilities and Fears," "Communicating as a Leader," and "Leading through Change." Starting in month seven of this ten-month class and twice in alternating months, teams of two are formed to review the course catalog, select a topic that addresses a specific area of skill development, and present their learning to the group. They share key points, along with a review of the course, noting what they liked and disliked about it. Individual learning is not limited to the classes or topics. All learners have access to the full catalog of programmes until the site license expires.

Effective Managing Series

The third BCPL succession management initiative is the Effective Managing Series. As outlined in the course description, the purpose of this series "is to provide an opportunity for less-seasoned supervisors and managers to come together as a learning community to explore and develop their unique management styles in the context of BCPL's culture and philosophy of effective management." This programme runs for ten months. With a little bit of theory but mostly lively discussion and practical application, it covers the following topics:

- Managing oneself
- Planning and evaluation
- Organizing oneself/time management
- Delegating
- Managing change
- Managing challenges, conflicts, and crises
- Managing one's boss/managing others
- Communication
- Decision making
- To be determined (as selected by the group)

These classes are facilitated by Mantegna, Fish, and experienced managers, who view it as an opportunity to give back, to model different managerial styles to participants, and to transfer their institutional knowledge to the next generation of BCPL leaders.

COLUMBUS METROPOLITAN LIBRARY

Though it is known for creating and even selling strong training and development programmes, Columbus Metropolitan Library did not have a standard curriculum to support managers and leaders or those aspiring to move up. Patrick Losinski, the library's executive director, and his staff went on a search for a programme of study and selected Business of People leadership training, based in Columbus. The programme focuses on how one uses oneself to develop the core foundational skills of leadership, acknowledging that each person is the most powerful force for change in her organization. The curriculum includes:

- Great people skills: contact skills (two sessions)
- Commitment to the ongoing enhancement of the managed group.
- Wearing two hats effectively: representing your people to leadership and leadership to your people
- Working with accountability as a personal development process; reviews, monitoring employee growth over the year.

- Understanding the managed group
- The skills of raising and maintaining high morale
- Commitment to your own training beyond the training
- Getting good buy-in, giving direction, dealing with spot problems, expecting response, and having a framework for dealing with lack of follow-through
- Integration of Business of People skills

In the first year, one hundred of the library's managers, in ten groups of ten, went through ten five-hour sessions each month. In the second year, fifty more managers will go through the programme—this time run by library staff who completed a train-the-trainer programme in partnership with trainers from Business of People. Outcomes, from Losinski's perspective, have been very positive: "It's the best thing we've ever done." In addition, all managers now have a common language and shared experiences. "Staff," Losinski notes, "are dealing with resistance and change far more effectively; they are also more empathetic and results-oriented as managers; their listening skills have been fine-tuned; they understand how to get buy-in from staff, give and accept feedback; and hold staff accountable. Trust has gone up and managers are feeling good about system wide decisions that are made. Staff are using the training, and using the language." According to Losinski, "It is sticking!"

CUYAHOGA COUNTY PUBLIC LIBRARY

Sometimes events or circumstances signal that it is time to do something differently. Cuyahoga County Public Library (CCPL) was at just such a point when the system lost five branch managers over a short period of time. The jobs were posted, but leadership did not see the calibre of candidates they expected. Applicants simply did not have the knowledge, experience, or understanding of the job. CCPL recruited branch managers externally, but library director Sari Feldman and deputy director Tracey Strobel thought the library system had not adequately developed internal candidates. They then put their heads together and, working with a consultant, designed the two-day Branch Leadership Academy to expose staff to the roles and expectations of a branch manager.

They expected ten to fifteen staff to apply; forty-eight librarians volunteered to attend the learning event.

Feldman and Strobel structured it as an opportunity for interested staff to learn the expectations, including competencies, of a branch manager in their system.

Context

Per its strategic plan, CCPL focuses on six priorities: connect with reading; ensure every child enters school ready to learn; help youth to reach maximum potential; put Cuyahoga County back to work; keep seniors healthy, happy, and independent; and connect with new Americans. One way to fulfill these priorities is through community partnerships. Therefore, it is no surprise that CCPL branch managers are expected to know their communities and local players well. Indeed, branch managers are expected to be proactively involved in the community and to be seen as important players at the community level.

For example, library staff and branch managers are expected to have an impact in and on workforce development, serve as a gateway for new immigrants, and take a leadership role in early childhood education. Strobel offered an example of difference in expectations for different levels of library staff: while it is anticipated that the adult librarian will serve as liaison with the senior center twice a month and have a connection with the senior center director, the branch manager is expected to be visible in the community, liaise with mayor and city council members, serve on a chamber of commerce board, and attend Rotary lunches, press briefings, and Kiwanis breakfasts, to name a few. The expectations and competencies flow directly from the library's mission statement.

Leadership Academy Application Process

All public service librarians and subject specialists with more than one year of experience were invited to apply. To be accepted into the Branch Leadership Academy, candidates were required to link their desire to attend with a commitment to, and experience with, CCPL's branch manager competencies (taken directly from the job description of branch manager). The agenda for the Leadership Academy included welcomes by Feldman and Strobel and discussions about the library's new customer service model, trends in libraries, and best practices for bosses. How-to sessions on analyzing library metrics and problem solving and risk taking were followed by exercises in which the potential branch managers could put into practice what they had just learned.

A panel of senior branch managers shared experiences of connecting with their community, and all engaged in an exercise called "community opportunity scenario." Later, after sharing information on circulation, holds, and other library data, Strobel described initiatives the library was planning over the next one to three years to create efficiencies and improve customer service. Participants learned about them here first. A few of the initiatives included changes in delivery models, online booking of meeting rooms managed centrally, online programme registration, system wide centralized selection of materials, floating collections, programming with experts, and a rethinking of materials security measures. It was truly added value that forty-eight system leaders were in on the new customer service model and other initiatives and, as a critical mass, could help move these initiatives forward. Evaluations showed that one of the most highly valued discussions took place at the end of the session when

Feldman and Strobel, along with two regional managers, shared their expectations of branch managers, took questions, and provided sincere answers about leadership.

Of the forty-eight attendees, five have become branch managers and eleven have received other promotions (nine at CCPL and two elsewhere). Eight or so participants decided either to slow down on the track to management or not to pursue a management position. Strobel speaks of the Branch Leadership Academy as a huge success, one that CCPL plans to offer again in the near future.

HARFORD COUNTY PUBLIC LIBRARY

Harford County Public Library (HCPL) used the changing economic climate to analyze its staff development programme. Library director Audra Caplan and HR director Terri Schell realized that limited funds would compel the library to hire and retain the right people in the right job with the right skills. The components of the library's programme are staff development, competencies, supervisory training, mentoring, and leadership development. Succession planning is one part of HCPL's staff development programme, which is designed "for cultivating knowledgeable and skilled staff, developing strong supervisors, managers, and administrators, and preparing emergent leaders for the libraries of tomorrow." HCPL begins its focus on staff development from an employee's first day on the job, indeed during the recruitment process.

Retention starts at orientation, and development is about continuous learning. HCPL builds staff knowledge and skills through both in-house and external efforts, using a variety of learning modalities. Mentoring is an opportunity provided to new supervisors, managers, administrators, and other professional staff. In 2000, HCPL developed a competency-based performance management system. Working with a committee and consultant, the system identified and defined seven core and four managerial competencies.

The core competencies, on which all employees are assessed, are sensitivity to internal and external customer service; communications skills; team player; dependability; efficient management of job responsibilities; knowledgeable of policies, procedures, and technology; and problem solver. Successful managers are expected to mentor and cross-train employees, recognize and reward employee performance, demonstrate leadership, and serve as an employee/system liaison. Staff are recruited and promoted on the basis of these competencies, and training is offered regularly. An HCPL-specific refresher course, "Concepts and Culture," is offered to incumbents twice per year. Also offered regularly are classes on innovation, a key organizational value articulated in the library's strategic plan. Caplan and Schell know that, for HCPL to remain a thriving twenty-first-century library, staff need to be developed into successful leaders—and that leadership occurs not just at the top but throughout the organization. Accordingly, the library system created and HR offers a basic supervision course for all supervisors and those considering a supervisory position. This course is offered as self-study and in the classroom.

Learners are provided with a video and new supervisor toolbox consisting of eight DVDs and a workbook. They are expected to review this material in advance and be prepared for classroom study by the time training begins. One advantage of this programme is that all supervisors go through it, thus enhancing consistency in practice, application, and language. An unanticipated outcome has been that some employees, peeking through the window of what is really involved in supervision, choose to opt out before making what might be a poor career choice. Many participants express a new appreciation of what a supervisor—their supervisor— actually does. This look into the backroom work of supervision, if nothing else, shows the library as a system leaving participants with a bigger picture of the library world. To support the transition into supervision and leadership, the library created a mentoring programme.

The programme received very positive feedback from its first group of thirteen mentoring pairs and helped acculturate leaders into their new roles. Succession planning is HCPL's most recent addition to staff development. The succession planning programme was purposefully developed as a proactive means to "prepare staff for promotional opportunities, allow for organizational education, manage anticipated personnel shortages in key positions, identify staff who have potential to become successful supervisors, managers, administrators and leadership, and develop individualized development plans to strengthen necessary skills." In thinking holistically about succession planning, HCPL realized that it did not really know how many employees were interested in staying in their current positions and how many aspired to a leadership role.

To learn more about staff wishes, they conducted a needs assessment and asked. To their surprise, findings indicated that many employees sought new responsibilities, including leadership roles. The next step for HR was to take supervisory training to the leadership and executive level. A leadership programme offering advanced information for senior staff to gain more experience was custom designed to meet HCPL's culture and strategic needs. It is a blended programme offered through print, online, and face-to-face meetings. It is designed for participants to L.E.A.D.: learn, experience, apply, and develop. Skills to be acquired include project management, facilitator training, and advanced leadership skills. Still in development, the programme offers nineteen topics to choose from, including public speaking, the Public Information Act, intellectual freedom, strategic planning, seeing the big picture, and completing ALA's Certified Public Library Administrator course. Mentoring by a senior library administrator is a key component of leadership development at HCPL, where leaders are expected to take a global approach, engaging in big-picture and systems thinking. To help them acquire this perspective, HCPL plans to structure rotational assignments for leaders to spend a month or more in other departments to learn what really happens throughout the system at the senior level.

HCPL's philosophy and approach are to develop all people and provide everyone the same opportunity to move to the next level. Until budget costs became prohibitive, HCPL provided tuition reimbursement for employees attending library school. At one time, graduates were automatically promoted to librarians; now, graduates compete for professional-level positions in order to ensure that the library is promoting those with the most leadership potential. Caplan and Schell realize that there will not be enough leadership positions for all employees ready, willing, and able to take the mantle, but they too are thinking globally—globally for all public libraries, knowing that talented employees might leave for another system. If they do, Caplan and Schell are proud of their contribution to leadership at other libraries.

PUBLIC LIBRARY OF CHARLOTTE AND MECKLENBURG COUNTY

The Public Library of Charlotte and Mecklenburg County (PLCMC) has engaged in three efforts to date that involve leadership development and succession planning: manager training, a leadership learning initiative for new supervisors and managers, and the "Build the Bench" mentoring programme described earlier. The manager curriculum was designed internally for all managers, is mandatory, and must be completed within eighteen months. The curriculum consists of nine courses designed to build the competencies of integrity, customer service, communication, individual leadership/influencing, teamwork and collaboration, planning, organizing and work management, visionary leadership, analysis/problem assessment, and maximizing performance. Most courses are taught by internal staff—senior members of the HR department.

Managers can register easily on a PeopleSoft module at their desk. Each course is scheduled for between two hours and one day. The curriculum includes these courses: New Employee Orientation; Communicating and Listening; Sexual Harassment: A Manager's Responsibility; Salary Administration; Ethics for Supervisors and Managers; Library Practices and Policies; Essentials of Leadership; Working through Conflict; and Behavioural Interviewing Techniques.

The plan going forward for this programme is the creation of virtual classrooms, to save both time and money. The goal of the manager training programme is to improve individual as well as organizational success and to develop future leaders for the organization. The Leadership Learning Initiative was created for newly hired managers and supervisors throughout the system.

Seeking a diversity of candidates, the library invited employees of all levels and with different types of experience to participate.

The initial iteration was a six-month programme built around Rachel Singer Gordon's *The Accidental Library Manager: Who Am I?* The core curriculum also focuses on developing managers in the areas of conflict resolution, building successful teams, and communications—competencies PLCMC finds to be the building blocks all supervisors and managers need to be successful. Multifaceted and multimedia, the curriculum consists of a combination of face-to-face meetings, virtual meetings, in-house speakers, and external community speakers. The pilot programme received rave reviews, and PLCMC plans to implement it again, and on an ongoing basis. The change they will make is to shorten it, keep the class size to twelve participants, offer classes more frequently, and eliminate redundancies that may occur with the manager training programme. New action learning projects pertaining to the system's mission, values, or strategic plan will be identified as the programme continues.

CREATE A DUAL CAREER LADDER SYSTEM FOR LIBRARIANS

Career ladders allow employees to focus on their expertise as, for example, an individual contributor (e.g., children's librarian) without having to take on a management role to earn more. In this scenario, an employee might advance from Librarian I to II by taking on more responsibility in collection development, conducting research, or designing new programmes in early childhood learning. Other options might include the Librarian I moving up by becoming a specialist in literacy, readers' advisory, information technology, or training.

Some libraries, such as Queens Borough (N.Y.) Public Library, have career ladders that extend through supervisory and management levels in order to prepare even senior managers to fill anticipated vacancies due to upcoming retirements. There are many ways to acknowledge and reward your staff for increasing their responsibility and value to the library outside advancement to a management position. Though the library may ultimately place the employee in a higher grade level and pay a higher salary, that amount will be far less than the cost of replacing her if she goes elsewhere or the cost of low morale and mistakes if she takes a management job she does not really desire, just to earn more.

OFFER COACHING TO MANAGERS AND LEADERS

Most employees are not ready to take on management/ leadership roles when first promoted to them. And why would they be? It is an entirely new role they were not taught in library school or as individual contributors. There are job content and process coaches. As the name implies, a job content coach helps the leader learn what the job entails. A process coach, on the other hand, focuses attention on how the leader affects others, creates roles and boundaries, creates an agenda, and works with a group to achieve results.

The coach especially works with the leader to gain an awareness of the special competencies needed at the new organizational level. Where do you find a coach? A staff member who is already experienced in that job, especially if her experience includes supervisory coaching for staff, can do most job content coaching. Process coaching requires some different skills, including the ability to maintain objectivity. Some HR departments provide process coaching. For some top leadership positions, the library may be willing to pay for an experienced process coach from outside the organization. There may be someone in your library that already has the right skills or is interested in developing them to fill a unique and valuable role; providing training for a "designated coach"—or a coaching team—may be a worthwhile investment. An excellent resource on coaching is Ruth Metz's *coaching in the Library.* The County of Los Angeles Public Library provides an external coach to its action learning teams, team leaders, and management.

The coach helps members through sticky situations and covers team effectiveness, presentation skills, and problem solving. Observing the teams allows the coach to see people in action, showing her who the high achievers are and who needs to develop which strengths; who talks a good game but has little substance; who is quiet but very capable. The process brings valuable input to management to augment the talent assessment process. The library's action learning teams typically work on their own once they are chartered; the executive team does not get involved unless asked. The coach, however, may suggest that a team or team member call the county librarian, for example, to ascertain direction or understand the politics of a course of action. Often teams' members say they "do not want to bother her," but of course they are missing a valuable resource and opportunity. An important learning experience results in either case.

PROMOTE MLS STUDENTS TO AN INTERIM GRADE LEVEL

After a student has successfully completed one-half of the degree, reclassify her job from library associate to librarian trainee or another title. Award a grade increase as well as a salary increase. The employee will value your appreciation and show it in her work as well as in her loyalty and decision to remain after graduation. Taking this approach can also have a downside. It is one thing to encourage someone with great potential to go to school; it is another thing entirely to promote anyone who completes a degree, whether or not she is someone you would hire to fill an MLS position. The disadvantage of paying for education rather than for job responsibilities is that you may find yourself paying for an MLS when the incumbent is not doing MLS-level work, or eventually paying someone an MLS salary when she is not someone you would have promoted into an MLS position. Another option is to encourage staff with demonstrated potential to apply for available MLS jobs even before they finish their coursework. Promote them and hire them at a provisional rate, giving them salary increases at milestones to degree completion. This is a useful practice when it is hard to recruit qualified MLS librarians and results in loyalty, too. Encouraging people to apply even if they have not completed the qualification helps them demonstrate their interest in advancement and gain skill in interviewing. You may discover previously hidden potential and then provide coaching or mentoring to help your students become stronger candidates for promotion.

The Carroll County Public Library has used this model to promote several MLS students into MLS jobs, with great success. Over the years they found that they were not seeing the quality of external candidates they wanted to fill entry-level MLS positions, yet they had several experienced bachelor's-prepared staff that demonstrated the library's core competencies (*e.g.*, customer service and teamwork) and were interested in developing themselves.

The library supported some staff in pursuit of MLS degrees in order to "grow their own" librarians, but there were not enough students graduating quickly enough to compete for vacancies coming available. So the library began to advertise to staff that students enrolled in an MLS programme would be considered for some (clearly identified) MLS jobs. Students began to apply for these jobs, and one or two staff members even enrolled in MLS programmes after seeing such job postings. Though it is never a given that an MLS student will be promoted, internal candidates who have demonstrated their interest have the advantage of having their work seen over time. Successful candidates have had several things in common:

- Relevant experience (such as supervisory experience) acquired from previous jobs
- Demonstrated competencies in the library's core areas, such as customer service or teamwork, and good progress in learning the technical competencies of their jobs (and sometimes of the jobs a level above theirs)
- Enough employment history with the library to have been identified (even informally) as Promotable or Emerging Talent

These librarians would be the first to admit that taking on a new and higher-level position while completing graduate school is not easy. Several of them have talked about "running to keep up" with all the competing demands on their time. Despite this, they have brought to the system a new energy level as their new ideas and new skills are put to use. It is important to note that not every MLS student gets a promotion, even after completing the degree. They must compete for vacant positions, sometimes against external candidates who already have an MLS. But even when a student is not promoted, the library gets a return on its investment, because it finds that students are engaged in learning and in applying what they learn to their work.

DEVELOP A PROGRAMME OF JOB ROTATION AND CROSS-TRAINING

Have staff swap jobs for three to six months. All will return with increased job knowledge, vitality, perspective, and appreciation of the library, its work, and the workforce. Do this as part of a structured programme in which staff members keep a journal or record questions they encounter and discuss their key learnings with their peers, a coach, or both. Alternately, job rotation can be less extensive. You can rotate library associates assigned to the central facility into a branch for a week or rotate employees among branches, if you have more than one building.

Cross-train public service, technical services, and business office employees. Not only do such assignments develop the individuals involved, they provide the library with a more flexible and capable workforce, reducing work stoppages or backlogs when vacation is taken or someone is out on extended sick leave. Employees undertaking a job rotation should develop an IDP that clarifies developmental goals for taking or seeking the assignment. The person is expected acquire new knowledge, skills, and abilities as an outcome of the job rotation.

"It's like springtime renewal when a person takes over a new area," says Patrick Losinski, executive director of Columbus Metropolitan Library. Columbus Metro also "switches deck chairs" around (as Losinski calls it), rotating or combining jobs. In one recent example, collection development staff and technical services staff were supervised by the marketing department.

This is one way to help someone see the bigger picture, in this case to support centralized collections. Losinski was able to report seeing new ways of thinking within three weeks. Switching deck chairs was also mandatory for five branch managers in order to provide lateral transfers, new challenges, and new ways of thinking.

Many of the branch managers in Cuyahoga County Public Library were reassigned when this twenty-eight-branch library system reorganized. The reorganization resulted in a rotational move for all branch managers with less than three years of tenure in their branch.

Yes, there were some tears and some opposition; a few branch managers even retired a little sooner than planned. Despite some short-term pain, library director Sari Feldman and her mover-and-shaker deputy Tracey Strobel report that the move was energizing overall. They see branch managers as pivotal to making the library's mission a reality, and according to Strobel this move "ramped everything up" across the system. The "jolt" re-energized the whole system, with staff rising to work with (and impress) their new bosses, managers looking at their new location and staff with fresh eyes, and all facing and growing from new challenges. New branch teams initiated many changes; more than a few of these resulted in higher efficiencies, improvement to effectiveness, increased circulation, higher door counts, and more.

TAKE ADVANTAGE OF TASK FORCES AND INTERIM JOB ASSIGNMENTS

Do not repeatedly ask the same people to serve on task forces or committees. For each new task force or job assignment, seek out a promising person who has not been given an opportunity to participate. Ask her to serve. If she agrees, provide support and watch her blossom. Fast teams are frequently used for problem solving and employee development at Santa Clara County Library. A fast team provides an intensive focus to an issue or problem facing the library. There are few people on fast teams, three to five, from targeted organizational units. Teams usually meet for no more than four weeks.

The team decides who will chair it, how many meetings are needed, and how communications up, down, and sideways will take place. One fast team rolled out chat reference. Another was tasked to provide the community with help getting connected with the library.

Charters for fast teams have a reasonable scope, and staff members provide their best thinking and research. The library has seen people rise to the challenge, and Melinda Cervantes, the library's executive director and county librarian, celebrates their success along with them. Shared leadership models such as task groups and committees are frequently used to develop employees at Fresno County Public Library.

A combination of employees having subject knowledge, those new to librarianship, and long-term staff participate on the same committee. For example, a task force was created to plan the events around the library's hundred-year anniversary as a county library. Fresno County Public Library also capitalizes on staff development under civil service regulations, even though they are often seen as limiting options.

For example, a special salary upgrade for up to nine months can be offered to an employee filling a temporary vacancy.

In this manner, a Librarian II who might have the years of experience to qualify as a Librarian III (supervisor) could work in a higher classification during a vacancy or leave. This not only helps the library provide continuous services but provides the librarian with the range of experiences needed to compete for promotion opportunities. County librarian Karen Bosch Cobb and training librarian Camille Turner have used this approach to create opportunities for all, resulting in staff with more competencies, trained and available for promotion.

ASSIGN MENTORS TO NEW AND LONGER-TERM EMPLOYEES

Mentoring can be a powerful tool in employee development, especially when an employee is promoted or assumes a new role. An effective mentoring process takes some thought and planning. It is important to match the mentor and the men tee carefully. Their personal styles and interests should be compatible. Allow a trial period for the relationship to settle in, and if there are problems make needed adjustments. Expectations for the mentoring relationship should be identified clearly. Define the results you expect and discuss responsibilities, roles, and expectations with both mentor and men tee.

Provide training for mentors. Monitor and evaluate progress, and reset expectations as the relationship grows and changes. The formal mentor/ men tee relationship is not intended to be permanent.

The final phase of the formal relationship should encourage independence at the appropriate time. Lois Zachary's *Mentor's Guide* is a wonderful resource for developing a mentoring programme or relationship. In this programme, a vice president of one division may mentor a young employee in another division. Both mentor and men tee learn from each other and build relationships that allow both to understand what happens in other parts of the organization as well.

The "Build the Bench" programme at the Public Library of Charlotte and Mecklenburg County (N.C.) created an "intimate type of learning environment" for high-potential managers. Rick Ricker, HR deputy director, told us that six high-potential managers were identified and paired with six senior managers, who were tasked to provide mentoring and one-on-one development as well as exposure to different management styles. All twelve were provided with mentor/ men tee training to help set goals and expectations. The programme offered collaborative project work and development over an eight-week period. Feedback was provided to the men tee managers and the executive leadership team about the potential for success and development needs of each participant.

Participants also worked on an action learning project: small groups were responsible for creating a section of a disaster recovery plan for the library and then cohesively working (inter group or across teams) to develop an effective plan. One manager from this group has since been promoted. All have created IDPs that will help them acquire the necessary knowledge, skills, and experiences to move towards their career goals. Mentoring is an ongoing activity at Santa Clara County Library. There is no formal programme, but mentoring is institutionalized and has helped many employees. Sarah Flowers is one:

- I was hired as a programme librarian at the Morgan Hill Library. I had a very good mentor in Catharine Fouts, who was the community librarian then. She spent a lot of time with me, talking about her own under standing of the system and her own philosophy of management. She was tremendously influential in my own development as a leader. Beyond that, though, probably the best thing she did for me was to take at least one four- to six-week vacation every year, leaving me in charge. After three years, she transferred to Los Altos and I was promoted to community librarian. I continued to call on her as a resource on how to do my new job, until she retired a couple of years later. Probably one of the biggest opportunities I was given during the time I was a community librarian was to be on the negotiating team for the SEIU contract negotiations. It was very helpful to have that background when I applied for the deputy county librarian job. I was asked to work out-of-class as deputy county librarian for six or eight weeks. That was a big help in preparing me too. I realized later that of course Julie knew she was leaving and wanted to start training someone for her job.

Nancy Howe is currently the deputy county librarian and has spent most of her library career with Santa Clara County. She has moved to a new position or been promoted six times during her fourteen-year tenure. Howe says that she has found ample opportunities for new challenges within the Santa Clara County Library.

- I spent most of my career working in the not-for-profit sector, and only came to the library when I was staying home raising my family. I started working as a substitute librarian, almost as a hobby, but quickly decided that my personal ambition was to bring my community and managerial experiences from my previous career to the library. Santa Clara County Library is large enough to have lots of movement and I always have been quick to raise my hand to take on a project, often that no one else wanted to do. I told my supervisors that I wanted to advance and I received lots of encouragement. In taking the deputy position, I really am stretching myself by managing the technology side of the library. I am grateful to Melinda as well as other people who have sensed my passion and believed in my abilities. From working as a substitute librarian in every one of our libraries, to a supervising librarian, adult services manager, staff development librarian, community librarian and now as deputy, I have a breadth and depth of experience that I can apply to future positions, either inside this system or elsewhere. I love the Santa Clara County Library for its values and am proud to be a part of it throughout my library career. It's my turn now to mentor many of our new hires, and one of my proudest accomplishments was having a hand in creating our intern programme that provides library school students with practical experience, often ending up with them working for us as librarians.

DEVELOPMENT AND COORDINATION OF LIBRARY SERVICES

In recent years the sise, complexity, pervasiveness and burgeoning growth of the federal government have made it a prime focus of the nation's news media, and it consequently has captured the attention of the general public. A similar expansion has occurred at the level of state government, but without as much commentary or analysis by the press.

One author refers to the "surprising discovery that the largest growth sector in the 1960s and 1970s is not national Defence, automobile manufacturing, or even the federal government" but is instead state and local government. When the broadened scope of responsibilities, services and agency functions are considered, the changing nature and importance of state government is even more impressive. Like the federal government, state governments have responded to the needs of a population beset by accelerating technological, social, economic, cultural, and political change. Thus there are state agencies, com- missions, committees, bureaus, councils, and departments whose responsibilities and concerns range from atomic energy to drug addiction treatment, and from medical care to the aged to the development of the arts.

This expanding scope of interests has meant that the business of state government, in all its facets, requires an expanding variety of information sources and services. Like the rest of society in this postindustrial era, state government has become heavily information-dependent. How have state libraries responded to the burgeoning information needs of state government? Almost every state library gives some kind of information service to other agencies of state government and, indeed, many have been doing so Since, the early days of the Republic. The standards for Library functions at the state level makes clear the state library's responsibility to provide quality services to other agencies of state government.

The ways in which state libraries fulfil this responsibility, the variety of services offered, the intensity of effort, and the degree of coordination with other agencies varies widely among the fifty states. As early as 1966, Phillip Monypenny noted a variety of provisions to supply service to legislative, executive and judicial branches of state government, with varying degrees of coordination between law libraries, historical societies, archives, departmental libraries, and general state library agencies.

Some indication of the variety of such services offered by state library agencies may be gained from the 1977 Simpson survey, where state library agencies listed the following: library services to state government, consultant services to state agency libraries, research library for state agencies, special collection for state agencies, cooperation with agency and departmental libraries, reference services to state agencies and officials, centralised purchasing for agency libraries, centralised processing for agency libraries, audiovisual production and direction for state agencies, legislative reference library, reference services to legislature, special administrative and legislative library, legislative research, computerised on- line bill status, state law library as part of state library, current awareness services, depository for state publications, depository for historical records, distribution of state publications, index of state publications, published checklist of state documents, records management service for state government, consultant services to state institutions, and library services to state institutions.

State library collections range in sise from the large and comprehensive libraries of New York, Illinois and California, to the more typical 100,000-200,000 volume collections held by many states. A few state libraries, such as Maryland's, do not maintain collections, but provide reference service by other means. In addition to the services and collections of the state library itself, agency or departmental libraries exist in many states. Although reliable and up to date data on these are difficult to obtain, a US Office of Education (USOE) survey conducted in late 1977 of special libraries serving state government will provide such data when compiled and published.

It is known, however, that the number of such libraries varies from state to state (New York has nearly fifty, Texas twenty-three, New Jersey thirteen). Similarly, the collection sise, budget and number and level of staffing will vary widely from state to state, from major and sizable libraries (most typically court or law libraries) to office collections with part- time or no library staff. The literature on the activities of state library agencies during the past fifteen years has clearly dealt more with statewide library development and extension services than with other functions.

A similar bias was observed by Ralph Blasingame in a survey of library studies conducted between 1965 and 1969 based on an ERIC bibliography. He reported that only seven of the eighty-nine studies listed were concerned with services to state institutions (none specifically with services to state government), while two-thirds were studies of public libraries. A reading of the literature indicates that information services to state government have not been the leading edge of "state library" Programme development during this period.

This emphasis on statewide library Programmes is not surprising in view of the passage of the Library Services Act of 1956, and the attendant in- flux of federal funds to support this type of development. Forced to respond to pressure from the field and anxious to seise the opportunity to effectuate long-sought improvements in statewide planning and library system development, many state libraries clearly have not given the same attention to the development of information services to state government. Regulations of the federal Library Services and Construction Act specifically prohibited use of federal funds for service to state government.

Several states, however, have commissioned studies during this period designed to improve information service to state government. Studies in South Dakota, Ohio, Indiana and New York do indicate a growing concern and offer recommendations for implementation of Programmes in this area. Michael Jackley, in a 1965 analysis of the functions of the South Dakota Library Commission, opted for greater centralisation. His recommendations take the form of central purchasing of library materials, with those appropriate to departmental libraries being placed on permanent loan with the departmental library as a branch of the central agency. Better access to materials held by archives, history and law would be promoted by close coordination with these agencies and the central library.

He suggested that those agencies of state government whose major function is research, such as the Legislative Research Council, should be housed with the state library on the Capitol grounds. Blasingame, in a 1968study for Ohio, advocated that the Information Resources and Services Division of the state library become a govern-mental service unit with three new staff positions. Each of these new staff members would work with a specific group of logically chosen state agencies in order to become knowledgeable about the concerns and problems of these groups. This would enable the state library to provide strong leadership in planning the development of information services in state agencies, and provide individual advice and assistance to those agencies with their own libraries.

Duplication of effort and materials would be avoided, and maximum exploitation of existing resources inspired. Recommendations by Genevieve Casey were made in 1970 in a study for the Indiana State Library.

Detailed recommendations for the coordination of services to the legislature and to state agencies include: consultant services to agencies desiring aid in cataloging and classifying materials; better circulation procedures; the provision of more sophisticated bibliographical services; centralised purchasing and processing; periodical print- outs and centralised records in the state library of the holdings of agencies; some form of current awareness service, with staff members working with administrators and librarians in the agencies assessing information needs and helping to establish acquisition policies; the use of existing TWX facilities by state employees; contracting for access to the collection and services of the Indiana University Medical Library for all state employees, especially those in the fields of health and environment; and the evaluation of the state library collection in terms of state government.

To provide guidance in establishing priorities for comprehensive information services, a council of persons responsible for department libraries and staff libraries in institutions would meet regularly with state library staff to discuss common problems and concerns. Work with large state agencies might be organised with small advisory councils within the agencies to work directly with the staff member from the state library responsible for that agency. Financial arrangements could take the form of either in- creased budget for the state library to support additional services to agencies, or an inter-accounting mechanism between the library agency and departments receiving special services. The state library would require additional funds in any case, primarily for new staff to implement these activities, but also for materials and equipment. In 1974, the New York State Library undertook a major review of information services to state government in other states. To obtain up- to-date information on existing patterns of service from the other forty- nine state library agencies, a brief but pointed questionnaire was developed and distributed in autumn 1974.

Follow up visits were made to Texas, North Carolina and Ohio in this study, and additional data were gathered from Washington State. These visits provided information on both innovative Programmes and the varying approaches to state agency services taken in each of the states.

The Texas State Library, employing a former public library consultant, has emphasised cooperative activities with other state agency libraries in Austin, resulting in the development of a lively organisation called State Agency Libraries of Texas (SALT). SALT publishes a news-letter, holds regular meetings and workshops, and has developed a number of cooperative projects, including a union list of serials and a Texas state documents project.

Building on the recommendations of the Blasingame report summarised above, the Ohio State Library has expanded its services in recent years through an aggressive campaign to create awareness. Acting Head, Information and Reference Division:

- Active marketing of the information provision capabilities of the State Library of Ohio is emphasised -through "sales calls," by pre-sentations before department groups, through orientation and familiarisation classes and tours, with follow-through in the form of individualised current awareness services which provide an ordering tool to the recipient. In the last year, more than a third of the circulation to state government personnel can be traced to the stimulus provided by the direct mail current awareness Programme. An important positive aspect is the system for delivery to the requestor whether he is remotely sited or contiguous to the library.

Like Texas and Ohio, the North Carolina State Library created a special unit to provide service to state agencies, entitled the "Library Services to State Agencies Branch." The Programme differs from Texas's and Ohio's reference-centered operations in that a considerable portion of the unit's thrust is in the area of technical services. In 1973-74, this unit provided cataloging, consultative and other support services to fourteen agency libraries, including the large Public Health Service library, the Department of Public Instruction, and newly organised libraries in the Labour and State Personnel departments.

In the latter instance, the state library provided the necessary in-service training to assist the agency in starting the new library and the department provided staff, furnishings, shelving and a card catalogue. Central to an understanding of the Washington State arrangement is the fact that the state librarian is a cabinet officer reporting directly to the governor, and the state library is responsible for all library services for state government (except law), no matter where the facility served is located. The former Washington State Librarian, described the Programme in refreshingly non-bureaucratic language:

- Some departments want us to operate fully and where they can generate federal funds for the service we enter into a "contract".... We pay no attention to the actual dollars so generated but render the service as needed. In some instances the department prefers to have the library staff on its payroll.... All materials are purchased and processed by us so that our catalog reflects the total information resource. The staffs are given orientation here so they realise we are back-up to their limited collection. The collections are weeded frequently and materials returned here for final decision as to retention. Some offices around the state have small collections but we encourage the employees to use their local public library and to call us directly. In addition to subscribing to key professional publications, we Xerox tables of contents and route them around. People write their names by the article desired and we send a Xerox copy which they can keep or throw away. It is a very wide ranging, flexible and effective programme.

Special consultative services are also available to state agencies by contract and have resulted in a comprehensive bibliography on disasters in Washington State for the Department of Emergency Services, and a combined subject index for environmental impact statements for the Department of Ecology.

The New York State Library, building on an 86-year history of special services to the legislature, established a Legislative and Governmental Services unit in 1977, directed by a member of the top-level administration.

This unit will promote library services to state agencies aggressively, provide special research and bibliographic support, and conduct orientation and other Programmes for legislative and agency staff. Publications currently issued by the unit include Legislative trends (an annotated list of state library acquisitions on topics of interest to the legislature), Spotlight (guides to basic resources in selected subject fields), Topics on top (short bibliographies on topics of current interest), and comprehensive literature searches on requested subjects. Resources offered include free search services on twenty-six computerised data banks.

Despite the considerable variety of state library Programmes, certain general norms or patterns emerge which suggest the following elements as essential in developing an effective Programme of state library services to state agencies:

- *Attitude:* An aggressive, outreach approach is needed, based on a commitment to service and a wide-ranging, well-defined Programme to meet the needs of state agencies, officials and employees.
- *Organisation:* The state library should serve as the hub or center of library activity for state government, and should create a special office or unit which will provide leadership, coordination and the necessary monitoring of the programme. At the least, it should assign one or more staff members to carry out this outreach Programme on a continuing and preferably full-time basis. Staff should be carefully chosen for many of the same qualities which characterise successful field consultants, as well as for their perception of reference and bibliographic needs, and of the operation and structure of state government.
- *Agency Involvement:* As many agencies as possible should be involved, not only in the planning of service patterns, but in their refinement and evaluation as well. Even if the cooperating agency has no library *per se*, it should assign someone to work with the state library coordinator.
- *Shared Activities/Shared Financing:* Services which are beyond the capability of the individual cooperating agency should be explored care- fully and implemented as practicable, including centralised ordering and processing of library materials, union lists and other methods of bibliographic control, central computerised data banks with terminal access as required, cooperative storage and materials retirement plans, etc. Shared financing on some unit cost basis, by means of contractual or other arrangements, is desirable and tends to stimulate mutual involvement, respect and commitment, and provides a basis for evaluating cost-effectiveness.
- *Visibility, Direct Contact with Administration:* In order to gain the support of the administration and the legislature, the state library and its Programme of service to state government needs visibility, a voice and some degree of clout. This may be achieved organisationally, with cabinet rank for the state librarian or with strong advisory groups who can make their voices heard by the power structure. It may like- wise be achieved personally, through the visibility and personal dynamics of the chief state library officer and the programme specialists; and functionally, through the provision of services of demonstrable value and reliable quality. All these avenues may be necessary and should be bulwarked with an effective public relations Programme including publicity, orientation workshops and appropriate accountability through regular reports.

The data assembled in this chapter indicate that state library agencies generally accept information service to state government as a primary responsibility. Although this function does not appear to have been the "leading edge" of state library Programme development in recent years, there is evidence of increased interest and innovative activity in a number of states. As state government expands its interests, as legislative, judicial and executive agencies become increasingly information dependent, and as the relationship of information availability to cost-effectiveness and productivity becomes clearer, it may be expected that information service to state government will become an increasingly critical area of state library agency activity.

8

Internet Training for Academic Library Staff

INTRODUCTION

Educational institutions are being encouraged by the Government and other organisations to upgrade their resources for research and education. Consequently the academic libraries of the higher education institutions are also being upgraded. Internet has proved to be boon in this endeavor. Internet has helped these libraries to be interconnected and share their resources and also to access resources in remote locations.

Internet connections have been growing in the recent years with good connectivity and access. But are these libraries fully geared up especially in terms of their employees' skills to be able to fully utilise the Internet for the benefit of the academic community?

It has already been widely discussed that training is essential for the staffs to work in a network and automated environment. The Library Association Working Party on Training cites in its Policy Statement that training "is of fundamental importance to all levels of staffs working in all types of library", contributing to "greater efficiency and continuity, with real cost benefits". Since, technology keeps on changing it becomes even more necessary for the staff to be trained in Internet.

OBJECTIVES

The present study aims to understand the status of Internet training for the academic library staff within greater Guwahati. Since, the importance of Internet is growing in today's academic environment therefore the issue of training the academic library staff in handling Internet is becoming important.

So this study will investigate the various training methods used in the academic libraries, the content of such training, problems encountered and whether any evaluation is undertaken for such training. The investigation will also try to reveal the attitudes of the library managers with regard to training their staff on Internet.

SCOPE

The present study was based on a sample of academic libraries from greater Guwahati selected randomly. Since, there are many academic libraries within greater Guwahati only those were selected which had a functional Internet connection. These include the following libraries:

- Hem Barua library (B.Borooah college).
- KKHandique Library (Gauhati University).
- Dr. BKB Library (Gauhati Commerce College).
- Central Library (IIT Guwahati).
- IASST Library (Institute of Advanced Studies in Science and technology).
- KC Das Commerce College Library.

METHODOLOGY

In order to understand the status of Internet training for the staffs of the academic libraries a sample of six academic libraries was taken. A questionnaire-based survey of the sample was conducted. The questionnaire contained both close-ended questions and open-ended questions. The questionnaire was prepared based on some existing studies already done on understanding the Internet training of academic library staff. Comprehending the importance of the study the author personally went to the respective libraries to collect the data.

INTERNET AND ITS USE IN ACADEMIC LIBRARIES

Many of us by now are familiar with Internet especially those working in the academic libraries. This is because the academic libraries have been the pioneer in the field of automation and Internet. Internet has become essential for today's education and research in the academic institutions. Library being a hub of research and academic activities are therefore being provided with Internet connections. The Internet is a unique information resource, bringing a wide range of material from around the world to a local machine. One of the earliest usages of the Internet was to access the OPAC, *i.e.*, the Online Public Access Catalogues of different libraries or within a campus.

The union catalogues which lists the holdings of several libraries was another important tool accessible through net. Another area of growing importance for academic libraries is that of electronic journals. Big publishing houses like Elsevier, Springer, ACM, etc., are providing packages of their journals to libraries in electronic form via Internet. So at nominal subscription the libraries can access to these costly journals, which are becoming increasingly popular with the users. Thus grew consortia based subscription in India.

INDEST, INFONET and CSIR Consortium are the examples of library consortia for sharing journals and bibliographic information. These consortia based journal subscription are available through the Internet. The Indian National Digital Library in Engineering Science and Technology, *i.e.*, INDEST was set up by the Ministry of Human resource Development (MHRD) for subscription to electronic resources for 38 institutions including IISc, IITs, NITs, IIMs, etc., Over 6000 e- journals are accessible through this consortium, which has its headquarters in IIT Delhi. Infonet Contortia is set up by UGC and operated through its INFLIBNET Centre, Ahmedabad. Over 100 Universities are its members.

It covers disciplines like Arts, Sciences, Mathematics and statistics, etc., About 4000 full text electronic journals from 25 publishers are currently accessible. CSIR e- journal Consortia provides access to 3300+ e- journals from 11 publishers to all CSIR SandT staff of different CSIR institutions located around India. These consortia not only provide full text access but they also give access to bibliographic databases like COMPENDEX, INSPEC SciFinder Scholar, and Web of Science, etc. Many open access materials important for education and research are available on the Internet. They are very useful in the context that they are not fee based and also don't have restricted access and are thus becoming very popular with students and researchers. Communicating with users is very important in academic libraries.

Widespread access to the Internet has also created new means of communicating with users. In some cases, Internet technologies are used to reproduce an existing service in another medium, such as online "suggestion boxes". However, there is "added value" to such a service as users can mail in their suggestions from terminals on or off campus at a time convenient to them. E-mail enquiry or reference services also represent an extension of mainstream library activity - although some academic librarians initially had concerns about being able to meet the demand of such a service. Reference and enquiry services in academic libraries in the main seek to teach their users how to search for information themselves, rather than answering the enquiries themselves, as is more likely to be the case in a special library.

A significant number of British academic libraries have adopted electronic mail enquiry or information services - at the University of Hull the "e-mail help line" is treated as an extension of the Enquiry Desk service. Anecdotal evidence suggests that electronic enquiry services are not overwhelmed, and most users do stay within the parameters of the service. The most successful e-mail enquiry services have developed their procedures and boundaries prior to the service going live. As many enquiries fall into the category of Frequently Asked Questions, these can thus be answered by existing position statements.

Electronic mail also has great potential to cut down on the mountain of paperwork involved in sending out recall notices, notifying readers that items can be collected, etc. Some library systems allow students to renew loans (provided no other reader is waiting for the book) directly via the OPAC or to request a renewal via e-mail. Similarly, weblogs or simply blogs are now becoming very popular on the Internet as a communication medium. A library weblog can be used to:

- Providing news information for users.
- Providing links to recommend internet sources.
- Book reviews, information about new books.
- Providing entertainment or amusement for users.
- Providing news or information for librarians.
- Book discussions.
- Provide news or information for the trustees.
- Provide research tips.
- Communication among the librarians (in a library system).

The library can make good use of the electronic mail system of Internet, *i.e.*, E-mail to communicate reservation alert, current awareness services like SDI, new arrivals of books and journals, receiving interlibrary loan request and sending overdue notices to the users. In addition to these specialist services academic librarians also make use of the Internet information that is available to all users. Much bibliographical and price information can be found from online bookstores and Web sites for professional organisations and publishers. A wide range of factual information from government and NGO sources is available too. Although librarians have more skepticism about the well-publicised Web search tools than most users, such services can be valuable, particularly for easily defined topics (such as names or abbreviations) and the sheer range of material indexed, subjects covered and the speed with which they search can make them useful when a clear starting point is not obvious.

They may not always retrieve a full answer, but may give helpful clues. Internet resources are just another information medium academic librarians are extending their skills to encompass it. So they may offer a current awareness service to teaching and research staff to inform them of new Web sites and discussion lists; they will apply established criteria to assessing the content of information sources or the effectiveness of secondary services like search tools. The hypertext nature of the Web makes it easy to make additional explanation or instruction for a resource as an optional choice. This concept of instruction at the point and time of use is harder to achieve in the physical library.

WHY INTERNET TRAINING IS NECESSARY

In the Internet age there is acute need of Internet specialists. These specialists will be armed with the necessary skills and training to help the users to locate their information pin pointedly and efficiently on the net. Libraries specially the academic libraries would have a great demand for these specialists. Internet connectivity in the academic libraries is growing day by day. So, the present administration of the academic institutions should take necessary steps to equip the library staff with the required skills and training on Internet. Training can help to understand many essential aspects of the Internet such as follows:

- Are we using the right type of Internet connection for our needs? Are we getting a good deal?
- How quickly can we find what we looking for on the Internet? We should be able to find useful information about virtually any topic in less than a minute. If you're taking longer, you're doing something wrong.
- How do we know if we are safe? Most people who contract viruses or other nastiest thought they were protected.
- Are we using e-mail correctly? Or are we really annoying we our colleagues and they are too polite to tell us? We might be unpleasantly surprised to learn the truth.
- How do we avoid those terrible pop-up windows?
- How do we know if information is real or a hoax?
- How can we make surfing faster?
- How can we get the maximum satisfaction without spending more time on net?

As noted by Paula L. Matthews while employing Internet in academic libraries one of the important issues for the administrator is the implementation library staff training.

"A lack of training can result in:

- Poor staff performance;
- Lack of motivation;
- High staff turnover;
- Resistance to change;
- Costly errors or accidents;
- Unfulfilled objectives;
- Undesirable low standards of service.

Academic librarians may well draw on training materials available on the Internet for the higher education community. Recently the issue of whether librarians should learn HTML (Hyper-Text Markup Language) was debated on a North American discussion list. The conclusion was that knowledge of basic HTML was necessary in order to prepare presentations and information guides, which are an integral part of the librarian's professional role. As an increasing number of academic libraries experience some measure of "convergence" with other academic support services, library staff has many opportunities to augment their IT skills and collaborate with colleagues in other services.

The combination of technical knowledge and the ability to evaluate information sources is a powerful argument for the continued need for LIS professionals in higher education. The users of the Academic libraries including some faculty member do not have net skills. In such cases the academic library staff has to come forward to help them. For readiness the staff should have some kind of net skills. The transition of traditional library resources to technology based library resources has put a lot of pressure on the academic library staff. Unless the staff is kept upto- date on Internet skills he will face more pressure to work in such conditions. So training of staff has become a necessity in today's context

SURVEY ANALYSIS AND DISCUSSION

Kirpatrik on his study on the training of academic library staff on IT found that a high 52.9 percent of the staff responded that they received individual training by coworker. This means that the most preferred method of training as founded on this study was internal training. Matthews has also found on his investigation that internal training was the most popular choice (100 per cent) of the 15 libraries that were included in his exploratory study. External training was least preferred. The high cost involved in external training was the cited as the chief cause for discouragement. Another factor was time. The library mangers cited lack of manpower as the reason for not preferring sending staff to receive external training. Commonly used training methods include both formal and informal. Formal training or off – the – job training involves practical courses on specific topics in a developed programme for new conceptual, analytical and problem solving skills whereas, on – the – job training is a basic training method where a trainee is being shown the ways a job can be done through instruction and supervision.

Table. Internal vs External Training Preference for Internet Training of Staff.

Sl.No.	Name of the Institution	Internal Training	External Training
1.	Hem Barua Library (B. Borooah College)	Yes	No
2.	KK Handique Library (Gauhati University)	Yes	No
3.	Dr. BKB Library (Gauhati Commerce College)	Yes	No
4.	Central Library (IITG)	Yes	No
5.	IASST Library	Yes	No
6.	KC Das Commerce College	Yes	No
	Percentage (percent)	**5/6 (83)**	**1/6 (17)**

The present study was however concentrated on the internal and external training methods. The internal training methods are basically on the job training. The internal training methods for Internet training includes lectures, presentations, demonstrations, workshops, tutorials, free search/browsing time and handouts. In the process of the above investigation as tabulate in Table. 1 it is found that 5 out of the 6 academic libraries, *i.e.*, 83 per cent of the respondents identified in Guwahati have undertaken internal Internet training.

Only 1 out of the 6 libraries has opted for external training citing it as more effective than internal training. Regarding the methods adopted or likely to be adopted in Internet training as tabulated in Table, majority 5/6 (83 per cent) has not preferred lecture as a good training.

A co-worker or the librarian himself gives lecture on specific topics. Demonstrations were another method found suitable for Internet training as it was opted by 5 (83 per cent) out of the total libraries surveyed. Other methods found popular among the libraries includes free searching or giving browsing time (67 per cent) to staffs.

This method although very effective is also difficult because the staff has to give sufficient time which may not be practical in difficult circumstances like busy schedule, budget constrains. It was surprising to find in the study that none of the libraries had opted handouts for internet training of staff (0 per cent). Because of the nature of Internet, which changes on a daily basis, guidance documentation is difficult to provide, as it can very soon be out of date. But as founded by Matthews *et al.* handouts are very popular and staff are often anxious to have a document they can refer to when they are no longer in a situation where help is at hand.

Table. Internet Training Method Employed/to be Empoyed.

Sl. No.	Name of Library/Institutions	Lectures	Presentations	Demonstrations	Workshops	Tutorials	Free Search/Browsing	Handouts
1.	Hem Barua library (B. Borooah collage)	N	N	N	N	N	Y	N
2.	K K Handique Library (Gauhati University)	N	N	Y	N	N	N	N
3.	Dr. BKB Library (Gauhati Commerce College)	N	Y	Y	N	Y	Y	N
4.	Central Library (IITG)	Y	Y	Y	Y	N	Y	N
5.	IASST Library	N	N	Y	N	N	N	N
6.	KC Das Commerce College Library	N	N	Y	N	N	Y	N
	Percentage (%)	Y = (17) N = (83)	Y = (83) N = (67)	Y = (83) N = (17)	Y = (17) N = (83)	Y = (17) N = (83)	Y = (67) N = (33)	Y = (0) N = (100)

Note:

(N = No, Y = Yes)

Workshops were also sparsely selected as a training method as only 17 per cent opted for it. The common disadvantage cited included time and budget constraints. Only 1 out of the 6 libraries has opted for external training citing it as more effective than internal training. Majority of the libraries cited cost as the main. Since, such Internet training in specifically applicable in libraries are not conducted locally. Mangers are ill prepared to send some staff to take training outside. The contents of the Internet training did not very much among the six surveyed libraries as show in Table. The common contents included E-mail, WWW and browsers. Those libraries, *i.e.*, mainly the college libraries felt that training on accessing e- journals were unnecessary as none of them had e-journals in their library.

IIT- Guwahati, IASST and Gauhati University which has a sufficient collection of e- journals had answered that they had trained or likely to train their staff on e-journals. Many of the staffs that got Internet training had developed the skills to use Internet as a reference tool and as a communication tool such as Internet.

Assisting users in Internet was another skill developed by such training. But none of the libraries reported on the development of publishing skills as an outcome of the training. The common reason cited was that it was felt too sophisticated in the present context. Information on Internet training was not available to the staff readily.

Many of the respondents felt that remoteness of this part of the world as factor for this. Only two of the respondents, *viz.* IIT- Guwahati and K. C. Das Commerce College cited that such information are readily available to them. The most common problem cited by the respondents was that the staff was mostly technically unqualified for Internet.

This was especially in the case of the college libraries where mostly no technical persons worked in the library. However none of the libraries had done any evaluation on the training of the staff in Internet. Workload and time constraints were sited as the major reason for not undertaking such evaluations. On the future plans majority of the respondents showed willingness on their part to participate in Internet training. However their viewpoint was that some local leading institutions like Gauhati University, IIT Guwahati or the likes of National Informatics Centre (NIC) should organise such skill development Programmes where they are ready to participate.

FINDINGS

- Nearly all the libraries reported that they did not have a formal programme on Internet training as they felt such training was not needed in the present context.
- In majority of the libraries internal training was the most preferred.
- E-mail, WWW, browsers were the most common contents included in the training.
- Majority of the respondents said that information on Internet training were mostly unavailable to them.
- Majority felt that publishing skills on internet were not required for them.

- Majority felt that basic skills developed by such training included ability to use Internet as a reference and communication tool and also ability to assist users.
- Majority cited that having non-technical staff in library as the main problem in Internet training.
- Constant electric failure was another problem cited by the respondents in conducting Internet training.
- No formal evaluation was done in any of the surveyed libraries.
- On future plans majority of the respondents had shown the willingness for Internet training provided that some reputed institutions of this reason comes forward in giving guidance for such training.

SUGGESTIONS

- Internet training of the staff should be given due importance.
- Individual libraries should develop a formal Programme for giving Internet training to their taff.
- Librarians should explore all the options including external training courses on the Internet.
- There is strong need for some leading Institutions of the region to take initiative where the staffs of academic libraries can be sent at periodic intervals to update their skills on Internet.
- Such Programmes are taking place outside Assam as in DRTC, INFLIBNET centres, etc., but institutions are not willing to sent staff for such training due to financial and other constraints.

IMPACT OF INTERNET ON LIBRARY AND INFORMATION SERVICES

Perhaps no other recent innovation has impacted the library profession to such a great extent as Internet. Not only is our world becoming an interconnected global community, but this early use of the Internet has changed the fundamental roles, paradigms, and organisational culture of libraries and librarians as well, which created profound impact on LandIS by offering new modes of information delivery and a vast information source.

There is a continuing evolution of the roles and functions of libraries and librarians, which appears to parallel the growth of acceptance and use of the Internet by library professionals. The innovative use of Internet technologies enable us to reach both local and distant users much more easily and effectively than hither to possible.

Technologies such as e-mail and Web provides tremendous opportunities for library and Inf. Scientists to deliver the information to the desktops of our users. Web offers significant advantage by integrating different library and information services with a common user interface offered by Web browsers.

Realising the potentials, many libraries are rushing to getting the connectivity. The following listing will give an idea of which various functions of libraries may take advantage from Internet and Web technologies.

Acquisition:

- Correspondance with Book seller and Publisher.
- Reminders, Price verification
- Biblographic details and downloading of bib. records etc
- Ordering, billing
- Bookshops are on-line, *e.g.,* amazon.com

Classification:

- Network resources
  - — Available on the net
  - — Subscribed or free or trial basis
- Dewey Online
- Maths. Classification System
- Engineering Electronics Lib. Classification
- Search engines – such as yahoo use DDC.

Collection Development:

- Ownership vs Access
- Subscribe in print or e-form
- Subscribe in print as well as in e-form
- Pay-per-use
- Consortial approach

Cataloguing:

- Cataloguing of network resources
- Online Catalogues
- WorldCat (OCLC)
- WebOPAC – web sites
- MARC adds 856 field
- OCLC Scorpian project- MARC and AACR2
- Metadata standards - Dublin core

Circulation:

- Remote login
- Status check
- OPAC access
- Reminder to users
- User requests
- Direct borrowing
- ILL

Resource Sharing:

- Union Catalogue
  - — Access, adding, downloading

- Access to databases over networks
  - Ohionet, ILLINET, WLN, OCLC, BID (UK)
  - Full text journals access, etc.

Services:

- ILL
- Document Delivery Service, *e.g.,* Ariel
- Reference/ Inf. Services
- CAS
  - Recent additions,
  - Contents pages
- SDI
  - From library collection
  - Databases
  - Internet Sources
- OPAC
- Database access
  - Bibliographical
  - Full text
  - Many vendors and organisations are moving to Internet (web) access

Subject Lists/ Gateways:

- Internet Public Library
- *EEVL* – Engineering
- *SOSIG* – Social Science
- *OMNI*- Medical
- *ADAM* – Arts, Design, etc.

User Education:

- Through E-mail
- Through Web
- Setting Intranet.

Preservation and Storage:

- The Internet is also a medium for the preservation and storage of information. In past, libraries were seen as the main storage facility of information. As society becomes increasingly more digital and more information resides on the Internet, the focus on storage and preservation is shifting. For example, some academic libraries are now faced with the problem of whether or not to purchase serials that can be just as easily accessed on-line. Preservation of these same media also becomes an issue of economics, not the 'just in case' preservation ideology of the past paradigm. Co joined to the function preservation is the destruction of information. Because the Internet can be seen as a medium for preserving information, the process of destruction of information also is affected. As more and more information is created and stored on the Internet, the capacity to store this information is also decreasing.

RETRIEVAL OF INFORMATION

Directories, Search Engines, Meta Search Engines and Information Gateways/Virtual Libraries etc are widely used to retrieve relevant information from Internet.

Search Engines:

- They are also called Meta crawlers or multi search engines
- Do not crawl the web compiling their own searchable databases
- Search the databases of multiple sets of individual search engines simultaneously from a single site and using the same interface.
- They function as intermediary
- Present the results of their searches in two ways
  - — Single lists
  - — Multiple Lists.
- There are three types of meta search engines,
  - — Listing
  - — Options
  - — Automatic
- While you query, options less
- Cover all major search engines
- Do not return all results retrieved, they take only top ones from the list.
- They are very fast.
- Use them when you are in a hurry
- Helpful when you want to have quick overview on a subject and/or unique term.
- Use them when you are,
  - — Conducting a relatively simple search
  - — Not having any luck pulling up documents in your search.

RESOURCES AVAILABLE ON THE INTERNET

The advent of IT and other communication technologies changed all means of information services and sources. The Internet has given the world numerous easy-to-use and inexpensive research tools. Internet is changing the way we view information sources. Information bundled in World Wide Web in the form of structured and Non-structured sources create huge problem for professionals who are dealing with information. The shift in publication process takes place as individuals, institutions, publishers, professional associations, business houses and many others are publishing information on Internet.

Electronic publishing is considered as the speedy, accurate and effective way of communication among academia and research community, and becoming a Favourite idea among information professionals to experiment with. The library and information professionals have a vital role to play in organising the information and bridging the *information gap*. Internet has become a part of library environment today. Internet for reference work in the library is gaining popularity. It can be successfully utilised for providing short-range and long-range reference service because various primary and secondary sources of information are available online from many sites. As information professionals, we can arrange the sources on net as we come across, in a structured manner. These can be;

- E-journals,
- E-books,
- Standards,
- E-TDs,
- Preprints,
- Library catalogue,
- Bibliographical Tools,
- Share wares,
- Old books,
- News papers,
- Dictionaries,
- Magazines,
- Encyclopaedias,
- Databases,
- Directories,
- Films,
- Maps,
- Technical reports,
- Audio/Video,
- Proceedings,
- Patents,
- Web sites of Companies, Institutions, Organisations, Associations, etc.

Evaluation of Information Sources

When we access or retrieve something on the Web, we need to decide whether the information is useful, reliable, and appropriate for our purposes. The resources identified can also occasionally contain inaccurate and misleading information. The nature of the Internet and WWW makes it easy for almost anyone to create and disperse information.

People also have considerable freedom and variety in the formats with which they publish information on the Web. We have to double -check the facts before giving it to users. Here we need to use some general guidelines or criteria when evaluating information sources. We should ask the following questions about whatever information we found:

- Who is the author or Institution?
- How current is the information?
- Who is the audience?
- Is the content accurate and objective?
- What is the purpose of the information?
- How easy to use it?

More than that, we can consider coverage, presentation and arrangement of information in the sources to find out its value. The tremendous increase in online information sources made the searching difficult, where organising skill is required for library and information professionals. Libraries role is also enhanced where they will have to adapt to changing environment. The scope is only limited to the imagination of information professionals, where they have to acquire thorough understanding of changes in their profession. Willingness to take up the challenges in information resource management is the need of the hour for us.

WEB SITE FOR A LIBRARY

The roles of libraries and the Internet in providing information in the 21st century are firmly intertwined. It behooves any librarian working today to understand not only how to find things on the World Wide Web, but to have a basic understanding of how it works. Librarians will be called on to become information architects, to be able to create Web sites with clearly stated goals, that are aesthetically pleasing and filled with relevent content and functionality.

As more and more libraries set up comprehensive Web sites, there becomes an increasing demand for librarians who have an understanding of HTML, as well as other types of Internet programming skills such as javascript, SQL, CGI, ASP, and Cold Fusion. Librarians should know the principles of setting up an efficient information resource. As the Internet becomes more interactive, there is a push Towards making databases accessible online; the best example of this is the library card catalog. Other interactive options include e-mail and bulletin board service, and moving from CD-ROMs to online subscriptions.

A library Web site is not merely establishing a presence on the Internet. It can be a virtual addition to the existing library structure, reaching out to patrons around the clock and providing valuable information resources. Additionally, a library's Web site is an important source of information about the library. The library's Internet policies, special programming, and new materials can all be made viewable at any time from the Web site. Libraries, too, should be designing their own Web sites that serve as portals to interesting sites that have been reviewed and annotated by professional librarians. Librarians will continue to play an important role as information professionals in the Information Age, well into the 21st century.

MARKETING OF LIBRARY SERVICES

In recent years, libraries of all types from all countries have found it necessary to compete for both money and clients as major changes have occurred. The Internet brings a whole new dimension of competition that public, academic, and special libraries are facing daily. Whereas budget problems have been around for some time, the recent competition from the Internet can translate into fewer users, despite the fact that the Internet is also a crucial tool used by librarians for research and marketing.

Because of all of these existing challenges and intensifying changes at least a handful of libraries have turned to 'tried and true' business models for improved planning and development, and that they are employing marketing plans as one method for moving forward. As time goes on, libraries must think about marketing of their services and resources to achieve goals. It is important to clarify what marketing means in a library environment.

Marketing is not so much about 'selling' information products to researchers, as it is more about spreading the word about potentially useful new tools. It is also about keeping users informed about library activities and involving them in collection development. It is more about integrating new research tools into existing, effective research processes, and in some way enhancing researchers' work, rather than selling the tool to users as an end in itself. As librarians market new tools, they should know how the tools may offer clarity, and not simply contribute to noise for the users. Effective marketing can only occur when librarians understand, at least in a broad sense, what the scientists, professors, and graduate students are already doing to keep informed, and what their research projects are about.

RECRUITING ON THE INTERNET

Using the Internet is faster and cheaper than many traditional methods of recruiting. Jobs can be posted on Internet sites for a modest amount, remain there for periods of thirty or sixty days or more - at no additional cost - and are available twenty-four hours a day. Candidates can view detailed information about the job and the organisation and then respond electronically.

Most homes and workplaces are now using computerised equipment for communication; the Internet is rapidly becoming the method of choice for accessing and sharing information. First-time job seekers are now more likely to search web sites for job postings than to peruse newspapers, magazines and journals. The prevalence of eadvertising has made it easier. The Internet speeds up the hiring process in three basis stages:

- Faster posting of jobs.
  - The submission of information to the media house and its appearance in print disappears. On the internet, the advertisement appears immediately and can be kept alive for as long as the recruiter requires it.
- Faster applicant response.
  - Jobs posted on the Internet and requiring responses via the same medium receive responses on the same day.
- Faster processing of résumés.
  - An applicant sending a résumé electronically can immediately have the application processed, receive an acknowledgement, be screened electronically, and have details of the application and résumé despatched to several managers at the same time.

On-line recruiting also provides access to passive job seekers, that is, individuals who already have a job but would apply for what appears a better one that is advertised on the Internet. These job seekers may be of a better quality Since, they are not desperate for a job change as are the active job seekers who may be frustrated, disgruntled workers looking for a new position. Companies that are likely to advertise on-line usually have a Web site that allows potential candidates to learn about the company before deciding whether to apply, thus lowering the incidence time-wasting through the submission of unsuitable applications.

The Web site can be used as a tool to encourage potential job seekers to build an interest in joining the organisation. Job web sites offer unlimited space which can be used, by management, to sell the organisation. The site can then be used, not only to post vacancies, but also to publicise the organisation. That will allow candidates to become more familiar with the company, know what skills the company is looking for and get to know about its culture. Most importantly, the system will provide a proper path to securing quick responses to job openings.

On-line recruiting facilitates the decentralisation of the hiring function by making it possible for other groups in the organisation to take responsibility for part of the function:

- Some applicants still place great value on face-to-face interactions in the hiring process. Such applicants are likely to ignore jobs posted, impersonally, on-line.
- Companies are overwhelmed by the volume of résumés posted on the Internet. This can, in fact, lengthen the short-listing process. If the screening process is not well done, the quantity of applications/ résumés logged-on may be more of a hindrance to the process that an aid to selection.

Job seekers who demand confidentiality in the recruitment process may be reluctant to use the Internet as a job search mechanism.

For effectiveness in the use of the strategy of e-Recruiting, companies are advised to:

- Use specialised Job Sites that cater to specific industries; interested in joining the company;
- Take advantage of the fact that Internet job advertisements have no space limitations so recruiters can use longer job descriptions to fully describe the company, job requirements and working conditions offered;
- Use valid Search Engines that will sort candidates effectively, but will not discriminate against any persons or groups;
- Create attention-grabbing newspaper advertisements that prompt people to visit the company's Web site. They will then see all vacancies that are advertised;
- Encourage employees to e-mail job advertisements to friends;
- Design and implement a successful e-Recruitment strategy.

COLLEGE RECRUITMENT

College recruiting – sending an employer's representatives to college campuses to prescreen applicants and create an applicant pool from that college's graduating class – is an important source of management trainees, promotable candidates, and professional and technical employees. To get the best out of this hiring strategy, the organisation and its career opportunities must be made to stand out.

Human resource professionals are aware that few college students and potential graduates know where their careers will take them over the next fifteen to twenty years. Therefore many of the an opportunity for recruiters to select the potential employees with the personal, technical and professional competencies they require in their organisation. The personal competencies identified may include, *inter alia*, a positive work ethic, strong interpersonal skills, leadership capacity and an ability to function well in a work team.

The opportunity to discuss a student's current strengths and potential future value to an organisation cannot be replicated in any other setting. Two major advantages of this strategy are the cost (which is higher than word-of-mouth recruiting but lower than advertising in the media or using an employment agency), and the convenience (Since, many candidates can be interviewed in a short time in the same location with space and administrative support provided by the college itself). Unfortunately, suitable candidates become available only at certain times of the year, which may not always suit the needs of the hiring organisation.

Another major disadvantage of college recruiting is the lack of experience and the inflated expectations of new graduates and the cost of hiring graduates for entry-level positions that may not require a college degree. To make college recruiting effective, the recruiting organisation must first determine how many and which schools should be targeted. It may prove cost-effective to do intensive recruiting in a few, carefully-selected institutions, establishing a presence and building the organisation's reputation among students and faculty.

Timely and frequent dissemination of literature, the offer of internships and the award of prises for academic and/or social prowess help to advertise the organisation as a preferred place of employment. Subsequent invitations to the organisation's offices, made to students identified as potential employees, may serve to solidify the firm's image. Public Service organisations are usually unable to compete financially with their Private Sector counterparts and are therefore less likely to pay competitive salaries.

However, most public service agencies provide their employees with a wealth and range of experiences that are available nowhere else. It is for that reason that many college graduates use the Public Service as an employer of first resort to gain the experiences that will make them marketable in the short term.

The strategies may not work as smoothly for public service recruiters, Since, the laws that govern their organisations' recruitment practices may be more stringent than those that apply in private sector companies. There may also be questions about the legality of the on-line application form. If this strategy were to be employed, public service recruiters must first decide on the criteria that should guide the process. The Public Service is seldom immediately seen as an attractive employer, mainly because salaries are uncompetitive.

Except for those students who have a commitment to public service, the top ten per cent of college graduates will select the Private Sector as the employer of choice, partly because of the prestige value but primarily because of the remuneration package and because the recruiters may have been more successful in marketing their company. Therefore, it is understood that many of the graduates who enter the Public Service will stay for a short time and either return to school or proceed to another sector once they have acquired the requisite skills and experience that make them marketable. Recruitment and retention strategies in the Public Service must, therefore, reflect this reality and efforts made to get the most out of college graduates before they move on; conversely, the organisation may need to plan to recruit those students whose academic records suggest that they will remain in an organisation that pays less.

Retention strategies will focus on ensuring opportunities for intense training and development for skill enhancement and personal satisfaction. College recruitment also offers opportunities for internships. These programmes may provide the organisations with quality employees at low cost per hire. Some interns are hired at low cost (perhaps minimum wage) and are offered work experience.

Interns are able to have business skills, check out potential employers, and learn more about employers' likes and dislikes before making final career choices. Some of the better interns are recruited after graduation. College recruitment is relatively expensive and time consuming for the recruiting company. The process involves screening the candidate, that is, determining whether he/she is worthy of further consideration and marketing the company as a preferred place of employment. An alternate strategy for college recruitment is the career planning workshop.

These activities are usually (but not exclusively) associated with adolescent school leavers. They do not immediately produce ready candidates for the job market but provide the opportunity for an organisation to present itself as an employer worthy of consideration. Co-ordinators of career planning workshops co-opt professionals and organisations to present career options to potential school leavers in a controlled setting so as to lay out the range of possibilities to young job seekers. Career planning workshops are used mainly as information-giving tools which the school leaver can use to make informed career choices. Some organisations use the workshops as a base for internships.

Job Fairs

The concept of a job fair is to bring those interested in finding a job into those companies who are searching for applicants. Job fairs are open fora at which employers can exhibit the best their companies have to offer so that job seekers can make informed choices. They are considered one of the most effective ways for job seekers to land jobs. At the job fair, employers have a large pool of candidates on which to draw, while job seekers have the opportunity to shop around for dozens – sometimes hundreds – of employers, all in one place.

Notwithstanding the fact that the atmosphere at the fair is more relaxed than at an interview, employers are still on the look out for qualified, potential employees who have interest, dedication and initiative.

Maintaining Fairness/Equity in the Recruitment Process

It is often difficult to ensure and maintain fairness/equity in the recruitment process although, in every jurisdiction, there are laws that protect individuals and vulnerable groups from the negative impact of discriminatory practices. Where necessary, systems, detailed procedures and processes exist or must be established to minimise discrimination.

Each country designates/identifies a group or groups for special notice; women, visible minorities and the disabled are usual targets. The Government of Canada, in articulating its "Employment Equity Act and Regulations", identified four designated groups as employment equity targets: women, Aboriginal people, members of visible minority groups, persons with disabilities.

In the legislation, managers' responsibilities for employment equity are stated as:

- Ensuring effective overall performance and continuous progress of the employment equity goals within the operation;
- Achieving, fostering and maintaining a representative workforce;
- Showing leadership in employment equity and demonstrating commitment to it by ensuring that discrimination and stereotyping are not tolerated; and
- Informing and educating employees in the organisation about employment equity and diversity.

The Australian Public Service Commission, in ensuring that there were no infringements against individuals rights, issued general guidelines on workplace diversity, some of which related to recruitment:

- Integrate workplace diversity with the agency's goals and business.
- Reflect agency workplace diversity objectives in workplace agreements and certified agreements.
- Integrate workplace diversity principles into human resources policies and practices.
- Include implementation of workplace diversity objectives in the corporate plan, business plan and client service charters.
- Ensure information about employment opportunities is available in accessible formats.
- Review recruitment and selection processes to ensure that current and potential employees are not discriminated against.

Gather information on demographics. It is the goal of every jurisdiction to minimise or eliminate any instance of obvious discrimination against individuals or groups. In discussing policies on employment equity, scholor explains: "Employment equity policies and Programmes are about fairness in the workplace, not about reverse discrimination. Fairness is achieved when no one is denied employment opportunity and no one benefits for reasons unrelated to ability. Employment equity Programmes attempt to change the composition of the Workforce so that employees better reflect the community. The facts (both historical and current) show that members of the four designated groups face discrimination, enjoy less access to educational Programmes and training, and are often denied employment and promotions even when they have the necessary skills and experience." The University's policies give special attention, *inter alia*, to the existence of systemic barriers and instances of intentional discrimination in the process of recruitment. Service Commissions were enshrined in the Independence Constitutions of the territories of the Commonwealth Caribbean and given *inter alia*, the power to recruit/appoint persons into the Public Service and, in so doing, reduce the influence of politicians on the staffing process.

In order to discharge their authority for making appointments, the Commissions have influenced the development of legislation and regulations that circumscribe the practice of recruitment, primarily to ensure that no discrimination attends the exercise. To this end, entry into the Public Service follows the procedures of:

- Application on prescribed forms;
- Selection on the basis of seniority of application; application of age limits for entry into certain defined grades/classes; the use of written examinations and/or competitive interviews as the basis for permanent appointment to certain grades/classes.

The rules established by the Commissions enforce compliance in an attempt to minimise or eliminate the possibility of bias in staffing on the basis of race/ethnicity, creed, age, social status or physical disability.

PROVISION OF TECHNICAL SUPPORT AND TRAINING FOR LIBRARY STAFF

Library networks are complex technical entities that support many users and applications; it is unreasonable to expect local library staff, especially those in smaller or rural libraries, to provide comprehensive technical support for the network. All the networks profiled here provide members with some level of technical support and training in how to solve technical problems.

The level of support ranges from handling all network problems to training local librarians in problem solving. Two of the networks—PLAN and Badger Net—continuously monitor network traffic and respond with solutions when they are needed. The case studies demonstrate several innovative approaches to supporting large networks:

- In a centralised model, OPLIN manages a support center that offers members a first line of defence for network troubleshooting.
- MSLN employs one circuit rider whose responsibilities include focusing on resource poor libraries with the most serious problems and developing technical skills among local library staff.
- SLN has network support staff in offices throughout the state and, like MSLN, works to develop the technical skills of library staff.
- In Wisconsin, regional library systems serve as the first point of contact to assist with troubleshooting and the installation of new equipment and software.
- In California, PLS meets the need for network-level support only; its member libraries all have technical support staff on site.

ROLE FOR LIBRARY REPRESENTATIVES IN NETWORK GOVERNANCE

The case study networks have widely varying governance and management structures. For example:

- The Maine Public Utilities Commission (MPUC) governs MSLN.
- Wisconsin's Department of Administration manages BadgerNet.
- The West Virginia Library Commission administers SLN.

All of these networks are dependent on the network's information technology (IT) staff for ensuring the day-to-day management of network operations. But just as there are differences in network management (*e.g.,* some may be outsourced), there are also differences in overall network governance and how much input the library community has to make decisions or to set network policy.

For example, the OPLIN governing board in Ohio consists solely of member library representatives. Wisconsin's BadgerNet Advisory Council includes representatives of all network users including libraries, K-12 schools, higher education and state government. The Advisory Council advises the state Administration Department in areas like member bandwidth needs and planning for the next generation network. California's PLS allows the technical staff of member libraries to be involved with network issues through a committee structure.

MULTIPLE FUNDING SOURCES

The networks profiled here rely on various revenue streams, such as grant funds, telecommunications settlement funds, universal service funds, state general funds, and local library funding. The five networks were established in economically favourable times, when state and other funds were more readily available for large capital projects than is the case today.

Nevertheless, all the networks face the challenge of securing ongoing funding. Even Maine, which has the most stable source of funding (state and federal universal service funds), struggles with balancing the need for increased network services with limited funding resources. The major sources of funding for the statewide networks have historically been state tax funds and universal service funds (both the federal E-rate programme and state-based programmes).

During the last year, however, tax revenues have decreased sharply in almost every state, and both OPLIN and SLN were in danger of losing significant state funding. California's PLS, funded primarily by member fees derived from local property taxes, has yet to see any significant reductions as assessments of property lag at least one year behind tax collections. Federal universal service funds are relatively stable. However, the total of applications for discounts is approaching fund availability, absent any policy intervention. Additionally, some organisations find the requirements for obtaining such funds to be onerous or contrary to their policies.

INVOLVEMENT OF THE STATE LIBRARY

One common characteristic of the statewide networks is the active involvement of the State Library:

- The State Library of Ohio has strong influence over OPLIN operations and development as a result of its authority to appoint all of the network's board members.

- The State Library in West Virginia operates SLN.
- In Wisconsin, the State Library influences BadgerNet planning and operations through its seat on the BadgerNet Council.

Although MSLN's governing board is the Maine Public Utilities Commission (MPUC), the state librarian is responsible for suggesting policy and for representing the interests of libraries before the MPUC. Furthermore, the Maine State Library has staff members responsible for assessing the needs of MSLN members and for preparing an annual report that outlines the network's needs and presents an annual budget request.

9

Managing Staff Development

There can be no doubt that the need for professional development, continuing education, or workplace learning in regard to technology is vital for today's libraries. Never before have the profession's tools undergone such extreme and rapid transformations, and these transformations are not about to cease, as illustrated in the various thesis compiled in Core *Technology Competencies for Librarians and Library Staff*.

It is, therefore, incumbent upon library administration to develop, implement, encourage, and support policies on staff competency and development. It is, also, necessary for both professional librarians and paraprofessionals to—at the very least— be proficient in the current trends of technology, if not embracing the changes by keeping pace with them. In short, with a little innovative leadership, learning options are endless, as well as accessible, user-friendly, and exciting.

HOW DO MANAGERS MANAGE?

The studies by researchers showed that from street gang leaders to the President of the United States, managers do not spend their time planning, organizing, coordinating, and controlling as the French industrialist, Henri Fayol said they did in 1916 and as most writers on management have continued to repeat ever since. They are not like the orchestra leader who directs the component parts of his organization with ease and precision. Instead, they spend their time reacting to crises, seizing special opportunities, attending meetings, negotiating, talking on the telephone, cultivating interpersonal and political relationships, gathering and disseminating information, and fulfilling a variety of ceremonial functions. Researcher says:

- I was struck during my study by the fact that the executives I was observing—all very competent by any standard—are fundamentally indistinguishable from their counterparts of a hundred years ago (or a thousand years ago. for that matter). The information they need differs, but they seek it in the same way—by word of mouth. Their decisions concern modem technology, but the procedures they use to make them are the same as the procedures of the 19th Century manager. Even the computer, so important for the specialized work of the organization, has apparently had no influence on the work procedures of general managers. In fact, the manager is in a kind of loop, with increasingly heavy work pressures but no aid forthcoming from management science.

The Mintzberg view is by no means unique. There is a growing number of management scholars who are questioning the conventional view of management and what managers do. In a critical review of *On Management*, a book of articles selected from 25 years of the *Harvard Business Review*, Albert Shapero, a management professor at the University of Texas, strikes a similar note:

- The term "management" conjures up images of control, rationality, systematics; but studies of what managers actually do depict behaviours and situations that are chaotic, unplanned, and charged with improvisation. The Managerial life at every level is reflexive—responding to calls, memos, personnel problems, fire drills, budget meetings, and personnel reviews. Occasionally, however, we find at managerial levels individuals who go 24 hours without being interrupted by meetings or phone calls. They are the longrange planners, the people in O.R., E.D.P., financial or market planning, or market research. Management is really for them. The bulk of the articles in *On Management* are concerned with ideas from the world of the staff functionary.

ARE MANAGEMENT SYSTEMS REALLY USED?

What about the claims of widespread use of new scientific management systems and techniques? Is it really true that managers in business, government, and other institutions are using them extensively while we library administrators are lagging far behind? Let's first look at what a few of the management experts say about the use of these systems in general, and then we will look at their use in libraries. William R, Dill, dean of the Graduate School of Business Administration at New York University, makes this sober assessment:

- For all the progress we have made in developing good approaches to planning, forecasting, budgeting, and control, and for all the enthusiasm we in schools of management have helped to build for these approaches, their use has been fitful and sporadic, even in the most analytically sophisticated and goal-oriented institutions. In corporations that are pointed out as models for what can be accomplished. the outputs of planning, budgeting, and modeling staffs are often quietly ignored by operating people when times are good: these outputs often seem irrelevant in times of sudden challenge or change. Analysis and planning are still far from foolproof ways to anticipate change and potential crises.

Aaron Wildavsky, dean of the Graduate School of Public Policy at the University of California, Berkeley, has written a number of articles in which he argues convincingly, citing evidence and authorities, that the major modern information systems like PERT, MBO, PPBS, Social Indicators, and Zero Based Budgeting have not worked and cannot work. About PERT (Programme Evaluation Review Technique), he says that: "the few studies that exist suggest that outside of construction, where one activity tends to follow another, PERT is rarely successful."

On MBO (Management by Objectives), he says: "The trouble with MBO is that the attempt to formalize procedures for choosing objectives without considering organizational dynamics leads to the opposite of what was intended—had management, irrational choice, and ineffective decision-making." "The main product of MBO, as experience in the United States federal government suggests, is, literally, a series of objectives. Aside from the unnecessary paper work, such exercises are self defeating because they become mechanisms for avoiding rather than making choices. Long lists of objectives are useless because rarely do resources remain beyond the first few."

On PPBS, Wildavsky is equally harsh. He says that "Programme budgeting does not work anywhere in the world it has been tried," and that "no one knows how to do programme budgeting." His assessments of Social Indicators and Zero Based Budgeting are in a similar vein.

These realistic assessments that we are getting from authorities like Mintzberg, Shapero, Dill. Wildavsky, and others should serve to remind us to maintain a healthy skepticism whenever we read about the effectiveness and widespread use of new management systems and techniques. We librarians should guard against the tendency we have to look for panaceas and to accept uncritically the claims and promises made on behalf of each new management theory or system that appears.

Consider the minimal impact on libraries as compared with the initial promise, for example, of PPBS, Operations Research, MBO, and even Participative Management. To the best of my knowledge, PPBS has not been successfully implemented in a single library and I doubt that it ever will be. Interest in it is rapidly waning.

The practical application of Operations Research in libraries has been extremely limited to date. One of the earliest and best known economic analyses of library decision making was done in the MIT Libraries in 1969. The report of that study came to this sobering conclusion: "Although helpful, an economic analysis of a university (or public) library is insufficient because libraries operate as political systems and thus improving libraries requires political analysis." In an excellent article on library decision making, Jeffrey Raffel, an economist and co-author of the MIT study begins by saying that "in general, the more important the decision, the less beneficial a cost-benefit analysis is to library decision makers," and concludes by saying that "it is time that we all recognized the politics of libraries and acted accordingly."

In a classic paper on Management by Objectives in academic libraries, James Michalko, after a thorough, critical review of the literature, recommends against the use of MBO in libraries on the grounds that it is a limited approach which is costly and difficult to implement and which yields uncertain results.

Participative management is another "new" management technique that has been particularly oversold in the last decade. In fact, it is considered by many librarians to be the perfect management system. Good management has always included consultation and participation, it is just the name, the faddishness, and some of the formal structures that are new. When used properly and honestly, participative management is a useful process at all levels, and not just by top managers on major decisions as is sometimes assumed. It is essential that there be appropriate consultation and participation of interested and competent staff members on important decisions affecting them. But participative management will not bring on the management millennium in libraries.

Participative management is not decision making by committee or by staff plebiscite. Good management requires that when all the facts have been gathered and analyzed and all the advice is in, the appropriate administrator has to make the decision and take responsibility for it. Knowing when and how to seek and take advantage of consultative advice and prior approval of decisions where appropriate is one of the most important managerial skills. Decisions should be made at the lowest competent level. The library's critical strategy decisions involve a world outside the library and must usually be made by the director and his chief associates. Staff committees can give good advice on such matters, but they simply do not have the information, the knowledge, or the perspective required to make those decisions—and they cannot take responsibility for the results.

One extreme form of participative management, the collegial or faculty system of governance, was developed for academic departments: it works badly there and worse or not at all in libraries. Where it appears to work, it is because those involved have tacitly made concessions to traditional hierarchical systems and the demands of the environment while preserving the collegial form. A library is not an academic department, it is a service organization and should be so administered. A librarian by any other name is still a librarian and it is time for mature acceptance of that fact. Perhaps the reason that participative management has been embraced so enthusiastically and uncritically by librarians in recent years is not because of its management benefits, but because it appears to be the model that best justifies faculty status.

It is assumed that because faculty members participate in a collegial academic decision-making process, that model is the appropriate one to use in libraries—if librarians are to achieve faculty status. Much of the library-based management literature since 1970 is self-serving and reflects a direct or indirect preoccupation with matters of staff status and benefits frequently hidden behind arguments for participative management. It is time that we recognized this natural bias and took steps to overcome it by giving more attention and weight to the more objective management literature from outside the library field.

Two recent articles on participative management in libraries, one by James Govan and the other by Dennis Dickenson, give encouraging evidence that the library profession is beginning to take a more realistic and balanced view of the advantages and limitations of participative management and collegial governance. Govan reminds us that:

> Librarians cannot afford to degrade services nor alienate their users in an effort, however enlightened or well-in-mentioned to make their jobs more challenging and satisfying. Participation and consultation cost time and money and often, like faculty deliberations, produce rather conservative results. In this connection, it is useful to remember Maslow's belief that Theory Y is possible only in periods of affluence. It is also healthy to recall Drucker's statement that service institutions do not operate for the people who work in them.

In his perceptive article, Dickenson tries to provide "an antidote for some of the more extreme and sometimes naive interpretations of participative management that appear from time to time in library literature."

Peter Drucker summed up an important truth about management when he said in response to an interviewer's question about the efficacy of new management techniques: "The young people today expect to see business run by theory, knowledge, concepts, and planning. But then they find it is run like the rest of the world—by experience and expediency, by who you know, and by the hydrostatic pressure in your bladder."

This is not just the way business is run, it is the way libraries are run as well. And it is the way they will continue to be run despite the current rhetoric about the managerial revolution that is being ushered in by the use of new quantitative and psychological management systems and theories. Why? Because a library operates in a political environment and nearly all the really important decisions that are made at the highest levels have an overriding political component. They are rarely the product of cost benefit analysis or Operations Research where the various factors are weighed and compared and the "best" or most cost-effective course is chosen. These management techniques can be useful sometimes to implement a programme or a project in the most effective manner after the political decision to proceed has been made. They can also be useful in providing a rationale to support some essentially political decision that is being proposed or advocated, or to impress higher authorities or constituents with the competence of the managers and the rationality of their decision making process. Management systems, particularly PPBS, ZBB, and PERT are used in government and military bureaucracies largely because they are mandated by law or regulation.

In the library world, as in education, business, and government, few major programme decisions are made solely or even largely on the basis of careful studies of needs and costs. Consider, for example, decisions to build a new library building, to open a new departmental or branch library, to achieve excellence in some special subject discipline, or to embark on a major automation programme. These programme decisions are usually the result of an initiative or vision by an imaginative and powerful person, perhaps a library director a dean, a president, a mayor, or other official. They are political, emotional, or even personal decisions—justified, rationalized, and perhaps implemented with the assistance of various kinds of analyses and studies, but seldom derived from them.

It is important that librarians understand how and why these really critical decisions are made so that they will not be disillusioned or discouraged when they discover that the "best." the most efficient, or the least expensive solution frequently loses out to the one that is the most politically expedient or attractive.

THE QUANTITATIVE APPROACH

Scholars think it is important to make a distinction between the claims made on behalf of complex quantitative management systems such as Operations Research and Cost-Benefit Analysis, and the collection and analysis of quantitative data in libraries to assist in rational decision making. Scholar is questioning the validity and usefulness of these complex systems, but scholar is not questioning the need for and use of quantitative studies for measuring and evaluating library services. Quite the contrary, we need to know more about libraries, their resources, and how they are actually used. We have relied historically upon input data, *e.g.*, the number of books acquired, the number of serials subscribed to, the number of books circulated, the dollars spent, etc. The qualitative characteristics of these data are dubious; we desperately need reliable measures of library effectiveness.

Following the pioneering work by Fremont Rider in 1940 on the growth of research libraries, there has been an increasing number of extremely valuable quantitative studies such as those by Fussier, Lancaster, Buckland. and other works of solid quality.

The findings of such studies provide the theoretical foundations and practical knowledge that working library managers need to draw on to help them think clearly and creatively about library management and to make sound decisions based on valid data. This is especially true in this time of transition when the conventional wisdom of our profession will not suffice to see us through.

As one of the library managers for whose benefit and use such studies are presumably made, researcher thanks the authors and urge them on to greater productivity and precision. Researcher also urge them to try to keep their studies as simple as possible and to summarize their findings in readable English.

Unfortunately, a good deal of the quantitative research that is done in the library field is unintelligible, irrelevant, or too complicated and theoretical for any practical use in libraries. Much of it is written in the language of higher mathematics which is incomprehensible to most managers. This is particularly true of studies that are made by academics outside the library field such as statisticians, economists, psychologists. Operations Research people, etc. Their goal is not necessarily to do studies that are useful, but to demonstrate their mathematical prowess, to test theories and methodologies, to get published, and to award doctoral degrees to deserving graduate students. They select the library as their laboratory because it is convenient and because they think it is virgin territory ready for easy exploitation. They are more interested in the process than in the results.

The most useful library research is done by librarians or others with a serious long-term interest and involvement in libraries who work with librarians in a spirit of genuine collaboration. They are trying to make an impact. It is the difference between a class assignment and the real thing, between war games and war.

A notable exception to this criticism of academics is the landmark work by William J. Baumol and Matityahu Marcus, Economics of Academic Libraries. These two economists went to unusual lengths to explain their statistical methods and to summarize their conclusions with refreshing brevity and clarity. As a consequence, their work is widely read and frequently cited.

Management scientists and other quantitatively oriented researchers frequently wonder why the results of quantitative research studies are not used more by practicing library managers in the decision making process. One reason is that the mathematics and the methodologies required are far too complex and difficult for operating managers to learn and apply in their busy work environments. Few senior library administrators have the kind of staff support needed to successfully carry out complex analyses. Another and equally important reason is that the quantitative approach does not and cannot take into sufficient account the complex of political, organizational, and psychological factors that characterize the real work where people are more potent than numbers or logic.

The quality of many decisions could be significantly improved if we had more and better data, but many of the more important decisions have a relatively small quantitative component. As a library director, I seldom have a critical need for more quantitative data than are available from regularly kept statistics or by having someone make a special and usually simple survey and analysis of the problem. When the data are simply not available or too difficult to assemble, researcher can usually find a satisfactory way to manage without them. My real problem has nearly always been to correctly assess the political rather than the economic or quantitative factors. It is fairly easy to determine the most cost-effective course of action with or without detailed data. It is much harder to map out and implement a successful strategy for achieving it, to assess how the various persons and groups affected will perceive the manager's intentions, and how they will react to the decision. Someone said that quantification is not synonymous with management. Finding the best or most cost-effective course of action is not the same as getting it accepted. Sometimes the quality of a decision is critical, other times, it is acceptance.

Effective decision-making processes in large academic and public libraries involve complex sets of policies, procedures, and problems which require a variety of different kinds of information and approaches. Some decisions will be authoritarian, some will be collegial, some will be made by committees, and some will be made by combinations of the above. Library directors are not all-knowing, nor are the collective judgemnts of library faculties and committees infallible. Different situations call for different approaches. There are no simple formulas and no easy answers.

The new management systems that we have been discussing in this article divide into two general categories. There are quantitative systems such as Operations Research, PPBS, and ZBB, and psychological or behavioural systems such as Theory Y (and its variants) and MBO. In each system, there are a number of concepts, ideas, tools, and techniques that have validity and can be used to advantage by library managers, but as comprehensive systems they are all far too theoretical, complex, and simplistic to be applied successfully by ordinary managers in the day-to-day work environment. Few managers have the time or the specialized knowledge and skills required to make these systems work, and those that do are probably astute enough to manage as well or better without them. In the hands of amateurs—and this is most of us— the quantitative systems frequently produce misleading and wrong solutions, while the psychological or behavioural systems can lead to the manipulation and misuse of people. The real danger with both kinds of management systems is that they offer mechanistic formulas for dealing with complex realities and keep us from thinking about and solving our management problems in practical, realistic, and common sense ways.

Despite the many claims to the contrary, management is not yet a science. It is still an art, but is very much an art that can and should be mastered and practiced by librarians.

BARRIERS TO LEARNING

The "graying" of today's library is perhaps the most cited obstacle for staff development in technology. Long and Applegate, for instance, provide statistical data that reveals the willingness to learn of library staff according to their generation. Many professional librarians who received their degrees prior to 1995, or before the study of computers in Library Science programmes in the United States, understand the importance of keeping up with technology, yet a surprisingly large percentage of support staff is unwilling to adapt to the technical changes or to explore the possibilities that new technology brings.

Time constraints are another barrier to staff development. Workers who are given the time to develop skills are more apt to do so. However, many employees say there is little time to complete their usual tasks, much less learn new skills, regardless of whether employers allow the time for it. One thing is clear and that is that management needs to understand their employee's learning needs, as a number of investigations note the lack of managerial support in staff development. In fact, even professionals must often be self-motivated and seek out learning opportunities on their own.

E-LEARNING, WEBINARS, AND LEARNING 2.0

E-Learning, or learning delivered through electronic tools, is clearly the most popular form of staff development today. Both professionals and paraprofessionals may choose from a myriad of sources for such learning. Among the many options are webinars from WebJunction, OCLC, EbscoHost, and Gale Cengage Learning, to name a few. However, Learning 2.0 has not only gained considerable attention, but it has also been implemented, studied, and documented, thereby, raising its stature and effectiveness.

Developed by Helen Blowers and based on Web 2.0 technology, Learning 2.0 is an incentive-based model programme for training library staff in new technologies. Students, who are self-directed, are asked to complete "23 Things," or online interactive projects on, for example, RSS feeds, flickr, wikis, podcasts, and LibraryThing. Kingsley and Jensen's paper on Learning 2.0's implementation at the University of Alaska Fairbanks Rasmuson Library stands as the most comprehensive study to date of the freely shared model, illustrating the programmes success rate and offering some concluding recommendations, such as making staff development mandatory.

ADMINISTRATION AND STAFF DEVELOPMENT

Not only are the tools with which library staff work changing, but so, too, are the philosophies and practices of management, especially in regard to staff competency and development. Mosley and Kaspar describe the challenges of hiring and retaining competent employees that can meet the ever-changing demands of library service. They suggest that management needs to look to the future by reconsidering job descriptions and job postings by avoiding the use of traditional library wording.

Management also must consider incentives when encouraging staff development. Incentives, such as the MP3s, PDAs, and laptops offered by Blower's pilot Learning 2.0 programme at the Public Library of Charlotte and Mecklenburg County, are not always possible, especially in the current economy. However, there are other methods of motivation. For instance, the University of Arizona Library restructured their monetary compensation, or wage, plans, which were based upon a traditional hierarchical scale. Their innovative and team-based "pay-for-skill" programme rewards employees for developing advanced capabilities, along with the willingness to learn and take on more responsibility.

ACADEMIC AND RESEARCH LIBRARIES

The application of computing to library work in India has a history of at least three decades because since the time the computer entered premier academic institutions and selected R and D facilities, it has been explored for improving information processing and management routines. *Information technology* (IT) enriched library services arrived initially for *science and technology* (SandT) information handling and for the special libraries attached to *research and development* (RandD) centres and academic libraries in higher education institutions.

In comparison to other libraries, academic and research libraries have better infrastructure and skilled manpower in greater numbers, making them able to offer information services comparable to advanced countries. Like qualified teaching and research personnel and well-equipped laboratories, the right information service is another vital element in the trinity which completes a fruitful academic or research environment.

MARKET-DRIVEN COLLABORATION

Academic and research libraries, especially in developing countries, are passing through a very challenging phase in their existence due to unfriendly trends in the emerging information market. On the one hand, these libraries are still left with many of the old problems such as poor budgetary support and weak infrastructure, as well as staff in fewer numbers and often with less expertise.

But the new information marketing techniques, like the possibilities of delivering and accessing electronic information in diverse channels, force these libraries to be very vigilant and cautious in their approach towards information acquisition and services. Libraries and professionals in India were quick to understand the emerging information environment was forcing their users to depend largely on those resources, which are becoming more expensive day by day due to the rise in production costs, fall in subscriptions and inflationary trends of Indian currency.

When individual libraries found that alone they are not in a position to satisfy the information requirements of their clients, they formulated various collaborative arrangements with other libraries such as,

- *Interlibrary loan* (ILL) services,
- *Document delivery services* (DDS),
- Resource-sharing, and
- Consortia-based subscriptions.

PRESENT PRACTICES AND EMERGING GOALS

The special libraries attached to research and higher education were lucky enough to garner resources to automate their in-house routine operations and for hosting online public access catalogues (OPACs); some of them also set up facilities to search electronic databases. A few of them evolved the desired infrastructure for Internet surfing, for hosting of full-text database access, and for setting up digital libraries. The major advantage of the progress in computerization is a considerable increase in the amount of information available online. We have experienced that at the start of computer applications only the surrogates (metadata) existed online, but some full-text content has been made accessible online in recent years.

These libraries are experiencing the virtues of electronic information in different forms such as e-journals, e-books, bibliographic/full-text electronic databases on CD-ROMs and through Web access. Due to publishers' 'electronic plus' policies, libraries are able to access electronic versions of printed sources such as journals either for free or by paying an additional fee. However the goal these libraries in specialized research and academic centres should have set for themselves is to enhance their information facilities to fully functional digital libraries, comparable with similar facilities in the developed countries.

CULTURES AND CONFLICTS FACED BY LIBRARIES

The fixed roles suggested by Levy for researchers, publishers and libraries are either overlapping or changing in the electronic scene. There are cases where an author or a library is acting as electronic publisher, and there are publishers providing a wide variety of information packages beyond the contents of printed journals.

The real question is: has the library really lost ground in the emerging information scene? Even the critics will not say so. The concerns expressed are only to revitalize the professional skills of librarians, rejuvenate the style of working and reorient the library towards its rightful place in effective dissemination of information. Maybe the common feeling that the library is a central place in the institution visited everyday by large numbers of users, like any public utility, has lost some ground in the electronic scene. Nonetheless, apart the continuing provision of information services for print sources, the electronic revolution has reaffirmed the library more as an information service and access centre than as an information storehouse.

TECHNOLOGY ADVANCES

The major technology breakthroughs in the context of libraries include:

- Advent of printing press and mass production of printed documents enabled democratization of information. Libraries had a major role in the print era, as no one can own a large number of books on a particular subject whereas libraries by their very purpose concentrated on doing so.
- Microforms helped to preserve less used information in a compact space and as a smoother delivery option for voluminous sources. Libraries had their unchallenged role even in the microform era as the special purpose readers for microfilms and microfiche were costly and exclusively housed in the library.
- The economical and affordable copying technology revolutionized the concept of information use as it spearheaded the trend of owning copies of relevant portions of library resources. The copying technology freed the user from sitting in the library for long duration for reading, since one can simply get a copy quickly and leave.
- Computing is the biggest technology revolution so far, as it is a major enabler in the information dissemination chain; also it is not a stand-alone technology unlike earlier technologies and can be networked and integrated with a whole lot of other devices and technologies. It not only revolutionized the production of books and microforms but also brought the arrival of online and CD-ROM databases, electronic information resources, Internet and the digital revolution.

PRODUCTS AND SERVICES

Adapting IT for library applications is an ongoing process, right from procuring or developing IT enabled information products through computer aided processing and management to delivering IT-enriched services. Library professionals in India are already exposed to the different offshoots of IT for library organization and information services.

LIBRARY AUTOMATION PACKAGES

The availability of a wide variety of library automation software to suit the varied needs of libraries themselves is a reflection of the progress libraries have made in automating the operations of procuring, processing and providing information sources. Procurement is the end of the story for many other software/databases used in a library, whereas library automation systems will open a floodgate of issues. What the vendor provides is a structure to build information concerning the collection and users, to conduct various aspects of organizing the collection and offering information services.

Thus software needs to be evaluated for its suitability for the target library before purchase. This may include case studies from other libraries using the software, evaluation of hardware and operating system required, computer awareness among staff and users, network as well as computer infrastructure in the institution, and above all estimation of cost and charges for after-sales support. Using suitable software for library automation will significantly reduce manual operations and enable professionals to dedicate more time for professional jobs.

CD-ROM AND ELECTRONIC DATABASES

Due to the poor communication infrastructure prevalent in India and to the immense costs involved, online database services were used only by few institutions. The distribution of the same content of online data repositories subsequently in CD-ROMs made it affordable to a larger number of institutions. While the library automation package gave search-and access facility to information sources present in the local collection, CD-ROM databases attempted consolidated access irrespective of holdings to the bibliographic data of publications in a discipline. CD-ROM databases have also freed library professionals from conducting searches and allowed the end user to conduct the searches. CD-ROM is so common nowadays that a library holds a good number of them not only for bibliographic, numeric and full-text databases, but also those received along with printed books and other reference sources. Managing and serving these high capacity discs was a problem earlier due to the stand-alone software required, whereas the onset of networking and hard-disk cached solutions provides an effective and functional way to enable access to them through the intranet.

WEB

Since the 1990s, the Internet has changed the dissemination of information, such as electronic copies of traditional paper-based journals and conference proceedings, free electronic-only refereed journals, haphazard copies of all kinds of material on home pages and a handful of electronic preprints archives. Most libraries in India now have a web site and they use the site to present the basic strengths of the library and to host services such as the OPAC and Web access to electronic information.

The 'size of the catalogue card' and the field lengths of primitive database technology are surpassed in the Web era. Types of information resources on the Web also vary from authentic primary information about the latest research results to ephemeral product catalogues. Issues worth consideration are often the content of the sites that are deleted, modified or changed to new machines without proper redirection and the extraction mechanism through search engines, when a flood of sources is retrieved against a query, of which few are relevant. The Internet and Web demonstrate that a large amount of electronic information can be hosted in a decentralized fashion in a cost-effective manner. The Web has also freed the user's dependence on library resources for finding information related to address and contact details of a person/institution, contents pages of books, journals, etc.

As far as possible, especially for reference and information services, looking at the Web has become an innovative trend in the reference service to complement dated print sources. Many publishers visibly feel the benefits and reach of the Web, and have considered it as an alternate medium for delivering information sources; some publishers even permit unrestricted access of tables of contents and abstracts of their primary journals. As a result of these initiatives, the 'print and distribute' paradigm is challenged by 'distribute and print' paradigm.

CONSORTIAL LICENCES

The term 'consortial licences' designates library groupings to negotiate access rights to electronic information with publishers and vendors aiming at enhanced access to more resources at better pricing. "Consortia can be a means to introduce products to a previously untapped market" for vendors and "consortia provide shared expertise, access to new electronic and print resources, professional development, new sources of funds, and safety in numbers" for libraries. In contrast to earlier library collaborative arrangements such as ILL and resource sharing, the publisher and trade community are parties in the consortial agreements.

In resource-sharing, libraries concentrate on collaborative subscriptions by avoiding duplication, where as in consortial licenses, the emphasis is to strike the 'best deals' even if the library suffers some duplication.

The publisher community experience is that increased subscription costs lead to a reduction in the total number of subscriptions, further raising the subscription cost every year. Publishers also found it difficult to enforce ownership rights with electronic sources, even after adopting the latest technology tools and forcing libraries to sign the toughest of the legal clauses.

The good marketing wisdom of the publisher and trade community prevailed to open up information access rights through consortial licenses for a large part of the product spectrum to at least those libraries or groups of libraries which procure products beyond a certain threshold value. The *Indian National Digital Library in Engineering Science and Technology* (INDEST) is the first and the major consortium in India. It is under the aegis of the *Ministry of Human Resource Development* (MHRD). Before the creation of the consortium, access to electronic journals in these institutions remained at 60per cent of subscribed titles, but the number of online journals has increased 10 times after the establishment of the consortium.

The rates for access offered to the consortium are lower by 50per cent to 90per cent depending upon the category of institution and the consortium paid only 11per cent of the list price to access these resources. Info net, another consortium, floated by the *University Grants Commission* (UGC) for Universities, is also gaining strength. Similar consortia are also operational for research institutions under the Council of Scientific and Industrial Research (CSIR) and the Department of Atomic Energy (DAE).

DIGITAL LIBRARIES

Libraries in India are engaged in the development of prototypes of digital information resources, as influenced by developments in other countries. There are certain types of content which lie inaccessible or less used in their present physical forms that can be put to more visible and enhanced use through digitization. Also heavily used content presently available in limited numbers of copies can be identified for conversion to electronic format.

The linear text in many of the print sources presents difficulties for providing a hypertext approach or a multimedia feeling, for simulating learning by doing; sustaining attention and interest for long duration calls for using electronic technologies to enable content to be more functional.

The static content in printed sources fails to attract users who are increasingly exposed to the widely appealing features of broadcasting and IT-intensive presentation tools. Multimedia-enabled digital information will be useful to a large percentage of illiterate and older population also.

There are cases such as papers in journals and conferences in print form that never get their deserved visibility and often end up with out reaching the target population. The digital dissemination of this content may lead to very effective teaching and more focused research in most areas.

To demonstrate the efficacy of digital libraries and collections, libraries must be able to identify materials in the public domain, sources generated in-house, and similar materials to overcome the constraints of copyright. Digital library (DL) development needs a two pronged strategy to digitize local content as well as to devise options for providing access to external resources obtained as free or as part of existing subscriptions or access licenses.

The typical academic or research library in-house digital library on an Intranet must include the following components:

- Consortial access to electronic journals and electronic databases;
- Free/paid Web access to journals subscribed in print format;
- Subject gateways and virtual libraries;

- Free/paid e-books from publishers and portals;
- Intranet access to bibliographic and full-text databases, and CD-ROM publications;
- Local archiving of free and paid e-books;
- LAN serving of e-supplements of purchased books;
- In-house digitization of copyright-owned and copyright- free printed books in the collection;
- Born-digital in-house publications such as research reports, annual reports, convocation reports, teaching materials, theses and dissertations, in-house journals, proceedings of conferences, seminars, workshops, etc., conducted by the institution;
- Preprints and post-prints of research papers sent for publication to journals, conferences, and books, especially with respect to the Open Archives Initiative gaining ground to provide further access to research published in toll journals and to make the results of publicly funded research available to those who need them;
- Publications in the public domain, such as government publications, publications from non-profit institutions, etc.

But many libraries are unable to provide these components due to lack of awareness or due to the hurdles invariably faced by libraries in India. The lack of interest on the part of parent institutions and the absence of action plans or priorities is the major hindrance.

Though computer and communication infrastructure is improving, their availability for information work is not appreciated in many organizations. Paschoud commented how several of the speakers and many of the delegates at the International Conference on Digital Libraries (ICDL) 2004 conference in New Delhi focussed on addressing what most European libraries would consider very basic issues such as network/Internet connectivity and management.

Even in places where infrastructure is available, there is an acute shortage of competent labour to take up the task of digitizing local content and evolving digital information repositories.

The students, faculty, curriculum and training methodology at the disposal of library schools have to be improved visibly to meet this challenge. Coupled with this is the need for continuing education for retraining the working professionals.

Institutions, individuals, or private publishers have rights over content, and motivating them to ease these rights when they are not inclined towards digitization is not a simple task.

Levying charges for access is a distant proposition; instead sponsorships from institutions, government bodies and library suppliers can be explored. Even when hosted as a free facility, enough security mechanisms must be evolved to prevent any trespassing by hackers. Selecting useful content requires careful review and evaluation by subject experts, as digitization will only help to preserve the record, and not its enhanced and continued access. Internet bandwidth in India has to be sufficiently augmented to allow faster access to Web content as more content is being hosted on the Web. The different funding agencies, research councils and institutions are not currently offering monetary support to the desired extent for digital library development.

10

Library Staff: Resource and Services

Library is the trinity of collection, staff and readers, where staff brings together other two elements. Qualified and adequate staff is pre-requisite for effective functioning of libraries.

LIBRARIANS

Libraries need the services of professionally qualified librarians for proper administration of the system. A library having good collection and adequate staff may not essentially provide effective library services, unless it is managed by a professionally qualified librarian having managerial capabilities. All the colleges, except UCE had sanctioned posts of librarians.

The UCE library had a post of an assistant librarian as incharge, which was lying vacant since the establishment of college in 2001. It was being managed by a library assistant. Two Goverment Colleges of Education (GCE) had two posts of librarians each. Out of these, in a college a post was vacant and one librarian was managing library. Table reveals the prevailing position of librarian's posts in colleges under study.

Table. Prevailing Position of Librarians Posts.

Sr. No.	Particulars	No. of Libraries	Percentage
1.	Permanent Librarians	13	72.22
2.	Adhoc based librarians	01	05.56
3.	Post vacant	04	22.22
	Total	**18**	**100.00**

It is evident from table that out of the 18 libraries having sanctioned posts of librarians, 13 (72.22per cent) libraries had permanent librarians, whereas, a goverment aided college appointed a librarian on adhoc basis. In 04 (22.22per cent) colleges posts of librarians were lying vacant.

Out of these, a goverment aided college appointed a professional and designated her as an assistant librarian, inspite of the fact that the college did not have any sanctioned post of an assistant librarian. The remaining three libraries were being run by restorers. The National Council for Teacher Education (NCTE) required each college to have a full time librarian. Analysis of the responses revealed that libraries of 06 (31.58per cent) colleges consisting of 04 Goverment. Aided Colleges of Education (GACE), one goverment college of education and UCE did not meet the NCTE norms about full time librarian.

EDUCATIONAL QUALIFICATION OF LIBRARIANS

Educational qualifications of librarians influence the organisational health of libraries. Higher academic and professional qualification leads to better library management, ultimately better library services.

Table. Educational Qualification of Librarians.

Sr. No.	Qualification		Number of Librarians	per cent
	Academic	Professional		
1.	M.A./M.Sc./ M.Ed./M.Com.	Ph.D.	01	06.67
2.	M.Phil/Ph.D.	B.Lib.and I.Sc.	01	06.67
3.	M.A./M.Sc.	M.Lib.and I.Sc.	04	26.66
4.	M.A./M.Sc.	B.Lib.and I.Sc.	06	40.00
5.	B.A./B.Sc.	M.Lib.and I.Sc.	03	20.00
	Total		**15**	**100.00**

Table shows that out of 15 librarians serving 14 libraries, 06 (40.00per cent) possessed master's degree in arts/science and bachelors' degree in Library and Information Science (LIS), while 04 (26.66per cent) librarians had master's degrees in arts/science in addition to masters' degree in LIS.

Three librarians had bachelors' degree in arts/science and master's degree in LIS. A librarian possessed Ph.D. degree in the subject of History and bachelor's degree in LIS.

Only one librarian had Ph.D. degree in LIS and master's degree in another discipline. Out of the 07 librarians having master's degree in LIS, 03 had qualified National Eligibility Test (NET) for Lectureship, while a librarian qualified State Eligibility Test (SET) for Lectureship.

It has been found that all 03 librarians serving GCE libraries had bachelor's degree in LIS, whereas all the librarians having master's degree in LIS were serving at GACE.

The NCTE has revised its norms regarding qualification of librarians. These are now only bachelors degree in Library and Information Science, whereas as per NCTE these were "As prescribed by State Government/UT Administration concerned.'

The qualifications laid by State Goverment were as per University Grant Commission. But the qualifications prescribed by NCTE are only B.Lib.and I.Sc. Therefore, this amounts to the degradation of librarians and eventually libraries.

EXPERIENCE OF LIBRARIANS

Table. Experience of Librarians.

Sr. No.	Experience in Years	No. of Librarians	Percentage
1.	Up to 5	02	13.33
2.	6-10	03	20.00
3.	11-15	—	—
4.	16-20	01	06.67
5.	21-25	03	20.00
6.	26-30	03	20.00
7.	More than 30	03	20.00
	Total	**15**	**100.00**

Table depicts that out of 15 librarians, 09 (60.00per cent) had experience of more than 20 years. Out of these, 07 librarians possessed bachelor's degree and 02 had master's degree in LIS. Five (33.33per cent) librarians had experience of less than 10 years, while a remaining librarian's experience ranged between 16-20 years. All three librarians serving GCE had experience of more than 20 years each. Analysis of the responses tabulated in tables reveals that all the librarians having only bachelor's degree in LIS were appointed more than 20 years ago. On the other hand, all the librarians appointed thereafter had master's degree in LIS.

REFRESHER COURSES ATTENDED

Librarians were asked if they had attended any refresher course, orientation programme, workshop, etc. Responses revealed that out of 15 librarians, 07 (46.67per cent) attended refresher courses, 02 (13.33) had attended orientation programmes and a librarian also participated in a workshop. It has been found that about 50per cent librarians had not participated in refresher courses and workshops, which are imperative for updating professionals and essential for Continuous Professional Development.

LIBRARY ASSISTANTS

The UCE and a goverment aided college had a post of library assistant each. Out of the two library assistants serving respective libraries, one possessed bachelors' degree in LIS, while another was only matriculate not having any degree or diploma in LIS.

LIBRARY RESTORERS

Thirteen (68.42per cent) libraries had sanctioned posts of restorers, while remaining 06 (31.58per cent) did not. In 12 (92.30per cent) of 13 libraries, restorers were working against the sanctioned posts, while in a goverment college library post was vacant. Two colleges out of the 06 not having sanctioned posts, appointed restorers on adhoc basis, while remaining 04 had not made such effort. All the GCE had sanctioned posts of restorers. About two-third of the library restorers serving libraries possessed either diploma or bachelor's degree in LIS, while remaining five did not.

LIBRARY ATTENDANTS

Eight (42.10per cent) libraries did not have sanctioned posts of library attendants. In two libraries, out of the 11 (57.90per cent) having sanctioned posts of attendants, posts were vacant. All the GCE had sanctioned posts of library attendants. But it was shocking to find that in Desh Bhagat Pandit Chetan Dev Goverment College of Education, Faridkot the previous principal had assigned the job of a 'gardener' to a graduate library attendant and replaced him with an illiterate peon in the library to provide library services to the users. This shows the ignorance and lack of importance of libraries on the part of authorities. Out of the 09 attendants serving libraries, one third had either degree or diploma in LIS, whereas, the remaining two third did not.

EXISTENCE OF LIBRARY COMMITTEES

LIBRARY COMMITTEE

Generally, library committee comprises of three types of authorities, principal as the chairman of committee, librarian as secretary and teachers and students as members. Keeping in view its significance, librarians were asked about the existence, structure and functions of library committees.

Out of a total 19 libraries, 18 (94.73per cent) had library committees, whereas a goverment aided college did not. In a college it was named as 'Book Purchase Committee'.

Table. Chairperson of Library Committee.

Sr. No.	Chairperson of Committee	No. of Libraries	Percentage
1.	Principal	12	66.67
2.	Librarian	02	11.11
3.	Lecturer	02	11.11
4.	No Chairman	02	11.11
	Total	**18**	**100.00**

Table reveals that in 12 (66.67per cent) libraries out of the 18 having library committees, principals were serving as the chairpersons of the committees, whereas in two GACE libraries, librarians themselves led these. In two colleges, lecturers were the heads of committees. Out of these, a college did not have regular principal. In two colleges, library committees did not have any chairman. In one of these, college principal was the convener of committee and librarian and lecturers were members, while in a remaining library, committee comprised of members only.

Table. Secretary of Library Committee.

Sr. No.	Secretary of Committee	No. of Libraries	per cent
1.	Librarian	08	44.44
2.	Lecturers	06	33.33
3.	No One	04	22.23
	Total	**18**	**100.00**

It is worth mentioning here that in majority of the libraries *i.e.* 08 (44.44per cent), librarians were serving as secretaries of the committees, while in 06 (33.33per cent) libraries lecturers did the job. Four libraries did not have any secretary of the library committees. In a library, it comprised of principal as convener and librarian and lecturers as members, while in two libraries these had only members including librarians. In a remaining library, where librarian was head of the committee, it consisted of lecturers as members. Survey revealed that only one library had students' representatives as members in the committee.

NATURE OF WORK OF LIBRARY COMMITTEE

In majority of the libraries forming 66.67 per cent, library committees were advisory bodies. In remaining one third libraries these were executive in nature because of lack of full time librarians.

SELECTION OF SUBJECT RELATED BOOKS

COLLECTION DEVELOPMENT

The Working Group on Libraries set up by National Know-ledge Commission (2007) emphasized for collection building based on the information needs of users. In its recommendations the Group added "To fulfill its role in the present and changing context, each library must have a well-rounded collection relevant to its user community". A balanced and need based collection, adequate to meet the present as well as future information needs of users depends upon a well prepared collection development policy. Library staff of ten colleges responded that they had prepared and were following collection development policy, while staff of remaining 09 libraries responded otherwise. It was very disappointing to find that none of the libraries had any written guidelines for collection development.

WHO MAKES SELECTION OF SUBJECT RELATED BOOKS

Subject books are meant to meet the curriculum based information needs of users and enable them to explore the concerned subjects in depth. Library staff was asked to give ranking in order of preference to the different authorities mentioned in Questionnaire-I, according to their role in selection of subject books.

Table. Selection of Subject Related Books.

Sr. No.	Persons who Select Books	Scores	Ranking
1.	Teachers	66	01
2.	Principal	60	02
3.	Library Committee	43	03
4.	Librarian	39	04
5.	Others (students and college management)	15	05

Sum total of the scores assigned to different options on the basis of ranking given by librarians reveals that teachers occupied the leading role in selection of subject books, followed by the principals and library committees respectively. Librarians attained the fourth position in order of ranking for subject related document selection, while others (students and college management) earned least scores.

GENERAL AND REFERENCE COLLECTION

As in case of subject books, scores have been assigned to the different authorities involved in selection of general and reference collection also, which are tabulated below:

Table. Selection of General and Reference Books.

Sr. No.	Persons who Select Books	Scores	Ranking
1.	Teachers	62	01
2.	Principal	60	02
3.	Librarian	45	03
4.	Library Committee	43	04
5.	Others (students and college management)	05	05

Table shows that teachers have earned the highest scores in selection of general and reference collection too. Principals and librarians were given second and third preferences, while library committees and others attained fourth and fifth positions respectively. Analysis of the responses given in tables makes it clear that the teachers and principals played a leading role in selection of subject related as well as general and reference collection.

DOCUMENT SELECTION TOOLS

Scores have been assigned to the various document selection tools listed in questionnaire-I on the basis of preference ranking given by librarians. Rank '1' was given the highest score '8' followed by others in descending order of 1 score at each stage. Table depicts that teacher's suggestions have earned the highest scores as sources of document selection, while publisher's catalogues and student's suggestions earned the second and third position respectively. Book reviews and other bibliographical tools were given least ranking as document selection tools.

Table. Document Selection Tools.

Sr. No.	Sources of Book Selection	Scores	Ranking
1.	Teachers' Suggestions	132	01
2.	Publishers' Catalogue	101	02
3.	Students' Suggestions	71	03
4.	Books on Approval	54	04
5.	Book Sellers' List	42	05
6.	Book Exhibitions	40	06
7.	Book Reviews	16	07
8.	Other Bibliographical Tools	11	08

BOOK COLLECTION OF LIBRARIES

Among three components of libraries *i.e.,* collection, staff and readers, collection occupies the key position. It is collection which determines the use of a library. Collection is a wider term covering books, periodicals, microforms, electronic form docu-ments, etc. Information was gathered about the nature and size of collection of libraries under study.

TOTAL BOOK COLLECTION

Responses received about the total collection of libraries were arranged into different ranges of 5000 each. It is evident from table that majority of the libraries under study *i.e.* 10 (52.63per cent) possessed 15,000-25,000 volumes, while 04 (21.06per cent) libraries had 10,000-15,000 books. Only two GCE libraries crossed the figure of 30,000 volumes. The UCE library had less than 5000 volumes due to its recent origin in 2001. The GCE were found rich in collection size than GACE and UCE. Main factor affecting this was that GCE received recurring grants for reading material from both the University Grants Commission (UGC) and the State Goverment, while GACE got grants for library from UGC only.

Table. Total Book Collection of Libraries.

Sr. No.	Total Number of Books Possessed	No. of Libraries	per cent
1.	0-5000	01	05.27
2.	5000-10000	02	10.53
3.	10000-15000	04	21.06
4.	15000-20000	05	26.31
5.	20000-25000	05	26.31
6.	25000-30000	—	—
7.	More than 30000	02	10.52
	Total	**19**	**100.00**

The NCTE (2007 and 2009) require each college to have a minimum 1000 titles and 3000 books for B.Ed. Course and minimum 2000 titles for M.Ed course in libraries to get recognition. The UCE had less than 5000 volumes though it was offering both B.Ed. and M.Ed. courses. The NCTE (2007 and 2009) further mentioned that a library should add 200 titles annually wherever B.Ed. course is being run. In addition it requires annual addition of '100 quality books' where M.Ed. course is also being run. It has been found that libraries of only two GACE were fulfilling the NCTE norms for M.Ed. course.

TEXT BOOK COLLECTION

Table shows the textbook collection of libraries of colleges of education in Punjab.

Table. Text Book Collection of Libraries.

Sr. No.	Number of Text Books Possessed	No. of Libraries	per cent
1.	0-4000	06	31.58
2.	4000-8000	07	36.84
3.	8000-12000	03	15.79
4.	12000-16000	03	15.79
	Total	**19**	**100.00**

Table reveals that majority of the libraries had 4000-8000 textbooks. Six libraries had less than 4000 volumes and 03 possessed 8000-12000 textbooks. Three libraries had 12000-16000 volumes of textbooks. It is evident from the table that textbooks constitute a large part of the total collection of libraries.

REFERENCE COLLECTION

A good reference collection is the soul for sound reference service. It has been observed that all libraries maintained separate reference parts. Responses received about the strength of reference collection are tabulated below.

Table. Reference Collection of Libraries.

Sr. No.	Number of Reference Books Possessed	No. of Libraries	per cent
1.	0-200	02	10.53
2.	200-500	05	26.31
3.	500-1000	02	10.53
4.	1000-1500	03	15.79
5.	1500-2500	03	15.79
6.	More than 2500	04	21.05
	Total	**19**	**100.00**

Table depicts that 05 (26.31per cent) libraries possessed 200-500 reference volumes, while other 05 had 500-1500 books. About 21.05per cent libraries had more than 2500 volumes in reference parts.

In majority of the libraries, the reference collection was found to be satisfactory in proportion to their total collection. It was noticed that though the libraries of two GCE were richest in their total collection, still libraries of 04 GACE had more volumes in reference parts.

BOOK BANK

Fifteen libraries (78.94per cent) had book banks to help poor and needy students, while remaining 04 did not. Out of the 15 libraries, 14 maintained separate book bank parts, while a librarian shared that they did not have any separate book bank part, but lend books to needy students for the full session from text books part. Table furnishes the number of volumes in book banks of 14 libraries.

Table. Size of Book Bank Collection.

Sr. No.	Number of Books in Book Bank	No. of Libraries	per cent
1.	0-500	04	28.58
2.	500-1000	04	28.58
3.	1000-2000	03	21.42
4.	2000-3000	01	07.14
5.	More than 3000	02	14.28
	Total	**14**	**100.00**

Table discloses that out of 14 libraries having separate book bank parts, 08 had less than 1000 volumes in their respective book banks. Four libraries had 1000-3000 books and 02 possessed more than 3000 volumes. It was learnt that majority of the libraries added only gifted books to book banks.

NON-BOOK MATERIAL

Non-book material constitutes an important source of information. The NCTE also requires libraries to have electronic publications (CD-ROMs) in collection. But, it has not gained the desired momentum in the libraries of colleges of education. It was found that only 09 libraries had non-book material in meagre quantity. Out of these, seven libraries possessed a few CD's and one had cassettes that came free with books. Another library had approximately 400 maps.

DISSERTATIONS

Out of 15 colleges running M.Ed. course, libraries of 13 had dissertations. Eight libraries possessed less than 300 dissertations and 03 had 300-400 titles. Two libraries possessed more than 400 dissertations. Number of the dissertations possessed by libraries varied according to the year of starting M.Ed. course. The University College of Education, Bathinda and SDS College of Education, Lopon (Moga) started M.Ed. courses during the academic sessions 2006-07 and 2007-08 respectively. Libraries of both of these colleges did not have dissertations.

PERIODICAL LITERATURE

Periodical publications serve the purpose of both information and recreation. These include journals, magazines and all other publications, which are issued at regular intervals.

JOURNALS

Journals are the subject specific periodicals, usually containing primary information. Table represents data about the number of journals on subscription of libraries.

Table. Number of Journals on Subscription.

Sr. No.	Number of Journals	No. of Libraries	per cent
1.	0-10	04	21.05
2.	11-20	10	52.63
3.	21-30	03	15.79
4.	More than 30	02	10.53
	Total	**19**	**100.00**

Table reveals that majority of the libraries forming 52.63 per cent were subscribing to 11-20 journals. Three libraries had 21-30 journals on subscription, while 02 libraries were subscribing to more than 30 journals. Only one library subscribed 02 international journals. A goverment aided college library was subscribing to merely two journals.

The NCTE (2007) has prescribed for B.Ed. and M.Ed. colleges to subscribe to a minimum of 10 and 15 journals respectively. But libraries of 02 colleges offering B.Ed. course and 03 colleges offering M.Ed. course in addition to B.Ed. also did not meet these standards. NCTE (2009) provided revised norms regarding journals for M.Ed. course. It requires each library to have subscription to at least one international publication.

BACK VOLUMES OF JOURNALS

Back volumes of journals are the vital sources of information for furtherance of research. All the libraries except one had back volumes of journals.

Table. Back Volume of Journals.

Sr. No.	Number of Volumes	No. of Libraries	per cent
1.	0-100	08	44.44
2.	100-200	03	16.67
3.	200-400	03	16.67
4.	More than 400	03	16.67
5.	No Response	01	05.55
	Total	**18**	**100.00**

Table depicts that 08 (44.44per cent) out of a total 18 libraries having back volumes of journals had less than 100 back volumes, while 03 (16.67per cent) had 100-200 volumes. Three libraries possessed 200-400 volumes, whereas other three libraries were having more than 400 back volumes of journals. One librarian had not specified the number of back volumes of journals available in library. Survey brought to notice that back volumes of journals were not properly organised as six libraries had loose issues, while in 03 libraries these were partially bound.

MAGAZINES

In addition to journals, libraries provide general magazines to users for reading. Majority of the of libraries *i.e.,* 13 (68.42per cent) were subscribing to less than 20 magazines, while 04 had 21-30 magazine titles on subscription. Two libraries were making available more than 30 magazine titles for users.

NEWSPAPERS

Sometimes, newspapers contain information not available from other sources. Fifteen libraries were subscribing to 05-10 newspaper titles, whereas two had 05 or less newspapers on subscription. A library was subscribing to more than 10 newspapers daily in English, Punjabi and Hindi.

BOOK EXHIBITIONS

Only 04 libraries were organising book exhibitions. Two librarians responded of organising these on the 'important occasions' *i.e.* Gandhi Jayanti, Maharishi Dayanand Anniversary etc. A library organised book exhibition on the occasion of annual convocation, while remaining one arranged that on the college functions. A few librarians invited booksellers to organise book exhibitions in their libraries. Three librarians responded of providing bibliographical services, while remaining responded otherwise.

PHOTOCOPY SERVICE

The NCTE provided in its norms and standards that a college library shall have photocopying facility. Only 08 (42.10per cent) libraries had provision of photocopy service, while remaining majority *i.e.* 11 (57.90per cent) did not. In majority of the libraries it was offered at a genuine rate of 50 paise to ₹1 per copy, whereas in a library photocopy charges were fixed @ ₹1.50 per copy for students and ₹1 for teachers. All libraries except one had no limit over number of pages a user could get copied at a time. The remaining library had fixed this limit to a maximum of 20 flashes.

RESOURCE SHARING

Resource sharing enables libraries to provide access to the users to the resources and services beyond their means and help to overcome the problem of paucity of funds. Only five libraries of GACE were participating in resource sharing programmes with other libraries. It has been found that resource sharing was limited to books only. These libraries were co-operating with the libraries of other institutes run by the same management.

REFERRAL SERVICE AND NEWSPAPER CLIPPING

Referral service is very useful as no library can acquire all the available information. Survey revealed that 14 libraries were providing referral service, while library staff of remaining 05 libraries responded otherwise. Staff of all libraries except one library had maintained newspaper clipping files of important newspaper articles on education and of news related to NCTE and their colleges.

ORIENTATION

Responses revealed that library staff of all libraries, except one was giving orientation to users towards libraries. Library staff was asked about the method of providing orientation.

It is evident from table that in 55.56 per cent of the 18 libraries giving orientation to users, it was provided through lecture method, while in 03 (16.67per cent) libraries users were taken around libraries. In three libraries, a combination of the aforesaid methods was used to give orientation. In UCE library users were given orientation individually at the time of giving them membership. Response received is tabulated below:

Table. Methods of Providing Orientation.

Sr. No.	Method Used	No. of Libraries	per cent
1.	Lecture	10	55.56
2.	Visit Around Library	03	16.67
3.	Notice Board	01	05.55
4.	Lecture and Visit Around Library	03	16.67
5.	Other Method	01	05.55
	Total	**18**	**100.00**

ACCESS

Open access is essential to facilitate maximum use of library collection. It gives users opportunities to browse documents on their own and enable them to find most relevant information. Survey brought to notice that only 05 libraries had open access system and 08 libraries were providing partially open access. The remaining 06 libraries had close access to collection. Fear of theft and lack of adequate number of staff members were the main reasons for following close access. During visit to DAV College of Education, Abohar it was observed that books were kept in almirahs touching the ceiling of library, leaving no scope for browsing.

USE OF COMPUTERS

The ICTs has greatly enhanced the efficiency of library services. Computers are used to provide various library services and perform the routine, repetitive and clerical jobs. The functioning of all types of libraries is influenced by this vital machine. Libraries of college of education are also adapting to this need of the day.

It was found that out of total 19 libraries, 10 libraries had computers, while remaining 09 did not. Eight libraries were using computers for automation, and one had two computers to provide the Internet service. In a library computer was kept aside in a corner without any use as library did not have any library automation software and the Internet connectivity.

Librarians were further asked to indicate the softwares being used for library automation. The responses received from library staff of 08 libraries using computers for library automation are discussed here.

Table shows that out of a total 08 libraries using computers for automation, 02 libraries were using locally developed softwares, while another implemented SOUL for automation. A library has implemented CDS/ISIS and other two were using WINSIS and Alice for Windows respectively. Two libraries had not used any library automation software but prepared databases of documents in 'Microsoft Word' and 'Microsoft Access' respectively.

Table. Softwares being Used for Automation of Libraries.

Sr. No.	Name of the Software	No. of Libraries	per cent
1.	SOUL	01	12.50
2.	CDS/ISIS	01	12.50
3.	WINSIS	01	12.50
4.	Alice for Windows	01	12.50
5.	Local	02	25.00
6.	Not Use Any Software	02	25.00
	Total	**08**	**100.00**

It was observed that majority of the libraries were using computer to perform housekeeping operations.

All libraries were using computers to create databases of books. Five of these also created databases of journals, magazines and newspapers in addition to databases of books.

INTERNET

Majority of the libraries did not have the Internet connectivity, though the NCTE requires a library to have computer with the Internet facility for the use of faculty and student-teachers. Only 06 libraries were providing the Internet service to users.

ATTEMPTS TO PROMOTE USE OF LIBRARIES

Library staff of 17 libraries responded of making efforts to promote use of libraries, whereas in remaining two libraries no such attempts were being made. Both of these libraries did not have librarians and these were being run by restorers.

Library staff of 17 libraries responded of ascertaining infor-mation needs of users to improve the resources and services to promote use of libraries. Responses revealed that in three libraries, the library staff displayed the lists of recent arrivals and in six libraries they displayed the recent acquisitions to promote use of libraries. Librarians were further asked to indicate the methods used to ascertain information needs of users.

Table. Methods used to Ascertain Information Needs of Users.

Sr. No.	Methods of Ascertain Information Needs	No. of Libraries	per cent
1.	Discussion with Users	17	100.00
2.	Maintain Suggestion Box	06	35.30
3.	Record Queries	03	17.64
4.	Conduct Survey	02	11.77

It is obvious from table that discussion with users was the most useful method to ascertain their information needs, as the staff of all 17 libraries ascertaining information needs of users was using this method. In addition, 06 libraries had maintained suggestion boxes. Two librarians reported about conducting user surveys to ascertain the information needs of their users and take necessary action wherever applicable. Three librarians responded of maintaining record of users' queries. Inadequate staff was the major problem faced by librarians in promoting use of libraries. Nine librarians expressed the need to appoint more staff to serve users effectively. A librarian of a goverment aided college not having adequate supporting staff in library commented "I remain busy in locking and unlocking almirahs throughout the day and do not get time for this.'

PROBLEMS FACED BY LIBRARIANS

Librarians were asked to express the problems being faced by them in managing libraries.

INADEQUATE STAFF

Lack of adequate staff was the major obstacle in functioning of libraries, influencing their organisation and administration. Nine librarians responded that they did not have adequate staff to serve the users. It has been found that three libraries were being run by restorers. Many GACE did not have the sanctioned posts of library restorers and library attendants. Librarians were overburdened with the non-professionals jobs due to lack of adequate staff.

PROBLEM OF SPACE

Some libraries including library of Goverment College of Educa-tion, Jalandhar were suffering from the problem of insufficient space. Only five libraries had separate reading room for users whereas, in remaining libraries chairs were arranged in stack area. A librarian complained of shortage of furniture.

PAUCITY OF FUNDS

Funds are the nerve centre of an organisation. Responses of the library staff of four colleges revealed that they were facing the problem of scarcity of funds for purchase of reading material. Purchase of documents largely depended upon the UGC grants. The administration of colleges contributed less towards libraries. A librarian shared that they did not have funds even to purchase catalogue cabinet and cards.

STATUS

Society has not recognized librarians equivalent to teachers. Three librarians complained that they were not given equal recognition with teaching staff. In spite of the higher academic and professional qualification they were thought as a part of clerical staff. One of the librarians went to the extent of saying that they were on a par with the teachers in terms of salary only but not in status.

LIBRARY BUILDING

Libraries are dynamic institutions which continue to grow in terms of collection, staff and readers. In order to tackle the resultant growth it becomes necessary to house a library in an independent, functional and modular building. Keeping in view the significance of library building, query was made to ascertain whether libraries have their own independent buildings. Responses revealed that only one goverment aided college library had an independent building used exclusively for library purpose.

The remaining 18 libraries were housed in buildings forming part of college premises. During visit, it was observed that library of GHG Khalsa College of Education, Gurusar Sadhar was sharing building with canteen. Library was located on first floor while canteen was sited on ground floor, causing disturbance to library users. Majority of the libraries *i.e.* 07 (36.84per cent) were housed in single rooms, while 06 (31.58per cent) libraries had two rooms each. Three libraries consisted of 04 rooms and one had more than 05 rooms.

It was astounding to find during visit to Khalsa College of Education, Mukatsar that a teacher was taking class in library. When asked, assistant librarian shared that it was a usual practice. That majority of the libraries were housed in one or two rooms, which can not be considered sufficient for effective functioning of libraries. The NCTE (2007 and 2009) norms about library building need to be revised. These require each college to have "a library-cum-reading room.'

SEPARATE READING ROOM

A separate reading room with sufficient seating capacity and free from disturbance is the essence of all types of libraries. Survey revealed that only 05 (26.31per cent) libraries had separate reading rooms for users, while in remaining libraries chairs were arranged within stack area. Similarly, five libraries had separate librarian's offices to perform the documentary work. In remaining libraries these were in the form of tables or cabins in corners of libraries.

USERS' VISIT TO LIBRARIES

Libraries exist to meet the information needs of users. The strength of users, their information needs and subjects of study, etc. greatly influence the resources and services of libraries. Table reveals the average number of visitors to libraries.

Table. Average Number of Visitors to Libraries.

Sr. No.	Number of Visitors	No. of Libraries	per cent
1.	0-40	03	15.79
2.	40-80	06	31.58
3.	80-120	06	31.58
4.	More than 120	04	21.05
	Total	**19**	**100.00**

It is evident from the table that 06 (31.58per cent) libraries were being visited by 80-120 users and other six libraries were visited by 40-80 users everyday. Four libraries were visited by more than 120 users daily on an average. In three libraries less than 40 users were visiting a day. The number of daily visitors to libraries varied due to variation in the students' strength with colleges.

SEATING CAPACITY

A library is supposed to provide adequate seating arrangement to users for reading inside library premises. Following table reveals the seating capacity of libraries.

Table shows that majority of the libraries had seating capacity for 26-50 users, while 04 libraries could accommodate 76-100 users at a time. Three libraries had less than 25 seats each for users. A library had seating arrangement for more than 100 users. Six libraries had separate seating arrangement for

M.Ed. students, while libraries of remaining 09 colleges offering M.Ed. course did not have such facility. Ten libraries had separate seating arrangement for teachers.

Table. Seating Capacity for Users.

Sr. No.	Number of Visitors	No. of Libraries	per cent
1.	0-25	03	15.79
2.	26-50	08	42.10
3.	51-75	03	15.79
4.	76-100	04	21.05
5.	More than 100	01	05.27
	Total	**19**	**100.00**

The NCTE (2007) prescribed for each college to provide seating arrangement in libraries for at least 25 per cent of their B.Ed. students and for 10 students of M.Ed. course, but 08 libraries did not meet this requirement. NCTE (2009) has revised norms regarding seating capacity of libraries for B.Ed course. It requires libraries to have seating arrangement for at least fifty per cent of B.Ed students. Only one library had drinking water facility for users. Similarly, Library of DAV College of Education, Abohar had toilet facility for faculty members. Students were not allowed to use that.

LIBRARY BUDGET AND SOURCES OF FINANCE

The impact of Information and Communication Technologies (ICTs) on libraries has brought structural changes to library practices. Effective library management and provision of services depends upon the availability of adequate funds. It was disappointing to find that none of the libraries except one had provision for library budget. Only UCE, Bathinda had provision of ₹50,000 each year for reading material. But since its establishment in 2001 no increase has been made in this amount. Libraries of GCE and GACE mainly depended up on the UGC grants. Moreover, NCTE (2007 and 2009) is silent about the financial provision for libraries. In libraries of colleges of education under study, the sources of finance varied considerably. Major sources of finance for purchase of reading material are given below:

- University Grants Commission (UGC) Grants;
- Library Fees;
- Library Development Funds; and
- Amalgamated Funds.

UGC GRANTS

The UGC plays a significant role in funding libraries through out the country. An attempt was made to find whether libraries have received any grant from UGC during the period 2002-2007. Only 13 (68.42per cent) libraries responded.

Table. Type of Grants Received from UGC.

Sr. No.	Type of Grant Received	No. of Libraries	per cent
1.	Recurring	10	76.92
2.	Non Recurring	01	07.70
3.	No Grant	02	15.38
	Total	**13**	**100.00**

Table shows that out of 13 libraries, 10 (76.92per cent) received recurring grants under tenth five year plan, while a library got non-recurring grant from UGC during the period 2002-2007. Office superintendent of the goverment aided college shared that the college had received special (non-recurring) grant for library meant for 'Backward District College'.

Libraries of two colleges including UCE and a goverment aided college had not received any recurring or non-recurring grant from UGC. The goverment aided college had not demanded grants from UGC because of the conflict between members of college management committee.

AMOUNT OF GRANTS RECEIVED BY LIBRARIES

Librarians were asked to mention the amount of grants received from UGC during the period 2002-2007. Responses received were arranged into different ranges of 1 lakh each.

Table. Extent of Grants Received.

Sr. No.	Amount of Grants Received	No. of Libraries	per cent
1.	Up to one Lakh	06	54.54
2.	1-2	04	36.36
3.	2-3	—	—
4.	3-4	01	09.10
	Total	**11**	**100.00**

Table reveals a considerable variation in the amount of grants received by 11 libraries. Majority of the libraries received less than ₹01 lakh as UGC grant for purchase of reading material under tenth five year plan, while 36.36per cent received 1-2 lakhs. A library received grant of more than 3 lakhs from UGC.

GRANTS FROM STATE GOVERNMENT

None of the libraries under study received grants from the State Goverment during the period 2002-2007. The State Goverment had earlier given grants to libraries of GCE only, as reported by librarians.

AMALGAMATED FUND

Amalgamated fund is collected from students each year at the time of admission to colleges. This amount is to be used for various purposes *i.e.* cultural activities, games, library and for some other similar purposes. Allocation of amalgamated funds towards library depends upon the discretion of the principals of colleges.

LIBRARY FEE AND LIBRARY DEVELOPMENT FUNDS

As like amalgamated fund, Library Fee and Library Development Fund are also charged from students at the time of admission to colleges. Out of the 13 responding colleges, 08 charged library fee at varying rates from ₹200-400. In 04 colleges it was termed as 'Books and Journals Fee'. Similarly 04 colleges charged library development fund from students at different rates of 100-200. In a goverment aided college it was being charged under the head 'Books Replacement Fund'.

OVERDUE FINE

The negligible amount of overdue fine can not be considered as reliable and sufficient source of funds for libraries. In UCE, the amount of overdue fine goes to the University Account.

TECHNICAL PROCESSING

Technical processing of documents takes place after accessioning. It covers all the activities related with their classi-fication, cataloguing and physical processing. Classification provides systematic order among documents and catalogue guide the users to retrieve needed documents easily from large collection, through various access points.

CLASSIFICATION

Collection has to be classified and the classification scheme has to be user friendly. Survey revealed that out of a total 19 libraries, 18 had classified their collection. On the other hand, in the library of Dev Samaj College of Education for Women, Ferozepur City that was established in 1942, collection was not classified at all. Almirah numbers were written on catalogue cards instead of call numbers. The following table furnishes data about the extent of classification of documents in libraries:

Table. Status of Classification of Collection.

Sr. No.	Extent of Classification	No. of Colleges	per cent
1.	Fully Classified	11	57.90
2.	Partially Classified	07	36.84
3.	Not At All Classified	01	05.26
	Total	**19**	**100.00**

Table reveals that in majority of the libraries *i.e.*, 11 (57.90per cent) collection was fully classified, while in 07 (36.84per cent) libraries it was classified partially. In a remaining library documents were not classified at all. It has been found that all libraries were using Dewey Decimal Classification (DDC) scheme ranging from 16th to 21st edition to classify collection.

Earlier UCE library was using Colon Classification (CC), but later on it switched over to DDC. Three librarians responded of facing problems in classifying collection. A librarian having 18th edition of DDC shared that the respective library had an old edition of DDC which did not contain detailed class numbers for the subject of Computer. Librarian of Goverment College of Education, Jalandhar said, "It becomes very difficult to decide the main class of a book in case of interdisciplinary subject books". A librarian stated lack of professionally qualified staff as one of the obstacles in organising collection.

CATALOGUING

Survey revealed that 11 (57.90per cent) libraries had partially catalogued their collection, not providing access points for all documents in possession. On the other hand, eight libraries had fully catalogued their holdings. Majority of the libraries *i.e.* 11 (57.90per cent) were following Anglo American Cataloguing Rules-II and remaining 08 (42.10per cent) libraries were using Anglo American Cataloguing Rules-I for cataloguing. This reflects the popularity of dictionary catalogue over classified catalogue among college libraries.

NUMBER OF ENTRIES PREPARED FOR EACH DOCUMENT

Users may approach a document through different access points *i.e.* subject, author, title, etc. Table shows the number of entries prepared for each volume in libraries to provide access to their holdings.

Table. Number of Entries for Each Document.

Sr. No.	No. of Entries Prepared	No. of Libraries	per cent
1.	One Entry	06	31.58
2.	Two Entries	09	47.37
3.	Three Entries	01	05.26
4.	All Possible Entries	03	15.79
	Total	**19**	**100.00**

Table reveals that in 09 (47.37per cent) libraries, only two entries (Author and Title), and in 06 libraries only one entry for each document was prepared. Three librarians responded that they prepared all possible entries for each book in possession. Librarians were further asked to state the time taken to process new arrivals. Table depicts that in 08 libraries, it was taking 1-2 weeks to process new arrivals, whereas, in other 08 libraries books were being processed with in a week. Three librarians responded of taking more than two weeks to process documents, due to inadequate staff. All libraries maintained card catalogue. Eight libraries using computers also prepared computer-based databases of books.

Table. Time Taken to Process Books from Date of Acquisition.

Sr. No.	Average Time Taken	No. of Libraries	per cent
1.	Less than a Week	08	42.11
2.	1-2 Weeks	08	42.11
3.	More than Two Weeks	03	15.78
	Total	**19**	**100.00**

Five librarians mentioned the problems they faced in cataloguing, whereas, remaining majority responded otherwise. Three librarians complained of lack of professional staff and one of them further added that his college principal did not sanction funds even to purchase catalogue cards and cabinet. A librarian responded that they did not have catalogue code to get clarity in case of any doubt about cataloguing rules, while another shared that their library did not have standard subject heading list and they faced problem in assigning subject headings.

Bibliography

Ajay Kumar Srivastav and Rajesh Kumar Singh: *Glossary of Library Information Communication and Technological Terms and Acronyms*, Shree Pub, 2007.

Ajit Singh Siwatch: *Encyclopedic Dictionary of Library and Information Science, Vols. I to III* , Shree Publishers, 2010.

Amjad Ali: *Ane's Encyclopedic Dictionary of Library and Information Science*, Ane Books India, 2006.

Anil Parnami: *Library Information : System and E-Journal Archiving*, Cyber Tech, 2011.

Bhupendra Narayan Singh: *Encyclopaedia of Library and Information Science in the Digital Age Vols. I to III*, Anmol Pub, 2011.

Bhupendra Narayan Singh: *Encyclopaedia of Library and Information Science in the Digital Age Vols. I to III*, Anmol Publication, Delhi, 2011.

Bikika Laloo Tariang: *Essays on Library and Information Science Education*, Ess Ess Publications, Delhi, 2012.

C.R. Karisiddappa: *Current Studies in Library and Information Science*, Manak Publication, Delhi, 1994.

Cherian Mathew: *Dynamics of Library and Information Science*, Cyber Tech Publicaitons, New Delhi, 2011.

D.B. Patil and M.M. Kooganuramath: *Library and Information Science*, APH Publication, Delhi, 2011.

G. Devarajan: *Applied Research in Library and Information Science*, Ess Ess Pub, 2005.

G. Devarajan: *Research in Library and Information Science*, Ess Ess Pub, 2002.

Kusum Verma: *Library Information Services and Systems*, Vista International Pub, 2008.

Kusum Verma: *Modern Practices of Library Information Services*, Vista International, 2006.

Mahendra Singh Sodhi: *Advancement in Library and Information Science*, Adhyayan Publication, Delhi, 2006.

Manisha Dawra: *Encyclopaedia of Modern Library and Information Science (5 Vols-Set)*, Rajat Publication, Delhi, 2003.

Purushotham Tiwari: *Dictionary of Library and Information Science*, A.P.H. Pub, 2011.

R P Bajpai: *Current Trends in Library and Information Science*, Shree Publication, Delhi, 2007.

R.G. Prasher: *Library and Information Science : Parameters and Perspectives : Essays in Honour of P.B. Mangla (2 Vols - set)*, Concept Publication, Delhi, 1997.

Shiv Ram Verma: *Foundations of Library and Information Science*, Shree, 2005.

Suryakant and O.S. Shekhar Singh: *Library and Information Science: Objective Questions Ability Tests For NET/SLET/JRF*, Ess Ess Pub, 2011.

T. Nasirudheen: *A Comprehensive Course in Library and Information Science*, Ess Ess Publications, 2012.

T. Saravanan: *Library and Information Science: UGC, JRF-SLETNET*, APH, 2008.

Vaishali Khaparde: *Advancement in Library and Information Science*, Ess Ess Publications, Delhi, 2012.

Vrushali Dandavate, Ajay Khatri and Pradip Umdale: *Application of Six Sigma in Library and Information Science*, Ess Ess Publications, Delhi, 2013.

Y.L. Chopra and Mamta Chopra: *Challenges Before Library and Information Science in New Millennium*, Ess Ess Publication, Delhi, 2001.

Index